Advance Praise for *Jesus Through Pagan Eyes*
by Reverend Mark Townsend

"There are certain words that just do [...] 'Pagan' most definitely fall into this ca[...] [...]ook, *Jesus through Pagan Eyes* addresses this [...] startling and inspirational way. Altogether the book is a [...] valuable contribution to understanding an important area of the contemporary spiritual quest. It is a 'must read' for anyone seeking insight into the modern encounter between these two ancient traditions."
—Simon Small,
Anglican priest and author

"*Jesus Through Pagan Eyes* is full of mystery and mysticism, with revelations that will mesmerize readers. I love how Mark peels back the Christian layers to remind us that Jesus was a Jewish Rabbi. Whether Pagan, Jewish, Christian, or other, you will be amazed and inspired by this book."
—Uri Geller, world-renowned mystic,
motivational speaker, and bestselling author

"This is a quite remarkable work, which reveals the figure of Jesus from most unusual and fascinating perspectives, likely to have value to convinced Christians, Pagans, and agnostics alike."—Prof. Ronald Hutton,
author of *The Triumph of the Moon*

"Mark skillfully and convincingly weaves oft-forgotten wisdom from early church leaders with modern Jesus scholarship and concepts from the Pagan and Druidic traditions into a beautiful tapestry of both the person of Jesus and the Christ-consciousness that he exhibited. As a lifelong Christian and a pastor to boot, I found much wisdom and beauty in this book and was introduced to aspects of Jesus that I had never been exposed to. I found myself asking, 'Why did I never see this before?'"
—Revd. Roger McClellan, co-founder and moderator
of The Progressive Christian Alliance

"For those of us who have discovered our spirituality outside churches, there remains the question of how to see and relate to Jesus, the man at the center of the religion that has dominated western culture and so infiltrated our sensibilities. Mark Townsend explores this question as a fellow seeker, as a Christian enriched by Paganism, creating bridges and inviting us to co-create meaning from what has always been true and essential in the stories of Jesus and our own deep knowing."—Oriah Mountain Dreamer, author of *The Invitation*

"Mark Townsend displays a remarkable breadth of knowledge, compassion, and common sense in the way he introduces contemporary Jesus scholarship to those who walk the Pagan path, and the way he introduces Christians to the delightful, humorous, and loving Pagan souls who appear in this book. A must-read for any Christian who is open to discovering the Pagan mysteries that inform so much of the Christian myth."
—Revd. Bruce Sanguin, author of
If Darwin Prayed: Prayers for Evolutionary Mystics

"It is no coincidence that Matthew Fox has written a foreword for this book. Like Fox, Mark Townsend resurrects the figure of Jesus, so vital, so wonderful to so many of us, and allows a risen Christ to speak after the death of the Doctrinal one."—Adrian Gibb, Coordinator of PAX (Progressive Anglican Christians), member of the Progressive Christian Alliance and the Christian Pagan Fellowship, and Co-admin of Hedge-Church

"*Jesus Through Pagan Eyes*, with its words about the Green Man and the Green Christ, enlarges our sympathies and extends our imaginations in our care for one another and creation."   —Revd. Donald Reeves

"There are knowledge transmitters—and then there are 'knowledge makers,' who have the courage, skill, and experience to put things together in new and revelatory ways. Knowledge makers re-configure our minds, our eyes, and our ears to receive bigger and better things. Mark Townsend is doing just that. We were not ready for Jesus, so some will not be ready for his followers either. Please don't be afraid!" —Fr. Richard Rohr, O.F.M., Center for Action and Contemplation in Albuquerque, New Mexico

Jesus *through* Pagan Eyes

About the Author

Reverend Mark Townsend is an ex-Church of England vicar, a professional (performance) magician, a member of the Order of Bards, Ovates, and Druids; and the author of five books, all of which combine the two areas of magic and religion.

He has studied both magic ("performance" and "real") and religion for at least twenty years. Rev. Townsend served as an Anglican priest for ten years, but within a continual love-hate relationship to the Church. Throughout that period he developed a deep desire for a more earth-centered/Pagan approach to spirituality. Rev. Townsend eventually resigned from his Christian ministry and quickly became involved in Pagan circles. He has been initiated into the Druid mysteries.

Rev. Townsend's previous book (*The Path of the Blue Raven*) caused something of a stir among the more traditionally minded because it was the first time he spoke openly about his path into Druidry while still an Anglican priest.

To Write to the Author

If you wish to contact the author or would like more information about this book, please write to the author in care of Llewellyn Worldwide, and we will forward your request. Both the author and publisher appreciate hearing from you and learning of your enjoyment of this book and how it has helped you. Llewellyn Worldwide cannot guarantee that every letter written to the author can be answered, but all will be forwarded. Please write to:

Reverend Mark Townsend
⁒ Llewellyn Worldwide
2143 Wooddale Drive
Woodbury, MN 55125-2989

Please enclose a self-addressed stamped envelope for reply,
or $1.00 to cover costs. If outside the USA, enclose
an international postal reply coupon.

Many of Llewellyn's authors have websites with additional information and resources. For more information, please visit our website at http://www.llewellyn.com.

Jesus *through* Pagan Eyes

*Bridging Neopagan Perspectives
with a Progressive Vision of Christ*

Reverend Mark Townsend

Preface by Barbara Erskine
Foreword by Matthew Fox

Llewellyn Publications
Woodbury, Minnesota

FIRST EDITION
First Printing, 2012

Book design by Bob Gaul
Editing by Laura Graves
Cover design by Adrienne Zimiga
Cover illustration by Steve McAfee
Cover image © iStockphoto.com/Jill Fromer
Part Page art © Lllewellyn art department

Llewellyn is a registered trademark of Llewellyn Worldwide Ltd.

Cataloging-in-Publication data for *Jesus Through Pagan Eyes*
(**ISBN**: 978-0-7387-2191-0) is on file at the Library of Congress

Llewellyn Worldwide Ltd. does not participate in, endorse, or have any authority
or responsibility concerning private business transactions between our authors and
the public.
   All mail addressed to the author is forwarded, but the publisher cannot, unless specifically instructed by the author, give out an address or phone number.
   Any Internet references contained in this work are current at publication time, but
the publisher cannot guarantee that a specific location will continue to be main-
tained. Please refer to the publisher's website for links to authors' websites and other
sources.

Llewellyn Publications
A Division of Llewellyn Worldwide Ltd.
2143 Wooddale Drive
Woodbury, MN 55125-2989
www.llewellyn.com

Printed in the United States of America

Contents

......

Part Two—Jesus Through Pagan Eyes: A Selection of Stories and Essays by Respected Pagan Elders

Part Three—Thirteen Interviews with Respected Pagan Elders

Jesus now has an honored place in my heart, and sometimes on my altar as well, but I remain a Pagan and a Wiccan, not a Christian.

—Gus DiZerega[1]

To Persephone's gift Sally, the sweet one who totally changed everything for me. Thank you from the bottom of my heart.

XXX

Acknowledgments

......

There are so many wonderful people to thank and acknowledge with regard to the creation of this book:

Firstly my children, Aisha and Jamie, for their patience and support. I am so proud of them both and learn far more *from* them than I could possibly have taught them. Llewellyn Worldwide, for their belief in my project and especially acquisitions editor, Elysia Gallo, who's been a delight to work with throughout the entire process.

Barbara Erskine, one of my very favourite novelists, for honouring me with her beautiful Preface, and for her generous friendship.

Matthew Fox, a longtime spiritual hero of mine, for his astonishing Foreword and for his encouragement in the light of my own problems with institutional Christianity.

The Pagan elders who gave so generously of their time and creativity in providing such a rich feast of essays: Emma Restall Orr, Reni, Adele Nozedar, Joyce Higginbotham, Christopher Penczak, Maria Ede-Weaving, Karen Tate, Rob Chapman, James Carrington, Stephen Critchley, John Michael Greer, Diana L. Paxson, Marcus Katz, Philip Carr-Gomm, Sarah Kral, and Erin Dragonsong.

The thirteen Pagan elders who allowed me into their lives with pen paper and a whole load of eccentric questions about Jesus: Maxine Sanders, Selena Fox, Raven Digitalis, Sorita D'Este, Caitlín Matthews, Janet Farrar, Gavin Bone, Oberon Zell-Ravenheart, Cassandra Eason, Raven Grimassi, Scott Blunt, Kerr Cuhulain, and Gill Edwards.

Others who've helped with advice, finding quotations and general support. Among them Raymond Buckland, Viviane Crowley, (and the late and great) IsaacBonewits.

My wonderful Facebook family and those at hedge-Church for the constant support, and those who were good enough to offer advice as proofreaders.

My sisters and brothers in The Order of Bards, Ovates, and Druids, The Druid Network; The Open Episcopal Church; The Progressive Christian Network Britain; The Progressive Christian Alliance; The Church of England; and all those from other religions, faiths, and paths who've accompanied me on my pilgrimage.

Finally the Source—God/Goddess/The Great Spirit/The Divine All. Thank you for the great adventure that never slows down or ceases to amaze. May the journey continue with your grace and presence by my side.

Preface

......

The affection in which Mark holds the figure of Jesus is obvious in every word of this book, which is an attempt to reconcile what might be to some irreconcilable: the world of the Christian and the world of the Pagan, and while doing so to explore the parameters within which the two spiritualities exist.

Mark addresses his book to two different groups of people: Pagans who nevertheless still hold some recessive affection for the figure of Jesus Christ, and Christians who find themselves uncomfortable with aspects of the church that took his name but have no wish to abandon it completely.

I come from the second group. I was a cradle Christian, carefully cocooning myself within a gentle and sheltered C of E (Church of England) world, the world of country churches, vicars who were poets and naturalists as much as priests, wheezing organs and cherished church mice, explaining away to myself the horrors of Christians tearing each other to shreds, by blaming narrow specifics such as the Inquisition, or Philip of Spain and Bloody Mary. As my studies progressed, however, I lost my faith if not in God then in the Church. Why was I even thinking about being part of something whose history was soaked in blood, marred by misogyny, and strangled by dogma, and which appeared to have lost sight of the man after whom it is named? I wanted the gentle Jesus of my childhood, but I also wanted mysticism and mystery. I wanted a god who fitted in my country, my mythos: Like so many others, as I was to discover later, I found it hard to relate to the remote and harsh Middle Eastern God of the Old Testament. I wanted a god who understood the world I knew and loved; a god not of sand and desert and olive groves, but a god of misty green isles and apple orchards and verdant forests.

I had to find for myself the Western Mystery Tradition, all but eradicated fifteen hundred years ago by the evangelizing Church, and work my way forward through the maze. I had to find a way of incorporating the female soul of the church which had been lost at the Reformation, an intellectualizing and rationalizing movement which was as misogynistic as that of the early church fathers. I, as a Protestant, had to discover the Virgin Mary, angels, beauty, and love rather than a stream of threats and the terror of a hell which could not feasibly be avoided. Above all I needed to know that nature was a part of God's world which we should protect and not ruthlessly exploit. A great many of my problems were semantic, I later discovered. They are all there; angels and promises and love—it was a matter of interpretation, and when my faith at last came back, unexpectedly and to a certain extent unsought, it was mediated through the gentle overview of Druidry. I had found my way alone through a tangle of doubt and confusion and ended up with a blend of two spiritualities: the Christianity of my childhood I had missed so much and the newly discovered philosophy and spirituality of Druidry. I was confused and hesitant, and there was no one I felt I could turn to for advice and to use as a sounding board. At the time, neither side seemed to want to talk about the other and I could see no way of joining them up. I wish I'd had Mark's book to guide and encourage me.

My quest has ended with the writing of a novel, *Time's Legacy*, putting Jesus fairly and squarely into "England's mountains green," as the poet, mystic, and Druid William Blake described it in his famous hymn, "Jerusalem." I didn't write the book with this in mind, but as it progressed I realised that I was working out my own theology in some way, the compromise and exploration of the theme which Mark addresses so comprehensively in this book. In my novel, the Christian characters—in this case, ordained members of the C of E, one of them a woman—are confronted by a Jesus who is a historical person…a real man with all the emotions and hang-ups of a real man. He is still in the process of preparing for his destiny and at this point, is doing so in the company of Druids. His divinity, or, if you prefer, his destiny as a Master and teacher, are hinted at but as yet he has not launched upon his final career, the three short years which will lead to the cross. Each character from their own perspective has to come to terms with the sudden presence in their lives in a way they had never considered possible—of a living, breathing Jesus.

••••••

In the first section of his book, Mark provides an erudite and loving picture of the Jesus I did not want to lose, discussing both the historical figure and that of the mystical Cosmic Christ. He considers whether they are one and the same or totally different, addressing many of the problems I and so many people like me have faced.

Following is a section of experiences of Jesus and of the Cosmic Christ by people who have walked the same road, personal and theoretical stories from well-known members of the Pagan community. Their expositions are thoughtful and assured; their learning and experience broad, scholarly, and deeply moving.

In part three, Mark has included the result of interviews with respected elders from various sections of the Pagan world on specific questions related to the book's theme.

I enjoyed Mark's book tremendously. I hope you do too. As you read it, it will speak to your soul.

—Barbara Erskine

Foreword

......

Welcoming This Book

I very much welcome this volume by Mark Townsend and his friends that celebrates the wisdom and the practice of so-called "pagan" ancestors. I say "so-called" because paganphobia has dominated for so long in the West, and those who identify with earth-based or pre-Biblical religions have endured the opprobrium of the dominant religious culture for so long that they may well find the term "pagan" suspect insofar as it is more a title given by the dominant culture. Indeed, the very invective that so often accompanies the term "pagan" belies the hatred of all things earthly that goes with it, since, as we all know, *paganus* simply means rural person. Why are those close to the land so threatening to those who no longer are?

Ernest Becker observed that "ancient man—unlike modern man—had not yet lost his awe of nature and being." There lies the depth of the gift of *pagani*, those close to the earth. Awe is as good a synonym for "mysticism" as any I know of. In our times of a shrinking globe, a rapid communication network worldwide, and the rise of interfaith or what I call "Deep Ecumenism," it is more important than ever that we listen to each other's religious journeys and hear from various religious lineages, including especially those who have not lost the awe of nature and of being. Our very survival as a species depends on deep listening and learning. As the Second Vatican Council put it in the sixties, the Holy Spirit has worked through *all cultures and all religions* through the human epoch. Instead of making war in the name of our gods or God or goddesses, it is wise to catch one's breath, breathe deep (in the Bible and many other languages around the world, the word for "breath" and "spirit" are identical), and learn rather than judge. It is often scandalous how "ecumenism" for some religious types means only sitting down with persons of the Book, ignoring sitting down with persons of the Book of Nature.

One thing we are learning is how much Jesus had in common with earth-based religions. Scholars now agree that the historical Jesus came from the wisdom tradition of Israel, and this tradition is not book-based but nature-based. He grew up in Galilee, the green belt and farming area of Israel, and his closeness to nature and her animals and her seasons and lessons is everywhere manifest in his parables and teachings. Wisdom is feminine, and she is cosmic and all about generativity and creativity in the Hebrew Scriptures. She is also a "friend of the prophets," and the prophetic tradition also spawned the historical Jesus who dared to take on religious hypocrisy and privilege in his day.

But Jesus's relationship to earth-based religions runs even deeper than that. Biblical scholar Bruce Chilton—author of *Rabbi Jesus, Rabbi Paul,* and *Mary Magdalene: A Biography*—makes the point that Jesus can rightly be understood *as a shaman.* Like shamans everywhere, Jesus withdrew periodically into the wilderness where, we are told in Mark, the oldest of the Gospels, he wrestled with spirits and the wild beasts came to succor him. (Mark 1:12, 13) His mentor, John the Baptist, with whom he probably spent his formative years as an adolescent, was very much a man of the wilderness.

Nor is Chilton alone in this assessment of Jesus as shaman. The late poet and ex-Dominican William Everson (also known as "Brother Antoninus") thought deeply about shamanism and he felt that Jesus "was perhaps the greatest of all shamans... Forty days in the desert, the carrying of the cross as a Sun Dance" and more.[2] He goes on: "The link would seem to be the Animal Powers. Christ would relate to the Animal Powers that preceded our more sophisticated religious impulses...Now when you press back, beyond this point, and try to bring those forces—the Animal Powers—into focus, it seems like it's whittling down even more on the Divinity of Christ, except that the infra-rational has its own Divinity, and it is by maintaining that continuity that the problem can be solved, I feel. In the arts, it will come in largely through the imagery."[3] Everson observes that the shaman descends into the "primordial wound," to recover a redeeming spirit.

It is interesting that Otto Rank talks about humans all being born with an "original wound" (as distinct from an "original sin"), and if Rank is right, then we see a powerful link between the very meaning of redemption and the work of the shaman. Rank also perceptively identifies our "original wound" as the separation from the womb that we all undergo and that is triggered again whenever other profound separations touch us. Wisely does Rank prescribe the medicine for this original wound as the "unio mystica," the mystical union that love and art restore.[4]

Everson talks of "the wounded buck" in one of his poems, but of course the psalms also offer similar imagery. The animals in their wild habitat easily "become a part of the religious persona because it invests us with a sense of the sacred." Shamans heal. They heal this visible world and the invisible one, they heal "the breach between sacred and profane, between divine and mortal, between eternal and contingent."[5] They heal because they have journeyed into their and society's wounds. David Paladin, a Navajo artist and healer, was tortured for years as a captured soldier in World War II to the point that when found, he was comatose and a paraplegic. Years later his elders told him that this suffering was his initiation into shamanhood, and he exclaimed: "Shamans know that those wounds are not theirs but the world's. Those pains are not theirs but Mother Earth's. You can gift the world as shaman because you're a wounded warrior. A wounded healer and a wounded warrior are one." The warrior-shaman rises above his own dead body and says, "I have died, too. Now let's dance. We're free. The spirit is ours because we have died. Now we are resurrected from the ashes."[6]

Paladin's wife explained to me that on more than one occasion dead artists would come to her husband in the middle of the night and request he paint something in their name. She showed me, for example, a painting signed "Paul Klee" that looked exactly like a Klee painting—"I remember the night he came to him," she told me. Yes, shamans live in several worlds at once.

One of the techniques shamans use to heal is the beat of the drum and the beat and rhythm of chant. Much of the shaman's work is to put people into a trance state. "The idea of trance [is] the basic psychological function of the shaman," notes Everson.[7] Silence also leads us into trance. The shaman we might say takes us deeper than language (left brain) into that area of the unconscious that is closer to animal communication, into what Meister Eckhart calls "the soil, the ground, the source of the God-head." Into the Godhead, not just into God. Into the lower chakras, where so many Westerners in the name of false religion and false education are afraid to journey. The first chakra is about our link to the earth, after all; all animals have feet that connect them to the earth. The second chakra is about our sexuality, another thing we share with all animals. And the third chakra includes our anger and moral outrage—it is *there* that we are grounded in the groundless Divinity, and it is there that compassion takes root. This is what shamanism evokes in us.

It is not only Everson who saw this but also the great nineteenth-century prophet Walt Whitman. Whitman reinvented poetry by taking it out of the classic European models of rhythm and rhyme and opening it up to the beat and to everyday language again (no compulsion to rhyme). He himself was aware that he was doing with language a shamanistic thing. He called his breakthrough the "breaking up of the crystalline structure of the classic mould."[8] His verse-technique was a method that liberated poetry itself. A telling story is shared of how, when he was ten years old, Whitman heard a Quaker preacher named Elias Hicks who was half black and half Native American. His words and cadence put Whitman into ecstasy. I am convinced that his shamanistic vocation began at that time, and notice—it did not come from books but from masters of oral traditions, an indigenous and African-American preacher. To this day and in its latest reincarnation as rap, the black religious impulse, like the Native American drum, beats its message, which is as much about sound and vibration as it is about content. It appeals to the lower chakras, not just the rarefied atmosphere of heady rationality.

Whitman scholar and Jungian psychotherapist Steven Herrmann says that for Whitman "the drum-beat works for him as a transport to the Divine." Whitman's journey is a journey of ecstasy, "an embodied sense of Ecstasy, ... he also sinks down into the bodily regions of soul, where body and soul cannot be distinguished: where soul *is* the body and body is the soul, and he speaks out of this oneness of the soul's body—*out of the language of the body which is the soul-language.*"9 Back into the lower chakras. (This is also what makes rave so enticing to the younger generation. It brings the first chakra into play. Our Cosmic Mass has demonstrated the power of this return to the body for worship, to dance as prayer.) Whitman, in a pre-modern way of seeing the world, celebrates how "everything without exception has an eternal soul! The trees have, rooted in the ground! The weeds of the sea have! The animals!"10

Whitman also celebrates the second chakra, our sexuality, for he sees sexuality "as the root impulse underlying all creation. He saw it ultimately as the means to spiritual development and union with the Self. It was from the animal heat generated during such a summer morning [of love making] that he became a bridge between the known and the Unknown, the ordinary experience of ecstasy and the shamanic state of Ecstasy, which cannot be symbolized."11

Whitman also sings of the sacred dance and how it leads to sacred trance: "I am a dance ... Play up there! The fit is whirling me fast." He tells us he beats his "serpent-skin drum" and again, "I hear the dance music of all nations…bathing me in bliss."[12] He is deeply ecumenical in his appreciation of putting the lower and sacred chakras to work when he calls explicitly on the music "of all nations." Herrmann summarizes Whitman's contribution this way: "Whitman's methods of vocalism and free verse are patterned on a shamanic technique of ecstasy that is archaic; its archaic function is to lead the reader to non-ordinary states whereby inflections from the Divine can be made imminent, and where the origin of all poems can be *experienced*. His religious vision is an outgrowth of shamanism; yet it cannot be limited to shamanism, or any established religions, for it is essentially contemporary, post-scientific and new."[13]

Whitman called for a "spiritual democracy" that would culminate in a political and economic democracy. In his way he was calling for "deep ecumenism" or the gathering of all religious tribes, none greater than the other. He also called for recognition of sexual diversity and indeed of homosexual marriage, an archetype now awakening all over the globe. In his appreciation of the mystical role of sexuality as well as spiritual democracy he was standing in opposition to "the Puritan myth [which] was based upon an unconscious projection of evil onto indigenous peoples, the lifeways of the two-spirits, and a bi-erotic image of the soul's wholeness."[14] His call for a new religion and a new Bible seems more real today than ever before.

Thomas Berry talks this way about the Shaman while comparing prophet and shaman. "While both Prophet and Shaman have special roles in their relation to the human community, the Shaman is more comprehensive in his field of consciousness. The prophet speaks somewhat directly in the name of God, the prophet is a message bearer, the prophet is interpreter of historical situations, and the prophet critiques the ruling powers. The Shaman functions in a less personal relationship with the divine. He is more cosmological, more primordial, personally more inventive in the source of his insight and his power."[15]

To bring earth back to religion and spirituality is to bring the body back and vice versa. It is also to bring sexuality back with its intimations of mystical encounter, the theophany of human love reconnected to divine love and the body. It is to take sexuality beyond the realm of mere moralizing into the kingdom of God-experience. Jesus would recognize this movement; it is the teaching of the "Song of Songs" in the Hebrew Bible. It is at the heart of a wisdom-based spirituality. Call it Pagan if you must. The Creator and those who claim to worship the Creator have no need to apologize for the ecstasies of creation, the re-emergence in the sacred wilderness that is ours to remember, ours to celebrate, ours to share. Those who do not dare to make the journey into their own depths or into the collective depths of the unconscious are today, as yesterday, standing on the sidelines shouting and throwing stones. But such fundamentalism has never been the religion of the future. It is a crutch for the fearful, and Gandhi warned us that a religion based on fear is no religion at all.

Part of the gift that indigenous peoples and the hunting-gathering religious genius bring to current spirituality is a profound sense of sacred ceremony. As Barbara Ehrenreich points out in her study *Dancing in the Streets,* the ancient rituals brought a "kind of spiritual merger with the group" that both healed and awakened joy. The dancing and the masks, the marking of the seasons and uniting with cosmos via the equinox and solstice, the painting of the body and the wearing of costumes inspired by the animal spirits all brought alive the human challenge and condition. It also brought defense insofar as many rituals were enacted to strengthen the hunters before they went out to risk life and limb on behalf of gathering food for the community.[16] Ritual was not just theater or piety—it was a survival mechanism. The great work of building a Stonehenge was motivated by the ancient realization of our necessary interdependence with the cycles of the cosmos. Macrocosm becomes microcosm and microcosm macrocosm in valiant rituals. While early Christianity saw itself in cosmic terms, the Christian church gradually lost that cosmic sense which indigenous ceremonies to this day still reenact and bring alive.

Speaking as a Christian who has been deeply blessed by undergoing indigenous rituals such as sweat lodges, sun dances, vision quests, and more, I know what these ceremonies bring to a psyche and a culture that is too cut off from the earth's ways and sounds.[17] The spirits of the animals are crying loudly today on behalf of mother earth with all her citizens in such peril. We need our shamans. We need our earth spirits. We need a vital exchange between those who honor the God of the Book and those who honor the God of the Book of Nature. There need be no split. Union and communion are beckoning us, and this volume is part of that invitation and calling.

A profound invitation to reconnect with Nature in our spiritual practices has everything to do with honoring the Divine Feminine. The goddess, as Marija Gimbutas reminds us, "in all her manifestations was a symbol of the unity of all life in Nature."[18] Native American religion has been called "aboriginal mother Love." Again, Wisdom, who is feminine, is speaking loudly today. Gaia is the new Christ being crucified by excessive yang forces (consider BP's recent assault on Gulf waters) of empire and corporate rape. The goddess is rising up in resistance and part of that resistance is incorporating (or re-incorporating) the Divine Feminine in all of our God talk and God action, including worship and education worthy of the name. The Divine Feminine deserves a worthy consort, however, and for that reason I believe the Sacred Masculine must also return—cleaned up and detoxicated. Only thus can we entertain again the Sacred Marriage of Divine Feminine and Sacred Masculine.[19]

It is not enough that we merely return to the past, however, to renew the relationship of self to nature and to the universe, for our understanding of the universe has altered profoundly thanks to contemporary science. As Thomas Berry puts it, "the small self of the individual reaches its completion in the Great Self of the universe," but we are not there yet. None of our religions are there yet. "To move from this abiding spatial context of personal identity to a sense of identity with an emergent universe is a transition that has, even now, not been accomplished in any comprehensive manner by any of the world's spiritual traditions."[20] Our work is cut out for us. This is why all traditions, earth-based and book-based, must work together and with science to forge an effective spiritual practice and rituals if our species is to become sustainable. Ceremonies that truly inspire and transform, that lead us from greed to community and from ravishing the planet to celebrating and healing it, are required. Can these fit into current ecclesial wine skins? I doubt it.

For this awakening to take root and for the Divine to truly become flesh again, we welcome earth-based and ancient ways of wisdom. We—that is our species—need all the help we can get.

As a person who has been received from my original Christian faith tradition by a welcoming Episcopal (Anglican) Church that offered me religious asylum when forces in Rome were hounding me, and now after sixteen years as an Episcopalian, I would like to offer a couple of observations apropos of the present volume. First, I became Episcopalian to work with young people (originally of the Planetary Mass in Sheffield, but after their sad and untimely demise exclusively in the United States) to reinvent forms of Western worship. Those forms, borrowed from rave culture, were also taken from pre-modern or indigenous, earth-based traditions for they are primarily about dance and the beat of the "urban drum" that lead us into our lower chakras. We have sponsored over ninety of these "Cosmic Masses," as we now call them, in various cities in North America from Vancouver to New York, from Houston to Boulder, from Kansas City to Portland, and especially in Oakland, California. We have learned much from this pilot project, and it is all positive—healings of a physical, religious, and psychic nature have occurred during these Masses which were appreciated not only by the young but by people of all ages. One eighteen-year-old said to me: "I have been attending raves every weekend for five years and I found here what I have been looking for: deep prayer and community and a heterogeneous community (rave is all one generation)." An eighty-four-year-old woman said to me while dancing away: "I have been waiting eighty-two years for someone to connect my love of prayer with my love of dance." We have proven that when you connect the genius of rave to a liturgical tradition, one does not need drugs to get high. Artists galore tumble out of the woodwork from VJs to DJs, from people on stilts to altar builders and rap artists. We have also learned that people of all faiths including Pagan traditions feel at home worshipping together in such a form. So I praise the Anglican Church for welcoming this connection between earth-based and liturgically based rituals. I would like to see much more of it happening.

I also praise the Episcopal Church for standing up for women priests and bishops as well as gay priests and bishops, and for fighting these battles for justice in the open and not behind closed doors.

But something else has transpired recently that should contribute to the Anglican Church taking on special leadership at this time in history. The Roman Catholic church, having abandoned so many principles of the Second Vatican Council under the past two papacies, so weighed down by the worldwide priestly pedophile scandal and above all its cover-up at the highest places of the all-boys club in the Vatican, is now purposely and deliberately raiding the Anglican Church in search of all homophobic and misogynist clergy to take them on board, married or not, into their for-men-only priesthood. What a blessing and a lightening of the load for the Anglican Church! Like a vacuum cleaner, the Vatican is sucking in all the sexist and gay-hating clerics of the Anglican Communion. A blessing indeed. And one wishes them well.

With every blessing comes responsibility, and I believe the Anglican Church should heed the lessons in this book. Now that it need not entertain sexist and homophobic clergy, and not pander to a Vatican that has turned very dark at this moment in history, it can and should turn itself with ever more vigor to the bigger issues of eco-justice, eco-spirituality, sexual mysticism along with sexual morality, and deep ecumenism shared with those earth-based traditions that were so badly treated in the past. A new relationship with indigenous and Pagan peoples is near. From this new and deeper alliance and from science whose sacred task it is to explore nature ever more deeply, much-needed wisdom can arise.

••••••

These are just a few of the reasons I rejoice at the arrival of this book.

—Matthew Fox

Introduction

......

"Divine" Babies and "Dirty" Bath Water

*Many millions throughout the ages have venerated the name of
Jesus, but few have understood him and fewer still have tried to
put into practise what he wanted to see done. His words have been
twisted and turned to mean everything, anything, and nothing.
His name has been used and abused to justify crimes, to frighten
children, and to inspire men and women to heroic foolishness. Jesus
has been more frequently honoured and worshipped for what he did
not mean than for what he did mean. The supreme irony is that
some of the things he opposed most strongly in the world of his time
were resurrected, preached, and spread more widely throughout the
world—in his name.*

—Albert Nolan[21]

Remarkably, the above words were composed by a Roman Catholic
monk of the Order of Preachers founded in 1216 by St. Dominic. The Dominicans were to become the monastic order most closely

1

associated with the infamous inquisitions of the medieval period. Yet here we see a Dominican priest expressing exactly what I've heard countless Pagans say: that the Church is often, by its beliefs and actions, in almost diametric opposition to the beliefs and actions of the one it claims to follow—Jesus of Nazareth.

This is a Jesus who, if he were here today, one could easily imagine getting in trouble for hanging out in the wrong joints and mixing with the wrong people. He might be seen turning up at a Druid Gorsedd or a New Age Festival, enjoying a pint of real ale, a spiritual discussion, and a chance to chat and make friends. I don't mean to suggest that he was a Pagan. Clearly he was not. He was a committed (if troublesome) first-century Jew, but one who had a dangerous habit of befriending those on the very edges of society, those who were often scorned and looked down upon by the religious and political elite.

However, suppose the religion Jesus was born into and challenged so powerfully was not first-century Palestinian Judaism but twenty-first-century Western Christianity, and suppose he practised the same ideology of inclusion now as then. If this were the case, could we not imagine him weeping the same tears of desolation over that institution's failure to truly share compassion? Could we not see him befriending those who'd been expelled from it or feared by it, and so threatening it that if it did not destroy him literally, it would most certainly try to do so in other ways?

$$\cdots\cdots$$

It's been fifteen years since I began my flirtation with the Pagan world, ten since I underwent a Native American–style vision quest in the New Mexican desert, and three since I became a member of a worldwide Druidic order. I was an Anglican vicar (parish minister) throughout most of it, but one whose spiritual life was on a slippery slope to disenchantment. I am still a priest but have come to the point where institutional Christianity makes very little sense. The hierarchical structures, heavy dogmatism, obsession with (perceived) sexual morality, and general sense of exclusivity have become stumbling blocks on my spiritual path. Doctrines such as original sin, blood atonement, and Christ as the one true way leave me cold, whereas walking with Druids and other Neopagans has injected a dose of pure magic into my life. I have glimpsed the world through a different set of eyes, and my whole perspective has been transformed.

For the last three years I've spoken at various Pagan gatherings, led workshops and quiet days, and had the privilege of befriending hundreds of Druids, Wiccans, and Heathens. I have never covered up the fact that I am an ordained Christian priest and, rather than being shunned or misunderstood, this has opened up deep and profound conversations. I am amazed by the amount of Pagans I meet who have a genuine respect, even love, for Jesus.

Of course, the vast majority of modern Western-world Pagans grew up within a Christian environment, and a large chunk of them were once churchgoers. I recently had the privilege of addressing a huge assembly of the Order of Bards, Ovates, and Druids at their gathering of the winter solstice at Glastonbury, England. The audience was a mixed crowd of more than two hundred Druids from various backgrounds and, because the atmosphere felt warm and hospitable, I decided to begin my session with a question; "How many of you originally came from a Christian tradition?" To my surprise well over two-thirds of the available hands shot up, and, after further enquiry with regard to specific denominations, it became clear that the majority of these ex-Christian Pagans had a Roman Catholic background. I found this fascinating and since then have had countless discussions with Pagans about Christianity and why so many of them rejected it. There are many reasons, but Jesus himself is not usually one of them. Rather it is the institutional Church that causes so much grief and disappointment. Interestingly, many told me that had the Church better reflected what they perceived to be the true spirit of Jesus, they may not have become so unhappy and disillusioned. Clearly these Pagans have a very different picture of Jesus than the one the Church usually presents.

During my discussions with ex-Christian Pagans I have discovered a number of new insights about Jesus. For some he is a wise man or teacher; for others a wizard or shaman; for still others an avatar or demigod but akin to the many mythic dying-rising deities of history. And there are those who simply do not know what to make of him anymore. They still feel an urge to have some kind of relationship with him, but do not know how to, or even whether they should.

While browsing on a Druid Internet forum recently, I came across a Pagan woman who moves back and forth in her opinion about Jesus. She's tried combining Christianity with Paganism but felt it did not work, yet still aches with feeling for this "god-man" she once gave her life to. She is a polytheistic Pagan who has been liberated from a very destructive form of Christianity and she cannot shake her connection to Jesus. She's tried to ignore him, but he always finds a way of creeping back into her psyche. In a recent email, she expressed how deeply she longs to find a way of remaining fully Pagan yet also have a place for the Jesus of her Christian past, outside of the "Churchianity" that so smothers him. It is for people like her that I offer this book. But it's not *just* for people like her. I also offer it to those who may be interested to know more of this now-metaphorically skyclad Jesus, who stands before us with all the clothes of Christendom stripped away.

· · · · ·

The book you hold is unique. It has never been done before. It is a book full of various pictures and insights about Jesus, written mainly by those who were once seen as his arch-enemies and many of whose spiritual ancestors were hanged or burned in his name. The Wiccans, Druids, and Heathens who've contributed to it will open eyes to a vision of Jesus few have ever seen before; one that is free from the unhelpful and often toxic baggage of religiosity; one that makes sense to the Pagan imagination.

By tapping into my own personal experiences and by conducting interviews with some of the most recognised names in the Neopagan world, I have uncovered a Jesus who can be a friend to all people without anyone having to join his "club." Therefore Pagans reading these words have no need to suspect an attempt at recapturing them for the Church. I have no desire to proselytize. There are no hidden agendas or ulterior motives. Rather, this is a book to enable fully Pagan folk to remain fully Pagan yet reclaim a long-lost friend, or perhaps make friends for the first time. Just as other great figures of the past like Confucius, Buddha, Socrates, and Lao Tzu, and modern gurus like Gandhi and the Dalai Lama have soul lessons for us all, so does this wisdom teacher of Galilee. And, like all those other gurus, his lessons do not require conversion in order to be embraced or learned from. Indeed to some his lessons, once understood, are more able to be authentically lived out within the modern Pagan world than Christendom.

Nevertheless I, personally, do not wish to formally renounce my own Christian ministerial orders. My ordination was quite beyond the realm of mere religious protocol. I was ordained in 1996 because I responded to a call; a call to recognise the divine light (known by Christians as "the Christ") in all, to serve that source, and to be a priest of the mysteries. I am still following that calling, but it is now leading me out from under the safety of the established ecclesiastical umbrella into the scary and unorganised open sky of raw Paganism (as well as Eastern mysticism, but that's another book!).

I do not feel the need to reject my past. I know many from that circle will consider my recent travels to be evidence of severe apostasy, and some may even demand my expulsion. And I am more than aware that a number of my new associates may also feel that an official break must be made if I am to be truly embraced by Paganism. Too bad—that won't happen. In fact, I find all such labels to be far too limiting. I simply see myself as a man who served the church as a liberal/progressive priest for ten years and who now travels in other places too. I am a priest at the edge, on the border between two worlds. I am, as my Druid friends call me, a hedgepriest!

The fact is I still love the founder of what became known as Christianity. I still love his stories, his metaphors, and his entrancing character. However I also feel liberated and (strangely) more able to truly get "under his human skin" now that I have had some space from the world of establishment Christianity. And what's more, my recent encounters have given me a whole new perspective into how he might be better understood. I have come to believe that, for my own pilgrimage, I can remain truer to the original intentions of this Galilean sage's teachings if I live within the space between these spiritual traditions, rather than within a purely Christian one.

This book is thus written for two different groups of people:

1. Pagans who still have some affection for the wandering teacher of Galilee, but who have left his Church for good (or were never part of it in the first place). Among this number are those who were told that it is incompatible to save a place for Christ on their Pagan altars, and who often ache to reconnect with him without having to reconnect to his church. I have met many such souls. Indeed my research for this book has put me in touch with ex–Roman Catholic nuns and missionaries who, while now following Druidry and Wicca, miss the long hours of devotion spent in front of their ornate church tabernacles and statues of the Sacred Heart. I wept while listening to a gay Alexandrian High Priest's tear-filled words as he told me of his deep love for the Jesus he misses so much. His story is made more painful by the fact that Jesus was wrenched out of his hands by a cruel and oppressive homophobic Church who told him he could not have it both ways. He described this forced parting as being like an involuntary divorce. If I can enable such people to reconnect with their long-lost friend and yet give up nothing of their liberating and refreshing Paganism, then I will indeed feel this work was worth all the blood, sweat, and tears.

2. Christians who are tired of the way the Church portrays its central figure and are open to new insights from a world far from their own. In fact, a large part of the source material used for the first section of this book comes from a world very close to their own, yet a world that remains largely invisible to most churchgoers—because it is too threatening.

I refer to the theological perspective known as Progressive Christianity. Progressive and liberal Christian groups are the main reason why I do not feel it necessary to remove my remaining foot from the Church world. These Christians take very seriously the work of modern biblical critical scholars and, in particular, the so-called quest for the historical Jesus—an attempt to uncover the historical man from the gospel traditions by removing apparent later theological interpretations. Pastors and preachers among them, unlike the majority of the ordained clergy, do not try to protect their congregations from what can be shell-shocking revelations but, rather, wake them up to the remarkable insights and discoveries of this work. It has been liberating and refreshing to get to know some of these brave men and women.

Of course every priest or minister who has attended a serious course of biblical and theological training will have been exposed to this scholarship, but the vast majority of those who end up in pulpits feel unable to pass it on and often end up forgetting the potentially liberating material in the process. They feel it is far safer to resort to the myth-made-facts of yesteryear instead. This is why the minority of public Christian leaders who do feel their congregations are mature enough for the truth are sadly labelled dangerous or heretical and to be avoided at all costs. I recently had the privilege of listening to Bishop John Shelby Spong who came to lecture at a church in my neighbourhood. The local press referred to him as "highly controversial" because he doubts the historicity of the virginal conception of Jesus. But as he said when he spoke, "There is not a credible biblical scholar on earth who believes it." It's not radical to doubt the virgin birth. It's old hat—*very* old hat.

I will be using many of the insights of the quest for the historical Jesus within the first part of this book because I have been astonished by how close the Jesus of my Pagan friends' imaginations corresponds to the picture emerging from this scholarly quest. I therefore hope to present a new Jesus for Pagans who would love to reconnect without ceasing to be Pagan, and for Christians who are tired of their own hierarchies protecting them.

In that sense it may build certain bridges—bridges of tolerance and respect between those who have been enemies for too long!

On that note there are also those who call themselves Christo-Pagans, folk who have already managed to somehow bridge the two worlds. An excellent book on this phenomenon is River and Joyce Higginbotham's *ChristoPaganism: An Inclusive Path.* However, like Paganism as a whole, it is impossible to adequately describe the practises and beliefs of Christo-Pagans because they are so varied. Some see themselves primarily as Pagan yet also view Christ as their patron deity, and others are primarily Christian yet employ certain Pagan practises or customs. I have encountered a number of Christian-Druids who have quite traditional beliefs about God, Jesus, and the Bible. Some have even struggled with my own progressive understanding of the Bible as myth. For this reason I felt it better to limit my interviews primarily to those who see themselves as wholly Pagan (of whatever form), not Christo-Pagan.

This book follows a three-fold pattern:

Part One begins by looking at Jesus as a human being and all the implications thereof. For this it relies largely on the work of modern biblical historians because (though nothing can be taken as one hundred percent accurate) their work is the most trustworthy and accurate available; as opposed to the mountain of Jesus books that come from romantic, conspiracy-based, speculative, or "channelled" sources. My feeling is that we need to begin on as solid ground as possible. After that we will then begin to allow ourselves into the realm of metaphor and mythology as we move from the Jesus of history to the notion of Christ. Thus the final two chapters of Part One look at the major attributes of the Christ story drawing new meaning from them, which will surprise and delight Pagan (and hopefully Christian) readers.

During my research I had the privilege of having discussions with and interviewing many respected elders of the Neopagan world. I've been astonished by their generosity and willingness to share their own personal stories and theories about Jesus. Part Two is a collection of their breathtaking essays, demonstrating that this god of the Christian Church indeed speaks, blesses, and inspires many who could never be part of his official family.

Part Three presents the results of the interviews I conducted. Through their words and insights I have discovered that the simple message of the historical Jesus is (ironically) much harder to harmonize with the modern Church world than it is with the modern Pagan world. This is precisely the message that I hope to uncover within the first section of the book and then re-present as the "Divine Baby" who was rather recklessly (yet understandably) chucked out with the dirty bath waters of Christendom.

May the journey begin.

Part One
The Naked Nazarene

☉ ✝ ☀ ∝ ✴ ✳ ☥ ✝

I see the historical Jesus a great teacher, a wise man, and a radical activist. In contrast to the person of Jesus, I understand the idea of the Christ to be the embodied God essence in us—a Christ consciousness, if you will.

—from an interview conducted
among Christo-Pagans by
Joyce and River Higginbotham

One

......

The Tri-part Jesus

He did not claim to be God; that would have blasphemed against
everything in the spiritual environment in which he lived and
taught. He called himself the Son of Man.

—Janet and Stewart Farrar [22]

Don't be shocked. We need to begin our journey with a naked Jesus, a Jesus stripped of his Christian clothing! He demands it, and when we've done so we must resist the temptation of re-clothing him with a "DaVinci Code" imagination. He requires brute honesty at this stage, not fantasy. There will be plenty of time for mythology later. All those wonderful legends about Jesus travelling to India, Egypt, or Britain are beautiful tales which can impart the deepest truths, but they are not provable history, so we must put them to one side for now.

This book must begin with facts, and as we will soon see, there are not many of which we can be certain regarding Jesus of Nazareth. However, once we have uncovered what we can and disentangled the historical man from the many layers of theological interpretation, we can then begin to do two things:

1. Get to know the man—the real person who challenged the political and religious world around him; a man who lived two thousand years ago in a Jewish backwater of the Roman Empire, and

2. Remove the negative layers of literalised mythology which have quenched the spirit of the man himself and, rather, turned him into something he never was. Then we might be better able to create a useful mythology that actually uplifts and inspires rather than burdens and cripples with guilt.

I started this project as a personal quest, an opportunity to try to understand Jesus in the light of my Pagan encounters. I wanted to push back the boundaries and ask myself, honestly, who I thought he was. But something strange has happened during the intense research. I have met not one but three different figures of Jesus. It's not that I'd never come across them before but that they were always a part of the one central personality know as *Jesus Christ*. I'm not referring to what Christians call the Holy Trinity; I'm referring to three separate religio-spiritual personalities:

1. The *human* Jesus of Nazareth

2. The *divinised* Jesus Christ of the Church (whom the scholars often refer to as the Christ of Faith)

3. The *universal* Mythic or Cosmic Christ

It was back in the days of pre-theological training that I first awoke to the shell-shocking realisation that the biblical portrait of Jesus is not historically accurate. My current research has led me even further down this path, and now I'm not only certain that parts of the New Testament are historically inaccurate but that the original Jesus and the Christ of the early Church are entirely different *personas*. Indeed they are different *categories* of person. One of them is a historical human being, and the other is an interpreted mythos. The Jesus of history may well be the historical figure *behind* the Christ of the Church, but the latter is a theologically constructed personality who began his life sometime between the middle and end of the first century CE, when Christian evangelists wrote stories and letters as a means of proclamation and teaching. The personality of this Christ of the Church then expanded and adapted over the decades until it was formally fixed in the fourth century during the period of the great ecclesiastical councils, when creeds were hammered out to combat heresy. This is who we might refer to as the Orthodox Christ.

On top of these two personas—the Jesus of history and the Christ of the Church—is the Cosmic Christ, or what I call the Mythic Christ. The term refers to the universal spark of deity manifested within all people and all things. This Cosmic Christ is not the possession of the Church. World-renowned Wiccan teachers Janet Farrar and Gavin Bone, who also speak of Three Christs, refer to the third one as the Astral Christ.

The more I discover, the more I become aware that the problem—the real stumbling block for Pagans—is not the human Jesus nor is it the Cosmic/Mythic Christ, but the Orthodox creedal Christ of the Church. And it would not have become such a problem were it not for one thing—it became a myth *literalised*. In other words, what was only ever intended to be symbolic was eventually regarded as factual.

In the early days of my priestly vocation I always pushed the boundaries, and often ended up in the ecclesiastical "dog house." I remember one particular clergy breakfast where I, the rookie, suggested that Jesus and Christ were two different aspects of the one we call God Incarnate and that they might be better understood separately. Suddenly one of the clergy shot out of his chair shouting, "Heretic! Do you think you know better than the earliest Catholic councils? Are you going to try to undo their work?" Well, heretic or not, and over a decade late, I now have the arrogance to answer that man, "Yes. I'm going to do precisely that. I'm going to split the one we know as Jesus Christ into two. For once we've temporarily separated this god-man, it will be easier to recognise what each part stands for."

I hasten to add that not all Christians see this as heretical. Indeed, some see it is a necessity. In a beautiful book called *Saving Jesus from the Church,* progressive Christian minister Robin R. Meyers suggests that the only way we can recover anything positive about Jesus is to go back to the point in history where (he believes) the Church took a wrong turn and created the Orthodox Christ. With uncompromising passion he says, "We have a sacred story that has been stolen from us, and in our time the thief is what passes for orthodoxy itself…"[23] The rest of the book re-presents the historical Jesus, stripped of his later Church-tailored garments, not as a savior to be believed in but a teacher to be learned from.

Jesus the man needs to be reclaimed, and the scholarship of the modern Jesus quest can help us do so. But Jesus the Christ also needs reclaiming as a universal mythos—something far beyond Christianity alone—something that points us to what is outside of everything and yet also strangely inside everything. This is a Pagan concept, and what really excites me is that we reach this "Pagan Christ" when the second and third personas of my "tri-part Jesus" have been merged.

Two

......

Will the Real Mr. Jesus
Please Stand Up!

Whether Christians or not, many people who have questions
about the historical Jesus can no longer accept the centuries-old
objection that historical curiosity about Jesus is shallow and irrel-
evant, that it is only the resurrected Christ that matters.

—Jacques Baldet[24]

Over the last few decades there's been an explosion of interest in the
quest for the historical Jesus. A brief Internet search will pull up
dozens of modern volumes on this project, each one from a different perspective. It's remarkable that the Church has happily attempted to follow
the one it calls the Christ for nearly two millennia yet has done so almost
entirely without the company of the historical Jesus. The quest to uncover
him only began about two centuries ago, and the vast majority of churchgoers since then have largely been protected from the results.

I remember attending a church service at the time when the infamous ex-Bishop of Durham, David Jenkins, told the press that there were no Magi who visited the infant Jesus near the time of that first Christmas. The vicar took a newspaper into the pulpit and allowed the congregation to see the headlines that decried this dreadful bishop. It was Midnight Mass and the preacher began what seemed like an attack on David Jenkins as he outlined what the liberal bishop had been trying to say. He spat the words out with theatrical venom, jabbing at the newspaper as he spoke. Finally he leaned over the pulpit and said in a booming voice, "Well now, let me tell you why he's right!" He had us riveted to our seats as he unpacked the metaphorical beauty of the New Testament legends and gave us a taste of the spiritual power of mythology. To him these were never literal stories and the Bishop of Durham had given him permission to say so. He was the only vicar I knew who took that line. The rest all poured scorn on poor old David Jenkins, a bishop who's only crime was to give the public just a little taste of what was, to anyone who'd done even a rudimentary course in basic Bible study, very old hat.

· · · · ·

The fact is that the Church has always found the *literalised* Christ more important than the Jesus of history. To biblical scholars, the man who wandered the dusty roads of first-century Palestine collecting disciples and challenging religious and political superiors is contrasted with the Christ of Faith—the incarnate God in human form, whom fourth-century creeds proclaimed to be fully God and fully man. This Christ of Faith is real in the sense that he exists inside the hearts and imaginations of millions of people, but he is not real in the sense of being a historical person. The Christ of Faith was formed as the Church gradually reflected upon the earliest memories in the context of their experiences. The Christ of Faith is an interpretation! He has many treasures, but, as that Midnight Mass vicar demonstrated, they are mythological, not literal.

The two-hundred-year-old quest has been an attempt to retrieve the Jesus who resides beneath his Christian vestments. By carefully scrutinising the ancient manuscripts of the gospels and by using advanced methods of textual analysis, these scholars have peeled away the theological and metaphorical layers that they believe were added to the very earliest sources. This work has seen three major periods of activity and is still alive and well today. The first two phases gave a great deal to the scholarly world, especially in terms of a highly useful set of criteria for discerning the historical authenticity of gospel passages. The first phase ended in the early twentieth century with the publication of Albert Schweitzer's monumental work *The Quest for the Historical Jesus.* His conclusions were, on the whole, rather depressing. Jesus was a Jewish radical who believed in the immanent end of the world and who taught an "interim ethic" which was, thus, only really relevant to those of his immediate cultural and historical context.

A few decades later, giant among twentieth-century New Testament experts Rudolf Bultman declared that the Jesus of History is irrelevant and that the Christ of Faith was the only importance to theology. He saw the quest as futile, which left other scholars feeling deeply unsatisfied. Ernst Kasemann and others felt that theology must be as least partially connected to this man of history, and they instinctively trusted that certain techniques could recover him, so the new quest was born. The most popular technique used within this phase was the so-called rule of discontinuity, where the scholars argued that for a man to stand out and be remembered he must have been at odds with his own culture. So they paid special attention to the texts and passages that portrayed Jesus in this light. However the resulting portrait of Jesus ended up totally detached from his Jewish roots and, consequently, sounded highly implausible, for how would someone so discontinuous and abnormal acquire such a following?

The most recent phase, the so-called third quest, while having the benefit of all the techniques and theories that went before has much else at its disposal; treasures that were not previously available. For example, the two great mid-twentieth-century discoveries of the Dead Sea Scrolls and the Nag Hammadi library have provided an astonishing amount of new insight into the Jewish culture of Jesus's day, and have broadened the picture of early Christianity. The Dead Sea Scrolls are a collection of about nine hundred documents that include texts from the Hebrew Bible. They are written in Hebrew, Aramaic, and Greek, and are dated from 150 BCE to 70 CE. While they don't mention Jesus in person, these scrolls have given scholars a much clearer picture of the type of Judaism that would have been his religious context. The Nag Hammadi library is a collection of just over fifty early Christian codices consisting mostly of Gnostic type texts written in Coptic, though probably translated from Greek. They have given us an enlightening glimpse into how various early Christian groups viewed Jesus—some of which hugely contrasted the orthodox traditions. They also gave us such important texts as the now famous Gospel of Thomas, a collection of Jesus's sayings a growing number of scholars regard as, in its earliest form, older than the four official Gospels of Matthew, Mark, Luke, and John.

The current quest includes scholars from right across the theological spectrum and is represented by Protestantism, Catholicism, Judaism, post-Christian thought, and the non-Theistic world. It has produced some wonderfully enticing portraits of Jesus, and, while no absolute consensus is on the horizon, there is universal agreement that the historical Jesus bears little resemblance to the early Church's Jesus, and even less to the Jesus of later Christian centuries. The actual man who lived in the first three decades of the first century CE gradually metamorphosed into the interpreted Jesus of the last three decades (when the Gospels were written) and finally climbed up onto the throne of the Orthodox Christ the Church still worships in the creeds. So when modern Christians say, "I believe in Jesus," it is this Christ of Faith they believe in, not the Jesus of history. Yet the current quest is now more optimistic that the pre-orthodox and pre-Easter Jesus is attainable. As one of the most widely respected modern Jesus experts, Marcus Borg, says, "Now scholars are more confident that we can, with a reasonable degree of probability, know something about the historical Jesus."[25]

While this book is not the place for a long and detailed analysis of the work of the quest scholars, I will give a broad and basic overview of some of the techniques and critical methods they use. For those who wish to explore this exciting field of study in more detail, please refer to the bibliography and suggestions for further study at the back of this book.

When discussing the work of the Jesus quest, it's important to remember that truth is never set in stone—it's always provisional. What this two-hundred-year project has done is not given us the absolute portrait of Jesus, but a method of reading the material about him, which is a clever filtering system. The primary material is what we know as the canonical gospels: Matthew, Mark, Luke, and (to a lesser degree) John. Incidentally, we do not know the identity of the original authors; the title names were added some time after their creation. More recently, certain scholars have been using the Gospel of Thomas as a primary source. (I will say more about Thomas and the reasons for its growing popularity later.) Archaeology is an important ingredient for understanding the historical and cultural setting of Jesus, and literature from other first-century sources is helpful, though notoriously limited and difficult in matters of proving reliability.

The scholars themselves have created their own reconstructions of Jesus—each one a little different from the others—but they have also given us tools which we can use ourselves. These tools (or rules) are referred to as "the criteria of historicity," the most central ones being the following (in a simplified form):

1. Criterion of embarrassment:

   The authors of the Gospels would not have willingly invented embarrassing incidents, such as the fleeing of Jesus's followers after his arrest[26] or the baptism of Jesus by John, thus making him seem subordinate.[27] Therefore such details would only have been included if they were true.

2. Criterion of dissimilarity:

   Following on from the reasoning detailed above, if a saying or action seems contrary or dissimilar to the views of the Judaism of Jesus's context or the ideals of the early Church, it can more confidently be regarded as authentic. On the other hand, if it is too similar it may have been added. For example, the notion of the

Divinity of Jesus was an established belief by the latter decades of the first century, so when it comes up in the Gospels it might be a theological reflection rather than remembered history.

3. Criterion of multiple attestation:

When two or more independent sources present consistent accounts, it is more likely that they are accurate reports of events or that they are reporting a tradition which pre-dates the sources themselves.

4. Criterion of coherence or historical congruency:

A source is far less credible if the account contradicts known historical facts, or if it conflicts with cultural practices common in the period in question. It has to fit the context. In other words, a '60s-era-type hippy with a benign message of love and peace to all would not have triggered the might of Rome into ordering an execution. Jesus really rocked the boat. His message was radical and dangerous.

·····

Often one of the first things to be noticed when studying gospel accounts critically is that there seems to be far too many similarities between the different authors' narratives. So many that one begins to suspect a little plagiarism. And that's precisely the word, for plagiarism was the name of the game. It's hard for twenty-first-century minds to comprehend, but back during the time period we're considering, copying and elaborating other people's work was not the taboo it is today. Indeed it was the norm. Hence, the vast majority of biblical scholars, from every theological perspective, agree on what they call "Marcan priority," that Mark's gospel was written first and the authors of Matthew and Luke copied it, using and adapting the material for their own. This is easy to spot when one sets out particular passages side by side in synopsis. In fact these three gospels are known as the synoptic Gospels—"seen together." Clearly Mark was the original because his words are often adapted and made more detailed (depending on their particular bias) by the other two.[28] On top of this, both Matthew and Luke clearly had at their disposal another source not known to Mark, for they contain nearly identical passages not found in Mark. This hypothetical source is known as "Q," the word *quelle* being German for "source."

A further problem is the distance of time between the event itself and the reporting of it. Jesus's words survived many years of oral transmission before they were gathered and formed into anything like Gospels, the earliest of which was not written until 35–40 years after his death (and we possess no originals of them). Over that period there would have been much adaptation and interpretation, which would have undoubtedly added to the final portrait. This is where the useful rule of dissimilarity can help. It would be unlikely for a writer to willingly make something up—he would be challenged over it. For example, in Luke 5:33–39 Jesus is questioned over fasting and drinking. His challengers point out that John the Baptist's disciples fast and pray whereas his eat and drink. This is quite out of character to both early Judaism and later Christianity (the former of which had strict rules in this area and the latter of which was far more aesthetic), suggesting there must be some historical truth to it.

Yet another problem to overcome is recognising author biases, and we all have them. Gospel authors were no more immune to bias than anyone else. In fact they were *especially* prone to it because their works were written for an explicit purpose—to convince other people to follow Jesus. But it's not just the writers who are biased; readers are too. One of the great problems of the quest for the historical Jesus is that, more often than not, each of its "phases" seemed to end up with a portrait of Jesus that looked very similar to the particular culture and perspectives of the scholars concerned. One of the most refreshing things about the current quest is that many of the scholars have recognised this and consequently tried as much as possible to put aside their particular biases. In fact many have even been prepared to have their own beliefs and assumptions radically altered as a result of their discoveries. The only important things are the facts of history. John Dominic Crossan, recognised by many as the preeminent of all modern Jesus scholars, is adamant that his singular intention was to reconstruct the historical Jesus with as much accuracy and honesty as possible. He states that his purpose was not motivated by any desire to find a Jesus whom he could like or dislike, agree or disagree with. He gives his readers an imaginary discussion between himself and Jesus, one which does not avoid a personal challenge to himself:

> *"I've read your book, Dominic, and it's quite good. So now you're ready to live by my vision and join me in my program?"*
> *"I don't think I have the courage, Jesus, but I did describe it quite well, didn't I, and the method was especially good, wasn't it?"*
> *"Thank you, Dominic, for not falsifying the message to suit your own incapacity. That at least is something."*
> *"Is it enough, Jesus?"*
> *"No, Dominic, it is not."* [29]

Another reason I decided to make use of so much current Christian critical scholarship for the first part of this book is that I wanted to introduce Pagans to something that many Christians have not even encountered, and if they did would probably find disconcerting. The few Christian groups that do value and use this material have consequently started to remodel their view of Jesus as well as their general theology. For example, there are now thousands of progressive and liberal Christians who do not feel they have to believe in a *literal* dual-nature Jesus of the creeds. There are those who are much more likely to see Jesus as a human teacher who points to the divine presence (Cosmic Christ) within all, than the Incarnate Son of God who was offered as a perfect sacrifice for sins. There are also many who see terms like the Incarnation as a metaphor. I will develop some of these insights in a later chapter. But first let's imagine a two-hundred-year-long archaeological dig, set not in some great desert or ancient ruins, but inside the walls of a research library. The metaphorical chisels and trowels have been momentarily placed to one side and, as the symbolic dust begins to settle, a figure gradually emerges. So what's he like, this de-Christened Jesus?

As I've said, there is no consensus, but there are some common agreements. In a nutshell, this is the sort of man we're talking about:

······

Jesus was a Galilean Jew, born most likely in Nazareth or the lesser-known *Galilean* Bethlehem, which was very close to Nazareth, unlike Judean Bethlehem, which is a few miles from Jerusalem.[30] He lived in the early part of the first century CE and was deeply connected to his own culture, seeing his mission as totally inseparable from it. In other words he did not envisage a new religion of Christianity, but wanted to extend the God-experience to those of his own culture and religion who were marginalised or somehow "outside the box." In this sense he was an anti-temple Jewish radical.

He did not preach himself as "the answer" but pointed to the "Kingdom of God" which many scholars now see not as a *coming* Kingdom, but as a Kingdom that is already present—even within us. It is a Kingdom of equality and openness.

In contrast to the periods of severe aestheticism and self-mortification within the Church, the historical Jesus shows signs of being very human and worldly, more interested in feasting than fasting, and knocking about with various misfits and outcasts whom regular society shuns. Jesus was a political reformer and a rebel against any form of inequality, be it from Jerusalem or Rome.

John the Baptist was a man of tremendous importance with regard to the formation of Jesus's own ministry. He was possibly originally one of John's followers.[31] Whether Jesus recognized his own messianic status is open to debate, but it is most unlikely that he saw himself as uniquely divine. If Jesus were somehow able to leap ahead to the council of Nicaea and heard himself being talked about as "fully God and fully man," he would have no idea what they were going on about.

Jesus was clearly some sort of holy man, healer, miracle maker, exorcist—whatever that all meant. Even non-Christian contemporary sources (like Josephus, a Romanised Jewish historian) agree with this,[32] and those who despise him do not charge him with being a fraud but able to achieve his miracles by the power of evil forces (witchcraft).[33]

Jesus was abandoned at his arrest, and only a few women remained there for him. His family seem to be suspicious of him and may have even thought he was mad. He was executed under Pontius Pilate, governor of Judea.

Three

......

The Naked Jesus

[T]he Gospels are the church's memories of the historical Jesus transformed by the community's experiences and reflection on the decades after Easter. They therefore tell us what these early Christian communities had come to believe about Jesus by the last third of the first century. They are not, first and foremost, reports of the ministry itself.

—Marcus Borg[34]

Once recovered, the pre-Christian historical Jesus begins to take on a powerful new significance, one that will greatly interest many within the modern Pagan world. In my experience, a large percentage of Pagans have huge problems with Jesus's divinity when it is spoken of *in an exclusive way*, even though they are intensely aware of the realm of spirit and deity. They are generally more than happy to see him as a person who was in some sense powerfully aware of and open to the divine, but this is quite different from the suggestion that he was uniquely divine in a way that the rest of the human world is not.

With the discoveries of the modern Jesus quest as a source, I will now put a little more flesh on the bones of my previous sketch.

Jesus the Spirit Person

There is almost universal scholarly agreement that Jesus was regarded as some sort of holy man who could heal and work miracles. In fact, however one understands them, some of the descriptions of his healing miracles pass all the tests of historical authenticity. As Jacques Baldet says, "The application of historical criteria can at times yield startling results. The most surprising for our present subject is that one of the most solidly established traditions speaks of 'miraculous' healings. This stands on more solid historical ground than other notable and often well-accepted traditions about Jesus's life, such as his working as a carpenter…"[35] Clearly something was going on with Jesus that was understood as stemming from a divine source. It appears that Jesus was recognised as being some sort of channel for the spirit. It might be a surprise to hear Jesus being referred to as a shaman or spirit person, but these are precisely some of the terms various modern scholars have been using for him. A giant among these is Marcus Borg.

Borg has given the Jesus quest some of the most widely respected books over the last couple of decades. His *Meeting Jesus for the First Time* became a bestseller and remains the biggest-selling modern book on the subject of the historical Jesus. Borg sees Jesus as a man infused directly by a divine or spiritual experience. He uses the term "spirit person" rather than the older equivalent "holy man" because not only does "person" make the concept non-gender-specific, but "spirit" rather than "holy" takes away any possible pious or sanctimonious connotations. One can't overemphasize how important Borg sees this aspect of Jesus's character. It is primary to everything else about him. In fact being a spirit person is not simply part of his character. It *is* his character. This is the starting point. Nothing else makes sense without it.

I find this especially convincing from personal experience. The religious leaders and teachers I've met whose beliefs seem authentic, alive, and relevant have themselves been touched by a deeply personal spiritual experience. They are not usually bound by religiosity or rules. They tend to come across as open, free, and humble. They do not see their way as the "right" way and all others as "wrong." They walk their talk. It's as if they become vessels for the flow of spirit that moves through them.

On the other hand, the religious leaders I've met who seem to think that the rules must be followed at any cost and come across as rather cold or lacking in compassion have usually not had such deeply transformative spiritual encounters, or if they have they were a thing of the past. Surprisingly, they are usually frightened of such experiences and their religion keeps them safely immune to them. They have to be in control and thus end up trying to control others too. This is one of the reasons why I have generally found the Pagan world a far easier place within which to explore spiritual things than mainstream Christianity. Granted, one does hear of certain "control freaks" that run some of the more closed Pagan groups, but the vast majority are unhappy with any form of strict hierarchy and are genuinely open to spirit wherever it comes from. There is an enormous difference between religious/pious people and spiritually aware/soulful people. Indeed one might suggest they are polar opposites. It's interesting that, for Jesus, the greatest obstacles always came from the religious law-abiders rather than those "at the edge."

Jesus's spiritual (divine) awareness was foundational to everything else. It meant that he saw the world through spirit-eyes or God-sight. Borg recognises that spirit persons are a cross-cultural phenomenon, showing up all over the world and experiencing this spirit dimension in a variety of ways. Some have visions, moments of seeing into other layers of reality; some seem to be able to journey into that other layer of reality—shamans; some sense that other reality coming upon them—being filled with the spirit; and some have momentary glimpses of a totally transfigured world—as if the other later rises to the surface and shines through. While exercising caution with regard to how he interprets what's going on within these experiences, Borg states that they *are* real. They are transformative experiences and bring with them a deep sense of *knowing*. "Spirit persons," he says, "are people who experience the sacred frequently and vividly…Sometimes they speak the word or will of God. Sometimes they mediate the power of God in the form of healings and/or exorcisms. Sometimes they function as game finders or rainmakers in hunting-and-gathering and early agricultural societies. Sometimes they become charismatic warriors or military leaders."[36]

Spirit people are still common throughout the world and were common in ancient Judaism. One only has to open the Old Testament at almost any point, and tales of those who (it is claimed) heard the voice of God, saw visions, performed miracles, and were somehow seen to be very close to their God are discovered.[37] This does not prove that these people could do all that was claimed, but it does prove that such people were believed to have existed. Historical records outside of the biblical materials also attest to there being some very powerful spirit people around near the time of Jesus.[38]

With all this in mind, Borg feels safely entitled to attribute the term "spirit person" to the historical Jesus—a term *very close* to that of "shaman."This alone has huge implications for Christian-Pagan dialogue, and it opens up new doorways of possibility for both groups. The idea that Jesus—the real, historical Jesus—was some sort of open shamanic vessel for the divine suddenly paints a very different portrait to the orthodox God-Incarnate of Christ. It becomes more credible and also makes Jesus far more accessible and, dare I say, relevant. It gives us a Jesus whom people do not have to believe in as the only way to heaven, but follow and learn from, so that they too might become shamanic vessels of the spirit.

Jesus as spirit person makes him one of us again, a fully human person, and yet it also makes him something of a mirror—a reflection—so that when we look at what he was able to make real in his life we see what can be real in our own experience. This is something over which both liberal-minded Christians and Pagans could quite easily agree, without either one having to step a single foot in the other's theological direction.

Another exciting quest scholar who portrays Jesus in a quasi-shamanic light is Bruce Chilton, who in *Rabbi Jesus* presents Jesus as Jewish mystic who devoted much time to contemplation and experiences of mystical communion. Chilton is an expert of languages of the ancient Near East and an authority on first-century Judaism. He explores the ancient esoteric practice of Merkabah (Chariot) mysticism (a discipline which is an ancestor of the Kabalah) and, with a mixture of historical reflection and intelligent guesses, suggests that Jesus practiced it. While Chilton's Jesus is a thoroughly orthodox Jew who sees his mission as entirely to his own people, his terminology has a very magical ring to it, something that will excite the Pagan imagination. For example, with regard to Jesus's first healing miracle, he says, "Jesus had spoken as a *chasid,* a rabbi who was able to dispense the mercy of God, and his words had resounded in heaven, unleashing a compassion greater than the paralysis."A paragraph later he says this about the Chasidim: "These rabbis cured sickness and relieved drought through prayer: that was the mark of divine compassion working through them. *Chasidim* were ancient Judaism's shamans, faith healers, witch doctors, and sorcerers. In one bold move, Jesus had joined their ranks. He had proved that he was anointed with the Holy Spirit: he was able to channel the energy of God."[39] (p.109)

Before moving on, what follows is a wonderful quotation from a man who served Jesus as an Episcopal (Anglican) priest before finding himself being drawn towards and then immersing himself within modern shamanism. In his book *Soul on Fire,* Peter Calhoun explains that he had to leave the Church in order to properly discover the true spiritual richness within. He now serves his Great Spirit as a shaman, and one who has come to know his old friend Jesus in a deeper way as a shaman than as an Episcopal priest. "A little more than three decades ago I began experiencing a spontaneous awakening of spiritual or paranormal abilities that I had always believed, if they actually existed, were exclusively reserved for native shamans or Eastern mystics. As a parish priest, in the Episcopal Church, I was no way prepared for what was happening to me. In fact, these bizarre changes had an unsettling effect on me, and I wondered if I were losing my grip on reality."[40] This was the stirring of his inner shamanic spirit and, as so many folk discover, he had to leave the confines of a religious institution to follow this inner calling. Within the shamanic tradition he was eventually able to make sense of, and use of, the strange spiritual stirrings within. He sees them as exactly the same as what Jesus was used to: "I discovered that many of these abilities that Christ said were inherent in each of us have always been recognised and described in story and myth and demonstrated by the holy men and holy women of various tribal traditions."[41]

Compassion and the Motherly God

The deep God-awareness of Jesus was tangibly expressed in an ever flowing stream of what Robin Meyers calls "pure, unbridled, reckless compassion."[42] Scholars hold that one of the most authentic Jesus sayings is "be compassionate as God is compassionate" (Luke 6:36). Jesus's experience of the compassion of God flowed outward, and when we look more carefully at this aspect of his character we see not only a man who saw his fellow humans in a remarkably different light to that of the general religious culture, but also see his God in a very original (and exciting) way to how we might imagine. Compassion means "to feel with." A similar term and one that in English Bible translations is often used in place of compassion, is "mercy." However, "mercy" implies a level of superiority that does not exist within compassion. Mercy also suggests that the person requiring it has done something wrong. "Compassion" has a very different resonance.

Etymological expert Phyllis Trible gives a marvellous insight into the Hebrew word for compassion. The root word *rchm* means "to have compassion." The noun is *racham* and its plural, *rachamim,* means "compassion" and the noun *rechem* is translated as "womb." The bodily organ of the woman, the womb, is thus associated with the act of compassion, evoking a profound female image. *Rachamim* could therefore be translated as womb-like compassion or even womb-love. It portrays the love of a mother for the child of her womb. It implies a range of feelings including goodness, tenderness, patience, and understanding. It expresses the tenderness of God's feminine love.[43]

The kind of God Jesus experiences is one who feels as a mother feels. There is a beautiful tenderness in how Jesus views the divine. Indeed even when he uses the more usual male pronouns for God he often does so in a very intimate way, which is quite counter-cultural. He refers to God as "father" using the Aramaic term *abba*, which is closer to the term "papa" or even "daddy." This was brought home to me when I visited Israel and overheard a little boy calling out to his father, "Abba, Abba." One could therefore argue that, for Jesus, God was both divine father and divine mother. Not only that, but God is a father and mother who feels, who oozes womb-like compassion. Many stories told about Jesus speak of God as having compassion or being moved by compassion. The feeling of compassion leads to an expression of compassion. To be compassionate is to feel for somebody as deeply as a mother feels for the child in her womb.

The discovery that Jesus used feminine imagery for the divine comes as a delightful surprise for Pagans and is yet another possible doorway for Pagan/Christian dialogue. Of course it does not necessarily follow that feminine deities ooze compassion and motherly warmth. Indeed I know more than a few Pagans who find any notion of goddesses or gods who love us (or even care at all about us) to be a totally alien concept. The gods are simply forces of nature personified and therefore will kill just as easily as bless. And in reality this is a perfectly reasonable conclusion. However, there are also many Pagans who feel some sense of underlying compassion or love when it comes to deity. This book is not an attempt to harmonise various Pagan beliefs, nor is it an attempt to qualify them. It is simply my desire to demonstrate how Jesus and his teachings can be complimentary to various forms of Paganism rather than antagonistic. A beautiful example of a world-respected Wiccan author writing on the notion of the loving nature of the dual-gender divine is from Scott Cunningham's best-seller *Wicca: A Guide for the Solitary Practitioner.* He says, "Wicca, in common with many other religions, recognizes deity as dual. It reveres both the Goddess and the God. They are equal, warm, and loving, not distant or resident in 'heaven,' but omnipresent throughout the universe."[44] Another lovely example comes from the excellent *Pagans & Christians: The Personal Spiritual Experience,* by Gus DiZerega, who describes an experience of suddenly feeling himself being immersed in a sea of perfect and limitless divine love: "There is no greater nor more perfect love than that from the Ultimate."[45] He also uses a term that I have heard many of the more progressive Christian teachers use when referring to Jesus's notion of God's love: "The experience [of divine love] encompasses complete understanding and unconditional acceptance, neither of which are purely human capacities." And, "Because divine love is unconditional, each being would be treasured and cherished, regardless of whether that love was returned."[46] This language of the unconditional love of God/dess is in perfect harmony with what countless progressive and liberal Christians see as a major teaching of Jesus and symbolised within the notion of the Christ. Bible scholar and Chair of the Progressive Christianity Network Britain, Rev. John Churcher talks of Jesus as someone who experienced "Perfect and Compassionate Love" within himself and whose mission was to awaken that divine source in others: "We have [within us] the sleeping giant of Perfect Unconditional Love waiting to be recognised, responded to and lived by us all."[47] With words that would sit very comfortably with many Pagans, Churcher refers to what Christians have commonly called the Incarnation (the becoming human of God in Jesus) in a wonderfully symbolic and non-exclusive way: "Evangelical Christians often proclaim that there is a 'God-shaped void in the heart of every human' and that only Jesus can fill this void. Surely there can be nothing further from the truth? Within each and every person, regardless of creed or religious experience, there is the Presence (not the void) of the Sacred. Even though this Presence of Perfect and Compassionate Love many not be recognized, it is the true spiritual Incarnation. It happened to Jesus, and it has happened to you and me. All the power of Perfect Love is incarnated within all people, for all are temples of the Spirit that is God. In my opinion, what was so special about Jesus was his living awareness of the Sacred Spirit within him."[48]

The compassionate and motherly image of deity is of course in huge contrast to the wrathful—and rather toxic—God images of certain Old Testament passages, as well as much of later Christian tradition (both Catholic and Protestant). The Jesus quest has shown quite clearly that the earliest and most original strands of the Jesus tradition portray a Jesus movement that had radically distanced itself away from God as apocalyptic judge to a gospel of healing and forgiveness. Jesus wandered the dusty streets, healing and exorcising the suffering peasants he met on his way. And he did not do so for any other reason that this: his life was an expression of compassion. He wanted to bring people back to themselves. He wanted to restore people to their rightful place as beloved by God. He wanted the ones who felt unloved and worthless to feel cherished. He cut across the orthodoxy of his day and refused to allow himself to perpetuate their manmade barriers. He was an astonishingly brave healer of religion-damaged souls. We are only now beginning to realise that the religion which now claims to own him as God is equally in need of his iconoclastic spirit.

Robin Meyers puts it like this: "Orthodoxy's front door is gilded, but the rusty back door of the early church remains ajar—the one leading to the kitchen behind the creedal looking glass. There sits Jesus, cross-legged, amid the steam and misery of the world … His message is non-judgmental presence. Without saying a word, the crowd gets it: we all matter; no exceptions."[49]

Iconoclast and Counter-Cultural Wisdom Teacher

The deep God-awareness that oozed out of Jesus in the form of motherly compassion and affected the way he viewed the world around him, also forced him to try to correct it in a more anarchistic manner. While, on the one hand, the most recent phase of the Jesus quest has rightly re-Judaised Jesus, it has also revealed a Jesus who was highly critical of the religious and political systems of his day. He was a reformer and an iconoclast, and it was this that cost him his life: " … unlike the claims of orthodoxy, Jesus did not come to die, rendering his life and teaching secondary. He died *because* of his life and teachings. He was killed *for* the things he said and did."[50]

Clearly Jesus sided with the oppressed, the downtrodden, those outside the box. He turned things on their head and accused those who were outwardly good of hypocrisy, while wrapping the so-called sinful and impure up in a robe of unconditional acceptance.

We know from modern therapeutic spiritual communities like Alcoholics Anonymous that unconditional acceptance contains a deeply healing and transformative quality. It enables real growth and change for the better, whereas forced attempts at holiness simply create very ugly self-righteousness. As Meyers says, "Reversing the categories of pure and impure, Jesus lifted up women (impure), leaven (also impure), and children (neither pure nor impure, just invisible). Most disturbing of all, he ate with outcasts, criminals, and prostitutes, proving that if we are known by the company we keep, then it is no wonder they called him a drunkard and a glutton."[51]

This is a Jesus who is far from that pious image we often have of a pure and holy do-gooder. This Jesus got his hands dirty. This Jesus loved real people and seemed to find the most "upright" to be a real pain in the arse. His lessons, paraphrased for the twenty-first century, might be along the lines of the following:

> *Be who you are, accept who you are, love who you are, and know*
> *that what you are is from a divine source. So do not attempt to con-*
> *vert to an alien religious perspective. Be what you are, and reclaim*
> *the deepest truth of your own tradition.*

I don't think it's overstating it to say that Jesus *hated* religious superiority and hypocrisy. He hated it because he saw where it led; he had firsthand experience of what such unbending religiosity did to people. It resulted in a system that totally contradicted his passion for a kingdom based on compassion. The warfare between Jesus and the so-called Pharisees was a war between compassion and their rigid purity codes and ideals of holiness. The strict laws and codes inevitably left many people outside of their own religion (God), and Jesus despised it. Indeed he tackled it head-on and often in a deliberately provocative way. For example, he chose the sacrosanct Sabbath as an issue over which to fight. He didn't have to but he chose to heal on the Sabbath, thus making an issue over it. Also the sharing of meals with those he should not eat with clearly demonstrates how compassion was more important to Jesus than religious obedience to purity codes.[52] This all made Jesus different from all other contemporary or preceding prophets.

·······

Through the new eyes given to us by the quest, the Jesus we are left with is one in whom we do not have to believe in for salvation, but listen to for wisdom. This is a figure more Buddha-like than God-like. He is human like you and I, yet filled with personal and divine awareness that overflows and affects those who meet him, putting them in contact with the same spiritual flow. In that sense he is a son of God—because he mirrors back to us our own naturally divine status.

Though Jesus—or to use his Aramaic name, Yeshua—was a proud Jew, much of his teaching and many of his practises were distinctly alternative to his own first-century Jewish culture. And the more I look at the ethos and actions that got him in trouble, the more they seem also to conflict with much of modern-day Christianity.

One of the most obvious ways Jesus blatantly ignored the religious customs of his day was by the company he kept. The three synoptic Gospels suggest that Jesus spent a large part of his time (perhaps because he had a natural fondness for them) with the "people of the earth," the peasants of rural Galilee.[53] As in most cultures, these peasants or country folk were looked down upon as inferior by the more urban and educated parts of the population. But even within this group, Jesus still seemed to single out for special attention the lowliest, most marginalised—often the so-called sinners, poor, and lame. These people had been shut out of society due to ritual impurity. By socialising with them, Jesus was contaminating himself in the eyes of the religious establishment.

Earlier in this chapter we saw that Jesus's motivation for this religious rule breaking came not out of some recklessly anarchic game but from a spirit-drenched soul and a heart full of divine compassion. He knew in his deepest self that all people were equal, worthy, and valuable, and he would not sit back and see them suffer in the misery of what felt to them like divine abandonment.

According to many scholars, Jesus probably began his own vocation as a member of John the Baptist's community with a John-like mission to warn of an approaching disaster. John's goal was to encourage people to undergo a baptism of repentance as preparation for judgement but, over time, Jesus's own ministry clearly modified and adapted this until it took on its own very distinct ethos and expression. Jesus, though John the Baptist's "successor," did not himself baptise, nor did he remain out in the desert pursuing some aesthetic life of denial. Rather, he left the wilderness and plugged himself back into the life of villages, towns, and cities, where he would befriend the disenfranchised, bringing the God experience to them directly. He turned his attention to the poor, the blind, the lame, the crippled, the lepers, the hungry, the sad, the persecuted, the downtrodden, the captives, the overburdened, the rabble, the law breakers, the crowds, the little ones, the least, the last, and the lost sheep of the house of Israel. Clearly Jesus saw his primary mission field as that unmistakable section of society, those on the margins, the unaccepted ones and the oppressed. As a Jewish religious preacher/teacher, this was astonishing behaviour, and many would have considered it suicidal in terms of an attempt to be granted any respect from the establishment. But Jesus didn't want respect. Jesus's heart was not concerned with propping up the establishment or being seen doing the right thing. His heart was motivated by love—love of God and love of fellow men and women made in the divine image. They were seen as sinners and thus outside the institution. Jesus, by embracing them, brought the divine-experience (which was the "possession" of the Temple and its official priesthood) directly into their lives, but the cost was enormous.

John the Baptist preached to these "sinners," other prophets tried to exorcise evil spirits from them, but Jesus *identified* with them. He deliberately mixed socially with beggars and prostitutes. He frequented their world, eating and drinking with them, thus breaking one of the biggest cultural taboos of all—table fellowship, the strict conventions of which people broke at their own peril. Ritual purity (which was at the heart of all such conventions) was symbolic of the purity of the relationship between God and his chosen people. Yet Jesus put human emotional and psychological needs on a higher level of importance than ritual purity. This was nothing short of blasphemous, but what treasure it imparted to these despised ones.

As Albert Nolan says, "The scandal Jesus caused in that society by mixing socially with sinners can hardly be imagined by most people in the modern world today. It meant that he accepted them and approved of them and that he actually wanted to be 'a *friend* of tax collectors and sinners' (Mt 11:19). The effect on the poor and the oppressed themselves was miraculous."[54] To these outcasts ("sinners") the fact that they were embraced and brought into a situation they were usually denied, gave them the experience of what some have called redemption—the healing of their own feeling of being unworthy and out of favour with God.

In first-century Palestine, sins were seen as debts owed to God—debts that had either been incurred because of law breaking (working on a Sabbath, etc.,) or contamination due to breaking of the purity codes (handling a corpse, perhaps). There were also those who'd been born into a state of permanent "impurity" (the lame, the lepers, the illegitimate). Their "sin" was viewed as having been passed down the family tree, so their "punishment" was not for anything they'd done personally but was their ancestors' unwanted inheritance to them. There was no way out of it, and it made for a highly toxic notion of God and religion. There were, of course, some "sinners" who were not in a permanent state of sin and who, if they went through the right set of procedures, could be forgiven and made clean, but they'd need to have the means to acquire it—class status and/or wealth.

Jesus sat down with these outcasts and brought them senses of being valued and made whole again. He often declared forgiveness over them even though he really had no place to do so. By doing this, he was not just at risk of "polluting" himself but putting himself in great physical danger. However, his compassion overrode any possible concerns about self-protection. The sense of liberation that must have been generated within those he befriended would have been life changing—nothing short of a de-toxification of a highly damaging God image. As a result, he himself became an enormous threat to the system itself.

This is an area where Jesus not only contradicts his own religious culture (by declaring people forgiven without them going through the usual temple-based mechanisms) but he also contradicts much of later Christian practise. When we look at Jesus in relation to the healing gift of forgiveness, it's crucially important we remember that later notions of substitutionary atonement or confession followed by a penance had not yet been invented. Jesus did not "forgive" people after they'd confessed their sins to a priest and pleaded the sacrificial benefits of his atoning blood sacrifice. He declared the forgiveness that was already theirs. With regard to the story of Jesus declaring the forgiveness of the "sinful woman" who washed Jesus's feet, Nolan says, "Jesus's faith in God's unconditional forgiveness had awakened the same faith in her."[55]

One of the most familiar stories that Jesus told (and which scholars generally believe goes back to the historical man himself) is the parable of the prodigal son. I call it the tale of two lost sons because it is about two brothers, each one failing to understand their father's unconditional love, though the more reckless one (the sinner) comes to discover and experience it in the end. This story is a pre-Christian, pre-atonement theology, a masterpiece of spiritual wisdom. This is not the place to do a complete text-by-text exposition or analysis; suffice it to say that the "God" in this parable (represented by the father) requires absolutely nothing from either of the two lost sons. What is his is theirs, and they can choose to be part of it or not. The son who insults his father by taking all his inheritance and blowing it on crap, only to return after losing everything and ending up feeling sorry for himself, is not punished or cursed or asked for any kind of penance or atoning sacrifice. He is simply loved, which brings him into a new sense of being. This ties in once more with Gus DiZerega's Wiccan view of the divine: "Because divine love is unconditional, each being would be treasured and cherished, regardless of whether that love was returned."[56]

This is the emotional/psychological effect Jesus had on people. He changed their lives—literally. They were brought into being again by his unconditional acceptance within a culture of punishments and rewards. Whether he knew the psychological implications of this or not, the effects were liberating. What he achieved in bringing a sense of forgiveness to these hurting people was deep inner healing, perhaps manifested in literal bodily cures. Scholars are divided as to whether his healings were physical as well as emotional/psychological, but they all agree on the fact that he enabled people to be brought back into an experience of wholeness they had not tasted for many years or perhaps ever. What we are really talking about here is, of course, self-forgiveness. By cutting across the conventions and rules of his day and bringing an actual experience of unearned and unconditional acceptance and forgiveness, Jesus brought these people back into a relationship with their God, their communities, and themselves. The important thing to remember is that he did not ask them to jump any hurdles or do anything religious at all. He did not give them something they did not already possess. He simply uncovered for them what was already there—oneness between them and the divine. *In other words, he used the language of religion "your sins are forgiven" to make redundant all such language.*

It was as if this man was so in touch with his own sense of being unconditionally accepted by the Divine that he was able to mingle with the broken and enable them to sparkle with their own god-light. And here, once again, we have a message that rings loud bells with the Pagan world. Self-forgiveness is a very close concept to that of self-awareness/self-knowledge (know thyself). We do not hear of rituals of repentance or requests to deity for forgiveness within Pagan circles. They take for granted the fact that there isn't and never has been any separation between the divine and the human. Jesus, from within a strictly religious culture, used the language and customs of that culture to say the same thing as modern Pagans—"friends, brothers, sisters, there is no separation between you and the divine." The following quote is from a book by a Roman Catholic priest who now co-leads an eclectic spiritual community which draws on Christian, Hindu, and Celtic wisdom. His name is Fr. Sean O'Laoire, and this is what he has to say about divine forgiveness. It is both provocative and strangely illuminating and, once again, touches that sacred space between the two traditions of Christianity and Paganism. Though he doesn't actually say that this is what Jesus believed about God and forgiveness, he does imply it. His vision of Jesus is very much that of an eastern wise man/ guru, not the dualistic heaven vs. earth Jesus of Christendom. It is a long passage but well worth quoting in full:

God is the only "person" in the universe, to use an anthropo-morphic term, who can't forgive and doesn't forgive. Because in order to forgive, He first has to hold a grudge against me and then subsequently let go of it. And since God, as the ineffable ground of being is totally incapable of holding a grudge, God is the only person who can't forgive. Forgiveness comes from inside each other.

It is very interesting to me that at the end of the Jewish year, before the book is closed, there is a ceremony called Kol Nidre. Kol Nidre is people acknowledging their misalignment, but none of it is about offending God. There is not a single statement in that entire liturgy about offending God. It's all about offending each other because you can't offend God. You can offend someone else, but you can't offend the transcendent, ineffable ground of our being. Forgiveness is never a question of asking God's pardon for having upset Her. Forgiveness is always coming to the realization that all sin is about failure to grow and that failure to grow affects my relationships, affects my culture and affects my world. And therefore those of whom I need to ask forgiveness are my brothers and sisters. All forgiveness is about the acknowledgement of the misalignment I've created between my essence and myself, and between myself and other selves; but I can't really be misaligned from the ultimate ground of my being."[57]

Apart from the so-called "sinners" and other untouchables mentioned above, another two groups that were treated as either inferior or invisible in Jesus's culture were women and children, yet he broke convention there too. First-century Palestinian women were regarded as valueless and the property of their father or husband, yet Jesus allowed women personal and intimate contact with him[58] and some women were numbered among his disciples.[59] Nolan puts it like this: "Jesus stood out amongst his contemporaries (and most of his subsequent followers) as someone who gave women exactly the same value and dignity as men."[60] Children were looked down upon as totally insignificant, yet Jesus takes a little child and places her in the centre of a crowd, pointing to her as the image of the kingdom of God.

But there was one group to whom Jesus showed astonishing acceptance which broke every conceivable boundary, the enemies—non-Jews, Samaritans, Romans, Gentiles, *Pagans*. Perhaps the most counter-cultural statement of all Jesus's radical teachings was "love your enemies." It seems to suggest (as do plenty of his actions) that Jesus, himself a Jew, was prepared to at least question one of the most foundational aspects of his own cultural faith—that of chosen-ness. Many scholars agree that his ministry was primarily or wholly directed towards the "lost sheep of the house of Israel," in other words, to his own Jewish people. Yet he also contradicted this time and time again by pointing to the complete outsider and using them as an example of true faith. For example, the well-known Parable of the Good Samaritan's clear message was that the true practitioner of neighbourliness came not from the religious establishment. Neither was he even a member of the pure Jewish community, but a despised and sub-Jewish Samaritan.[61] There is also the account of a Pagan Roman centurion who sends a message to Jesus asking that his slave be healed. Jesus responds and commends the man for his display of true faith.[62] And there is the highly uncomfortable passage of when Jesus was confronted by a Gentile woman, whom he refers to as a "gentile dog." She persists and Jesus helps her.[63]

Perhaps his attitude modified over time as he stumbled across more and more who did not fit inside the "chosen" box, and yet who impressed him with their faith and humanity. There are certainly many gospel passages suggesting that Jesus's God did not seem to be interested in favourites anymore. In fact, if anything this God was more likely to be experienced within the lives of those outside the box, outside the chosen-ness and favouritism of the system.

While I was working on this particular section of the book, I had an experience I felt necessary to write about and add, for it enabled me to come to a deeper insight about that which I was trying to express. I often find that my morning walks in the countryside open me to the oft locked-up inner voice of the spirit within. It is as if the clutter and background noise of the head and mind are somehow quietened when one is embraced by nature, and the desk, PC, and phone are a long ways off. Occasionally I jot down my experiences. This was one of them:

> *I'm standing on the brow of a small hill. I'm beginning to find these daily morning walks invaluable. I talk to the divine constantly, which often turns into dialogue. It's as if the deepest inner "God-voice" (Self) somehow awakens when I'm free from the constraints of home, office, or other pressures. The voices of nature—the crows call, the wind through the trees, the cows in the distance—seem to speak to a place within my soul that triggers what some may call innate wisdom. We all have this. We all do it. We just don't usually notice.*
>
> *This morning I know I will learn something new—something profound. Here I stand, open to nature in all her glory, at peace with God/dess and self. I start thinking about Jesus, which is probably triggered by the "orthodoxy test" I'm preparing for where I'll have to answer doctrinal questions about the nature of Jesus Christ.*
>
> *As I stand here, I hear myself saying that Jesus is indeed still something of a powerful gateway to the God experience. For me he breaks down barriers that I have set up in my own head between myself and the divine. Ironically, many of those barriers were erected*

in and through the world of Christianity, the religion that attempts to follow him. He always was an iconoclast, fearlessly tackling anything that was set up to obstruct or deny people's God-given right to know the divine. The religious institution of his day was very good at doing precisely that, as is the religious institution of our day.

Often when I stand here I can hear the "sanctus bell" of the church I used to pastor. In many ways it triggers nostalgia, yet it is also a metaphorical sign of something different, a necessary change in my own spiritual understanding and growth. This experience of being here and hearing that sound somehow symbolizes the two approaches to the divine. Here I stand, a free spirit, out in God/dess country, outside the box, nothing between deity and me. And my good friend Jesus is here too, for neither can he be boxed up. And there, down in the town, the bell speaks of a God who descends into bread and wine... and who is then (a little later) boxed up inside a wall tabernacle. The folk who are meeting their deity there are genuinely meeting him, but it's inside a structure that I often feel constricts, protects, and confines. I'm happier, by far, out here on the hill.

I still love the Mass when I occasionally go and hope, some day, to celebrate it myself again but it has become a sacrament of exclusivity and boxed up-ness rather than one of unity and opening out.

This is the difference between the wilderness God and the God of the Temple. Which did Jesus point to? Possibly both, but he most certainly did not wish the temple structures to get in the way for people.

I still love Jesus. I love him as a special friend who lives within my heart (through what we call Christos) not as the ONLY way to God or the sole door to heaven, but as someone who challenged ALL so-called only doors to heaven. He is for me a gateway to divine experience because of his challenges to religion and his beautiful pointers to deity. He reminds me that God is within, that Grace is God's way, that unconditional acceptance is the name of the game. He reminds me that all such attempts to bargain, buy, or earn one's way into heaven are futile. Why? Because we are already there.

Jesus often used the phrase "the Kingdom of God." For me this is his term for a spiritual experience of overcoming all such separationist doctrines and dogmas, where everyone is held by divine love and where there are no inequalities based on class, gender, background, or status. As Rex Weyler says in his book on Jesus's authentic sayings, "Jesus taught that unadorned, unconditional compassion is the kingdom made manifest."[64]

Many modern quest scholars have broken tradition with their predecessors and now see Jesus as pointing not to some future coming Kingdom, but to the fact that it is here already, on a level of reality that remains hidden to most. The kingdom of God, for Jesus, is clearly not a future "place" or "destiny," but a possible present state where all are valued equally and where folk lean on the God that is found within them, a society where there is no prestige, no status, no class divides or separation between inferior and superior categories. Everyone is valued, loved, and respected, and not because of their education, wealth, ancestry, or other achievements.

The Kingdom of God has also been described as an internal experience, which is yet another area where there are some healthy Christian and Pagan parallel understandings. In the next chapter we will look at this and other areas of Jesus's alternative wisdom that are counter-cultural to much of modern Christianity, yet perfectly in line with large parts of Paganism.

One of the most enlightening books I've ever read about Jesus is by a man named Brother John Martin Sahajananda, *You Are the Light: Rediscovering the Eastern Jesus.* Brother Martin was one of the monks of the astonishing Benedictine spiritual teacher Fr. Bede Griffiths, who for decades ran a Hindu-Catholic ashram in India. The book is an amazing fusion of Catholic and Indian/Hindu spirituality, and it has a most enlightening approach to understanding Jesus's "Kingdom of God" which I will get to shortly.

The basic thesis is that the Christian Church (of which is the author is clearly a part) has yet to discover the good news (gospel) about Jesus. Human beings, he believes, are greater than all religions, and God is not locked away inside any one of them, but is everywhere and in all things, a little like an ocean to the fish that swim in it (we being the fish). Brother

Martin teaches that All is God and that God is in All, and that Jesus, far from being the only Son of God, was a symbol of what is true for us all. He quotes John's Gospel where its author has Jesus say, "I and the father are one," but rather than the usual orthodox interpretation which assumes that this is only true for Jesus, Brother Martin believes that it is true for all humanity at the deepest level—they just have not woken up to it yet.

In the first chapter the reader is asked the question, "How is Jesus good news?" In order to answer and explain this, the author then goes on to show that Jesus's message of good news had three parts to it. The gospels tell us that Jesus preached a message of the "Kingdom of God," that it was "at hand," and that to find it one must "repent." Three parts: Kingdom, at hand, and repent. To Brother Martin, "Kingdom of God" neither meant a new, physical messianic state, nor a future spiritual kingdom beyond this world but one that is as Jesus said, "at hand," which means close enough to touch. He puts it like this: "The kingdom of God is the dynamic aspect of God. It means that God is everywhere, God is among us, within us, and outside us, and we are all already in God. In saying that the kingdom of God is at hand, Jesus was announcing an eternal and universal truth."[65] But how do we realise this truth? How do we make real the experience of discovering that God's Kingdom (the divine realm) is as close as breath? One word—"repent." Before suffering the usual knee-jerk reaction against such an overused and "toxic" word, however, let's allow Brother Martin to expound upon its more esoteric meaning. For while we might normally associate this word with ideas of unworthiness and sin, the actual word can mean something quite different. As he says:

> "[T]he Gospels were written in Greek and the Greek word used for repentance is metanoia, which has the meaning of a radical change of mind. But metanoia also has a much more profound meaning. The word comes from Platonic philosophy in which reality is seen on four levels. The first is the body, the second is the individual soul, the third is the universal soul or nous, and the fourth is One, of God. The word meta means to transcend or to go beyond. For example,

we can say that metaphysics is that which transcends physics of the physical world. So metanoia *means 'to go beyond the nous.' To find God, each person has to transcend his or her identification with the body, with the individual soul, and even with the universal soul, and only then can the "One," God or kingdom of God be found.*"[66]

The monk then goes on to give an astonishing explanation of what it means to repent—i.e., to go beyond the dualisms of the individual me to the oneness of all, and, shockingly, it does not mean to *do* anything but, on the contrary, to *stop doing.* It is about letting go, not striving to "be a better person." He continues, "It is important to realise that the word 'repent' does not imply a positive action, a movement towards a positive goal. Rather it implies a negative action. It is like the little fish in the ocean that does not know that it is in the ocean and is searching for the ocean. The little fish asks a big fish, 'Tell me, where is the ocean?' The big fish responds by saying, 'My dear little one, the ocean is everywhere. You are living and moving and have your being in it. You cannot live one minute without the ocean. Stop all your searching and realize that you are already in the ocean.' In the same way Jesus announced the eternal truth to humanity that God is like an infinite ocean and we are all like little fish in the ocean searching for God. We cannot find God through movement, by going hither and thither. What we have to do is stop all our movements and realise that we are already in God."[67]

Clearly for Brother Martin, Jesus's message of "repent, the kingdom of God is at hand" is far more like that of an Eastern enlightenment teacher who cries "wake up out of your illusion of separateness" than a prophet of salvation from sin. Not only that, his Jesus also has close correlations to Borg's spirit person. As he says, "Jesus had to experience the good news of the kingdom of God in his own life before he could proclaim it."[68] And, as we shall see in a later chapter, Brother Martin's Jesus has not only woken up to the kingdom himself and shared that experience with his followers, but his own "Christ status" is also something that is not just his own, but belongs to all—*the Cosmic Christ.*

Four

......

I Am *Not* the Way (and Other "Alternative to the Church" Jesus Wisdom)

One of the stumbling-blocks, of course, is the Christians' insistence that Jesus was God Incarnate; that the carpenter of Nazareth, the man who wavered over his destiny in the Garden of Gethsemane, was in fact the creator of the cosmos. Even accepting that the gospels are a reasonably accurate account of his sayings, we cannot find that he ever claimed to be God.

—Janet and Stewart Farrar[69]

It may come as a surprise to hear a "man of the cloth" say this, but I honestly and truly believe that Jesus would never have claimed to have been the *only* way to God literally, nor did he think of himself as the only incarnate son of God. I am not for one minute suggesting that these theological texts of John's Gospel (and elsewhere) are wrong or untruthful but that they are metaphorical We will look at how we might reclaim some of this "literalised metaphor" in a later chapter.

From what we now know of the actual man who walked first-century Palestinian earth, it is simply impossible to imagine him making such extraordinary claims about his own divinity. It is completely out of character. As Baldet points out: "What's so striking and worth emphasising in these synoptic extracts is that in those sayings that satisfy the criterion of multiple attestation, Jesus never claims a central role for himself in an event or in his teaching. He never presents himself as someone worthy of worship, never as the Son of the Almighty, or as God Incarnate."[70] Borg puts it this way: "Jesus was in all likelihood *nonmessianic*... His message was not about believing in him. Rather, the pre-Easter Jesus consistently pointed away from himself to God. His message was *theocentric,* not christocentric—centred in God, not centred in a messianic proclamation about himself."[71]

And it's not just the fact that the earliest and most authentic sayings of Jesus do not have him claiming divinity; it's his whole style of teaching and what he taught that makes the enormous "I am" statements so historically unlikely. In his teaching Jesus was consistently pointing away from himself, either to God or to his listeners themselves as the place to look for wisdom.[72] His parables were wonderfully constructed koan-like-stories which did not give "answers" or produce devotion from his audiences. In fact, he did not even speak with any supposed divine authority. Nolan sees it like this: "Nothing could be more unauthoritative than the parables of Jesus. Their whole purpose is to enable the listener to discover something for himself. They are not illustrations of revealed doctrines; they are works of art which reveal or uncover the truth about life. They awaken faith in the listener so that he can 'see' the truth for himself."[73]

Jesus simply did not require people to believe in him. He wanted folk to listen to him and make use of his teachings that they might come to know inner freedom and transformation in themselves, not to bow down and worship him or become the so-called "saved" of evangelistic rallies. The subtitle of Robin Meyers's book is *"How to Stop Worshipping Christ and Start Following Jesus."* As I've said, it is a gem of a book and is written from the perspective of a progressive Christian leader. One of the most brilliant observations of Meyers is with regard to this contrast between Jesus as Sacrificial Son of God in whom people must simply believe in order to be saved and Jesus as Teacher of Transformative Wisdom, whom folk follow and are changed. Like all such progressive clergy and leaders, Meyers is passionate about Jesus. He oozes with excited admiration for this Galilean master whose sermon on the mount, as the great Gandhi knew, could have literally changed the world if only its teachings were applied and not rejected for Churchianity. Meyers cleverly enlightens his readers to the shocking fact that in the space of a few centuries Christianity changed from being a group of followers of the radical teachings of this nonviolent genius into an institution where the teachings were submerged under weighty doctrines and dogmas. In other words, it stopped being action-based and became belief-centred. It changed from following Jesus to worshipping Christ. Meyers puts it like this: "Consider this: there is not a single word in that sermon [on the mount] about what to *believe,* only words about what to *do.* It is a behavioural manifesto, not a propositional one. Yet three centuries later, when the Nicene Creed became the official oath of Christendom, there was not a single word in it about what to do, only words about what to believe."[74]

The Gospel of Thomas

Jesus said, "If those who lead you say, 'See, the Kingdom is in the sky,' then the birds of the sky will precede you. If they say to you, 'It is in the sea,' then the fish will precede you. Rather, the Kingdom is inside of you, and it is outside of you. When you come to know yourselves, then you will become known, and you will realize that it is you who are the sons of the living Father. But if you will not know yourselves, you dwell in poverty and it is you who are that poverty.[75]

—Thomas Saying 3

In a previous chapter I mentioned that certain Jesus scholars now tend to place the Gospel of Thomas alongside the three synoptic Gospels as an equally reliable source. Indeed some have dated its original edition as early at 50–60 CE, which is earlier than the estimated date for Mark, the earliest of the three synoptics. Others believe it is more likely to be early to mid second century, like John's Gospel. Whatever the actual date, one can't deny the fact that it paints a very different portrait of Jesus to the heavily divinised later Gospel of John.

One of the most well-respected authorities on the Nag Hammadi library and, in particular, the Gospel of Thomas, is Elaine Pagels. In the second chapter of her remarkable book *Beyond Belief: The Secret Gospel of Thomas*, she cross-compares the two Gospels of Thomas and John. She, along with many other Thomas and non-canonical gospel scholars, holds that were Thomas kept and not banned by the early Church, Christianity would have developed into a very different animal than what it is.

No other important early Christian text has caused as much heated debate and disagreement as Thomas. To many it is falsely termed a gospel. Rather it is a short manuscript of Jesus sayings, similar to how many New Testament scholars imagine the hypothetical "Q" document to have looked.[76]

·····

Unlike the four canonical Gospels, Thomas has no narrative or context for the sayings of Jesus. There are no miracle accounts or Christological titles such as "Christ" or "Son of God." There are no references to his birth, death, resurrection, or second coming. Dating the document is notoriously difficult. There are, however, some clues. For example, if the Thomas we have today is (basically) the original, it cannot really have been written before 70 CE, for it gives reference to the destruction of the Jerusalem Temple (which occurred in 70 CE). The majority of scholars would not place it much after the end of the second century because there are references to it within other early third-century Christian writings. However, a certain amount of Jesus scholars actually date it earlier than

70 CE, for they believe that there was an earlier edition which was added to at a later date. Among the reasons for this assertion are two things: The simple (even primitive) style of lists of sayings seems to suggest an earlier method of writing than the more narrative-based Gospels of Mark, Matthew, Luke, and John. Thomas looks a lot like what scholars hope to some day discover as "Q," which clearly preceded the other gospels, for they used it as a source. The other thing is that roughly half of Thomas's sayings are also found in the canonical gospels, though their order in Thomas is completely independent of the biblical material. This suggests an author not borrowing from narrative-based Gospel stories but, on the contrary, that those authors inserted Jesus sayings into their own narratives, taking them from Thomas or an independent common source.

I'm not concerned here with proving one view or another. Rather I'm excited by the fact that a very early Christian text about Jesus paints a very different portrait of him to the one the Church has taught for almost two thousand years, a portrait which has strong Pagan connotations. This at least proves that, in early centuries, there were a number of ways of viewing Jesus and his role. Over time the Orthodox way became the only official line and wiped out the rest. But thankfully we are now discovering something of this, up until now, previously hidden Jesus.

The Jesus one encounters in Thomas is a spiritual teacher whose words hold the secret to eternal life. Interestingly, the philosophy is very close to that of the non-dualistic Eastern Christianity of Brother John Martin Sahanjananda we looked at in the previous chapter. Knowing oneself and having direct and personal experience of the divine without need of a mediator is where Thomas attempts to lead his readers, and being made aware of and drawn into the "Kingdom" means going beyond all duality. One can easily say that Thomas gives a very different picture of Christianity to that of Christian orthodoxy. It is a mystical and esoteric approach rather than dogmatic and exoteric.

A central teaching in Thomas, and one which is in huge contrast to most of the canonical New Testament is with regard to "finding the inner light." There has been a constant denominational argument over the New

Testament's apparently mutually exclusive concept of salvation by works as opposed to salvation by grace.[77] Thomas is unconcerned with either. Rather, he points to something which on the whole sounds more Buddhist, the way of insight: finding the light within so one can become a light in the world.[78]

Elaine Pagels talks about her own revelation when reading some of Thomas's Jesus sayings which point us to what's within rather than to beliefs about this or that doctrine. She says that Thomas's Jesus "does not tell us what to believe but challenges us to discover what lies hidden within ourselves; and, with a shock of recognition, I realized that this perspective seemed to me self-evidently true."[79]

As I mentioned above, Pagels examines Thomas's and John's Gospels together. One striking similarity between them (which sets them apart from the three synoptic Gospels) is their notion of Jesus as "the light." John's Gospel contains the highest Christology of any. He presents Jesus as the incarnation of the pre-existent logos (the word of God). On top of this, he is the light of God which comes into this darkened world to illuminate it and bring salvation. We've seen Thomas also advocate a strong "light" ethos; however, for him the light is not reserved for Jesus alone, but is found in all things. With reference to this similarity yet distinction between John and Thomas, Pagels says this: "What might have been complementary interpretations of God's presence on earth became, instead, rival ones; for by claiming that Jesus alone embodies the divine light, John challenges Thomas's claim that this light might be present in everyone. John's views, of course, prevailed, and have shaped Christian thought ever since."[80]

For John, Jesus points to himself as the light and the way. For Thomas, Jesus points his followers to themselves, to discover the light within and to know their true selves as in some sense divine. This corresponds very closely to the often quoted Pagan phrase "know thyself." The Gospel of John's Jesus is not even a human being at all, but a divine presence who takes on a human form. If humans believe in this divine incarnation then they are saved, but if they do not they are damned and will not enter the kingdom of God. But in Thomas, far from setting up an enormous chasm of separation between the human followers of Jesus and Jesus himself, he actually bridges that divide by suggesting that Jesus and his followers are in fact one. Elaine Pagels points out, at a very deep and profound level, that whoever reads the gospel is in fact a twin of Jesus—identical twins. The book claims to be written by "the twin, Didymous Judas Thomas." Interestingly Thomas is Hebrew for "twin," and Didymous is Greek for "twin." This, according to Pagels, is symbolic language. As she explains, "By encountering the 'living Jesus,' as Thomas suggests, one may come to recognize oneself and Jesus as, so to speak, identical twins."[81]

My own reflection on the distinction between the Gospels of Thomas and John has led me to the conclusion that John's "Logos" is the Cosmic Christ and not Jesus at all. Rather it is the pre-existent "word" which John sees as manifested in Jesus (but not identical with him). Jesus is the "in time and space" limited human form of the "eternal" unlimited Christ. I believe that the term Christ would never have become such a great difficulty were it not for the fact of being literalized throughout much of Christian history, to the extent that it almost became Jesus the human's surname. I will come back to this very important notion in a later chapter on the Cosmic Christ.

Five

......

Jesus and the
Tarot Twelve Card

The first thing we might notice about this card is the title. Well,
no. The first thing people see is that he's upside down. Give a
Tarot deck to people new to the cards, and let them leaf through
it. When they get to card twelve, they usually will turn it around.
This, then, becomes a fundamental meaning of the Hanged
Man—to seem, at least, upside down, the wrong way around. To
give others the irresistible urge to turn us around so that we look
and think and act like everyone else.

—Rachel Pollack[82]

Inspiration comes from the most unexpected places and often out of the
most difficult (even painful) circumstances. I had many such experiences during the writing of this book. My research had taken me on an
exciting journey into the discoveries of the Jesus quest, and as a result I
had been brought face to face with a man who was far more captivating

and relevant than I had ever known before. But the constant emotional cost of this effort was draining; at the same time, I was being tested by the Church for unorthodoxy (*heresy*). The cost of being true to myself had, three years previously, robbed me of my job as a full-time clergyman, along with many other things—home, security, pension, and so much more. I still saw myself as a priest (though unlicensed) and offered myself as a freelance celebrant of rites of passage and other ceremonies for those outside the officialdom of formal religion. As I've made clear in this book, I had no intention of resigning my actual orders. In fact, I wanted very much to be seen (by the Church) as a progressive priest who had a deep love and connection for Paganism, and an ability to swim in both rivers. But the only way the Church would consider having me as a licensed "priest at the edge" was to test my orthodoxy and see if I could still fit under the breadth of the Anglican tradition. There are plenty of clergy who are far less "orthodox" than me, and some have passed such "tests for orthodoxy" by a clever use of semantics and half truths. I could not employ such tactics; I needed to be totally honest—totally myself. Integrity and authenticity is what caused me to lose my job in the first place. If I allowed myself to play the semantics game at this stage, well, the previous three years of shit would have been for nothing. Besides, I'm really not clever enough.

In the end, I was actually given back my "Permission to Officiate" as an official Church of England priest, but I decided not to accept it. I still loved the Church of England from the bottom of my heart (and do to this day) but thought I'd rather be a friend of it on the outside, than an antagonist on the inside. Even though life was tremendously tough—especially financially—I knew I had to remain true to myself and continue to live outside the institution.

All this turmoil from the ecclesiastical powers that be as well as the trauma of the past three years had taken its toll on my life in the most devastating way. The book writing and necessary inspiration thus became harder to find. My life was becoming burdensome and stunted my creativity and openness to spirit. When I reached this particular chapter (I didn't know it was going to be about the twelfth tarot card, the Hanged

Man at that point), I had nothing left. I'd come to a dead end. Indeed, I was beginning to feel as if I'd died within, and something like a dark night descended. And the book's first-draft deadline rapidly approached.

Yet then came a ray of light, as it does so often through the cracks of coming to the end of one's own resources. I put out a little note on my Facebook page, stating that the Muses had left me, my Awen had dried up. And, after an hour or so, a response came:

There once was an Xtian bard
Who was finding a chapter quite hard
He looked to the tower
On top grew a flower
Why not pick a tarot card?

It was from my good friend Adele, who had herself submitted a lovely story for this book. I read the rhyme, and chuckled to myself as I reached for my Rider-Waite deck. I pulled a card. As I turned it over and saw what it was, I knew immediately that Adele had become my impromptu Muse, and that the card had become my gateway. I replied with a rhyme of my own.

The Xtian bard was delighted
The card that he picked his world lighted
For the archetype found
Was a hanged man, yet crowned
With a halo—Twas Jesus he sighted…

And so I had my inspiration, and it appeared in the most remarkable way. The death of the historical Jesus came to me depicted by a strange deck of cards usually associated with the Pagan (or at least the magical) community. But not only that; through this Hanged Man–Jesus card my own story had also been powerfully connected. The suffering I had been going through gave way to inspiration, just as all suffering can often make way for magic. Suffering can often enable us to see things from a very different perspective. It turns everything on its head, upside down like the Hanged Man.

This is one of the more esoteric meanings of the cross which we will come to in the next part of the book. For now, however, let's turn our minds to the way the historical Jesus story ended.

Jesus died upon a torturous cross of wood—this is a fact. We do not know any more than that, but we do know that much. There is even non-biblical literary evidence to support his.[83] As far as the doctrine and theology of the Cross (Atonement) go, we'll have to leave them for the next chapter, where we will try to unpack some of the Christian mythology surrounding Jesus. For now, I want us to stay with this image of a man dying on a cross, a real human being who was put there because he was a threat to the religious and political powers that be.

Jesus of Nazareth's execution was the price he paid for taking the risks he did. His compassion—his expressed love—turned out to be truly sacrificial, yet not in the sense that later doctrine suggested. It was love that spilled out of his veins as they were opened by whip, nail, and fist. And while this was happening, there were no Christians praising God for the sacrifice that was being offered upon the altar of the sacred Cross. There was nothing sacred about that cross. It was a disgusting instrument of torture and death, and Jesus's mission to be true to the message within him and to teach others to be true to themselves, ended there.

The theology/mythology of the Cross is a later development, and it still has a power of its own, but here, pre-Easter, pre-Church, we just see the pitiless depths to which humanity is prepared to go to destroy a gift. We also see the courage, the resolve, the sacrificial authenticity of a man who knows what he had to do—simply because his heart will not allow him to betray his own deepest self.

Jesus the hanged man is a sign to all people of any faith or none that being true to one's own deepest truth is of more importance than anything else. It is the symbol of the martyr, of the nonviolent protestor, of all those who have stood against anyone or anything that tries to rob them of their dignity, of their message, of themselves—especially of those whose life is lived for the sake of freeing others. Gandhi, Martin Luther King, Sadat, et al. all stand in this stream, this powerful tradition. And they do become more powerful after their death. They do live on. Not in the sense of coming back to life literally, but in the sense that their own selfless and authentic courage gives hope, strength, and meaning to those who try to emulate their practise. Jesus the human being should never have been turned into a "god who did it all for us." His message was not "You don't need to bother because I've paid the price for you." Rather, it was closer to this: "Be true to YOU, do the work, go through the process, and let it lead you to the place of true freedom and true selfhood. For there you will find your inner god-self."

This now essentially leads us onto the next persona of my "tri-part Christ." The historical Jesus's story ended as a naked, bleeding man, paying the price for his own authentic walk. It is inevitable that such profound images begin to transmute into myth and metaphor. It is a perfectly natural phenomenon. The only problem when this happened with the story of Jesus is (as I've been consistently claiming) that it was then re-literalised to give the world what is essentially a supernatural hero figure but equated with real history. Jesus himself was indeed a man of history but Christ was an added metaphorical layer thus creating a mythos. Yes, I believe that God was in Jesus of Nazareth and yes I believe that Christ is what we call this phenomenon of deity embodied in humanity—spirit in matter. But God/Christ are also in every other human being that lives on this planet. Jesus shows us what we all are.

For Pagans, Jesus the man holds a great fascination. He seems to emulate their dream of authenticity along with many of their beliefs and understandings about the realm of spirit and their own divinity. However, Jesus *Christ* shouts at them with an exclusive message of "I am the way, the truth, and the Life, no one comes to the Father but by me." Once we understand this Christ-ness of Jesus as a natural metaphoricalization of an amazingly important man and as a profound symbol of what is true for all humankind, a whole new world of theological possibilities will open up. And once we re-mythologize what has been literalised by the Church, we are left with another divine-man image which can unlock many profound and universal truths.

Six

......

Reclaiming Jesus Christ

Instead of thinking that wisdom is unique to the Messiah, we should take Jesus literally when he says, "You are the light of the world." Jesus is describing our destiny as equal to his own. God-consciousness is offering to open a path for us.

—Deepak Chopra[84]

So does this de-Christed Jesus now mean we must dispense with the theological and symbolic stories that surround him because they are historically unreliable? Must we read only the handful of New Testament passages that have passed the biblical scholars' criteria of historicity? Must we ignore the creedal statements about being born of a virgin and purge from our minds the weighty concepts of incarnation, atonement, and resurrection? Can we never again enjoy our children's school Christmas nativity plays or literalistic films like *Ben Hur* or *Jesus of Nazareth*?

The answer is of course we can continue to enjoy and find meaning in all the above. We do not need to avoid the one called Jesus Christ just because his life has been clothed with so much mythology. Rather, we simply need to remythologize those aspects of his story that were literalised and upon which some of the more exclusive religious traditions have been allowed to develop. Eastern mystics often say that once a person recognises an illusion, it loses its negative power. Psychologists hold that once the reality of the shadow is acknowledged, it loosens its grip on a person's life. The same is true for literalised myth. Once it has been recognised as mythology, it loses its narrowness and becomes a far more positive and life-affirming force.

With Jesus Christ, once we recognise the difference between what the quest scholars term the Jesus of History and the Christ of Faith, he becomes a totally different reality—he moves from the position of being a privatised god-man of a single religion to a mythic figure of universal significance and relevance. Some of the Pagans I interviewed for this book see Christ as another mythic deity in a long line of Christ-type figures from various cultures. Others see him as the Astral or Cosmic Christ—the spark of deity in all things. They have therefore been able to gain spiritual meaning from Christ without having to join or be part the religion named after him.

The fact that the story of Jesus Christ (though based on a historical figure) is layered with theological interpretation added during the gospel writing in no way means that it is untrue or valueless—far from it. Indeed even the ancient Creeds are perfectly acceptable as long as we see them for what they are: early stages of development in Christian theological understanding. They are primarily metaphorical. I suggested in an earlier chapter that the reason why the creedal or orthodox Jesus Christ has been so problematic is that the Church has by and large viewed this Jesus Christ in purely literal terms. The metaphor has been literalized, resulting in the scenario that means most Christians see the Jesus Christ of the Creeds as the same as the historical Jesus. In fact, we have seen that even the Jesus of parts of the New Testament is not the same as the historical Jesus!

Therefore we will now take another look at a few of the characteristics within the story of this creedal Christ (the Church's Jesus Christ) and see what metaphorical gold it offers to the people of the Pagan world. Trust me when I say that there are treasure troves full. "Life, death, and re-birth" is a commonly heard phrase within modern Pagan gatherings. Indeed the cyclical nature of the eight seasonal festivals takes the Pagan community on a constant spiral-like journey through each year, which in itself celebrates the life, death, and re-birth of the natural world and cosmos. Clearly the story of Jesus Christ, along with the celebrations and customs that mark that story, also follows this pattern. The three most central themes within the story of Jesus Christ are his miraculous birth, his sacrificial death, and his rising to new life. These three events also have theological terms attached to them—Incarnation, Atonement (or Redemption), and Resurrection—and they are marked by the Christian festivals of Christmas, Good Friday, and Easter. The three natural stages of life, death, and rebirth form a perfect pattern on which to place the Jesus Christ story as we draw Pagan meaning from these oft-exclusive Christian theological beliefs.

Birth/Incarnation

When Christians believe in a literal Jesus Christ and see his Incarnation as the only Begotten Son of God in totally historical terms, there is little hope of fruitful dialogue with Pagans, or any non-Christian for that matter. However when seen as metaphor, a whole new world of possibility opens up. We've already seen how the historical Jesus was so filled with his own God-awareness as a spirit person that he naturally enabled those he encountered to find it (spirit) within themselves. As we saw earlier, he was ever pointing away from himself to others. Thus the language of Incarnation was eventually attributed to him because people began to see him as a gateway to divine experience. In fact, I will take this a step further. I am quite happy to use terms like "God Incarnate" and "Son of God" for Jesus Christ because I am happy to use such terms for the human family as a whole. We will look more closely as this when we come to the notion of Cosmic Christ, but what we celebrate when we speak of Jesus Christ being Incarnate—true God and true man—we celebrate about each and every one of us. In *The Meaning of Jesus*, Marcus Borg explains how he feels perfectly able to see Jesus as a real human being who was limited by all the usual human characteristics, and yet also as "the embodiment or incarnation of God."[85] He explains that there are basically two different ways of understanding God and His relationship to the world. On the one hand is supernatural theism, which has always been popular through the Church's life span wherein it views the creedal statements quite literally. Within this framework God is seen as "out there" and usually absent. Thus when God sends Jesus, He (God) is present among us literally but only for as long as the life of the incarnate God Jesus.[86] In contrast to this is panentheism or "dialectic theism," which sees God (Deity) as not just "out there" but "right here" and "more than right here, both immanent and transcendent."[87] Jesus, as a man totally open to this immanent and transcendent God, becomes the spirit person we've already mentioned and thus an embodiment of the God who is already here, rather than the human-God who is not usually here. So in Jesus the human we can also see God, and more than that, we can see the God who is also in us. This is a metaphorical way of using the terms *embodiment* or *incarnation*, but that is not to say it is not real. Borg goes on to list the special (Christological) titles given to Jesus in the New Testament: door, vine, Son of God, Word of God, and so on. He explains that they are clearly metaphors. Jesus was not literally a door or a vine, but his followers are helped in their understanding of him if they see him that way. To see Jesus as God Incarnate is also a metaphor and a symbol of what's potentially true for the whole human family. God (deity) and humanity are symbolically one through this metaphor of the god-man Jesus Christ.

It may come as a surprise to learn that is quite acceptable within the more academic Christian traditions to view the Incarnation of God in Jesus as a metaphor or myth. Indeed, I even passed an "orthodoxy test" by talking about Jesus Christ in this way. Two decades ago, while attending theological college, I was introduced to a book by the Christian theologian John Hick called *The Metaphor of God Incarnate*. Hick wanted to find a way of holding to the truth of the Incarnation but in a way that was reasonable and believable. He considered it a mistake to think of the term

Incarnation as something that could be proved as a scientific proposition, but thought it could still be seen as truth metaphorically or symbolically.

One of the most beautiful experiences I ever enjoyed as a Christian parish priest was baptising babies. Even though in the early Church (as well as in certain current Protestant denominations) adult baptisms were the norm, most modern baptisms are performed for babies or toddlers. They are thus as much celebrations of birth as they are celebrations of entry to the Church. I never saw them in magical terms, as if somehow the water literally washed away a dark stain upon a baby's soul or made them children of God as if they were not before. They were always, for me, opportunities to emphasise what is true for all human beings—that we have divine origins, sacred DNA. This sounds Pagan and corresponds to the Wiccan statement "thou art god/thou art goddess." Yet it's the authentic Judeo-Christian tradition too, even if most Christians seem to have forgotten it. The very first book of the Hebrew Scriptures tells us that God created men and women in God's image and likeness (the Imago Dei). Baptism became a way that I could claim this more universal understanding of Incarnation and apply it to those who brought their children to me for the rite of passage. The birth of Jesus Christ as an Incarnation—a becoming flesh of God—thus points to each of our Incarnations as manifested deity. Every human birthday is yet another expression of the Incarnate God/dess who lives within human clothing.

I find it quite synchronistic that I am writing these very words in the late fall, the "season of good will" being just around the corner. For some reason I've always been obsessed by Christmas. As far back as I can remember, the winter season and the period running up to and including Christmas Day had an almost magical ability to shift my usual boredom with life into an intensely magical experience. It has never left me.

For those of us who live in the Northern Hemisphere, Christmas is always a celebration of light during the darkest period of the year. It is one of the great festivals of light (like the Hindu Diwali and the Jewish Chanukah). Its roots go back to a period before the one whose name (or more properly, title) it is identified with, Christ. For centuries the human family has celebrated the solstices, those mysterious cosmic moments when the sun seems to stand still on its eternal back-and-forth journey across the horizon. The summer solstice marks the longest day, where there is the most daylight within a twenty-four-hour period, and the winter solstice marks the opposite, the shortest day. The winter solstice occurs around December 22, so the symbolic birthday of Jesus Christ (December 25) occurs at the point when the light is just beginning to refill the dark sky again. There was thus a symbolic reason for his birthday being fixed at that date as well as a political reason. The biggest competitor to Jesus Christ in the earliest period of the Church's history was the Persian sun god and lord of light, Mithras, whose birthday was celebrated at the winter solstice and who had become a major god image for the Roman world.

There have been dozens of popular and academic books written on the fascinating phenomena of ancient Near Eastern Pagan deities that clearly have parallels to the story of Jesus Christ. An excellent summary of this can be found in chapter 4 of *ChristoPaganism* by Joyce and River Higginbotham. There are two extremes of opinion concerning the Jesus story and how much of it has its roots in the deities of various Pagan mystery religions. On the one hand are those who take a totally non-historical view, seeing the whole Jesus Christ story as an invented mythos based largely on Pagan (and Jewish) mythology. To these people, Jesus never existed. On the other hand are the far more conservative groupings that see this as preposterous fantasy and hold that no such copycat plagiarism went on. One of the problems the non-historical group has to face is that some of the more popular books that represent this theory have been accused of basing much of their scholarship on outdated or even dubious works, such as James Frazer's *The Golden Bough* and Kersey Graves's *The World's Sixteen Crucified Saviours*. Consequently one needs to tread carefully and not get carried away with it all without checking and balancing the detail. On top of this it has to be recognised that the vast majority of critical scholars and historians do believe that Jesus existed as a first-century Jewish figure.

My own belief is that Jesus did exist, but (while being cautious with regard to where I look for the evidence) I also accept the rather obvious fact that large parts of the narrative of Jesus Christ and later Christian ritual and belief do have striking similarities and parallels with earlier Near Eastern and classical Paganism. Therefore I do see the figure of Jesus Christ as, at least in part, influenced by Pagan religions. As you will see from the collection of essays and interviews with modern Pagan writers and teachers in parts two and three of this book, today's Pagans are very clued up about these connections. However, Christians, on the whole, are not.

This is not the place to go too deeply into the whole question of the similarities between Jesus Christ and his Pagan counterparts; suffice to say that many of the major ingredients/details within the story of Jesus Christ can also be found within earlier Near Eastern and Mediterranean god-man epics. So similar are some of these Pagan myths that early Christian apologists found themselves having to explain their existence and did so by suggesting that the devil has prepared them ahead of time in order to confuse and ensnare possible latter day Christians who might read them. Possibly the most renowned Church father and Christian apologist who employs this means of explanation was Justin Martyr (CE 100–165). Justin was a gentile ex-Pagan of Samaria who'd become a Christian. In chapters 14 and 15 of his First Apology he sets out many arguments concerning the Pagan "imitations" of Christianity:

> Be well assured, then, Trypho, that I am established in the knowledge of and faith in the Scriptures by those counterfeits which he who is called the Devil is said to have performed among the Greeks; just as some were wrought by the Magi in Egypt, and others by the false prophets in Elijah's days. For when they tell that Bacchus, son of Jupiter, was begotten by [Jupiter's] intercourse with Semele, and that he was the discoverer of the vine; and when they relate, that being torn in pieces, and having died, he rose again, and ascended to heaven; and when they introduce wine into his mysteries, do I not perceive that [the devil] has imitated the prophecy announced by the patriarch Jacob, and recorded by Moses?... And when he [the devil] brings forward Aesculapius as the raiser of the dead and healer of all diseases,

may I not say in this matter likewise he has imitated the prophecies
about Christ?... And when I hear that Perseus was begotten of a vir-
gin, I understand that the deceiving serpent counterfeited this also.

—Justin Martyr[88]

Many of the Pagan writers who've either submitted their own essays or been interviewed for this book will allude to this parallel between Jesus Christ and ancient Pagan deities in a latter part of the book.

Death/Atonement

As I sit hunched up at the bottom of my staircase in a house that is cold, small, and could soon be taken away from me, I feel the pressure of living in such a precarious, wounded, and at times hostile world. Sometimes life—daily life—feels like death. Sometimes one reaches the very end of his or her resources and literally crashes in a broken heap. I alluded to some of the darker aspects of my own journey within the chapter on the Hanged Man. It has not been an easy ride of late and, because of certain devastating events of the last few months, I've already missed the deadline for handing in the first draft of this very book. (The publishers were extremely generous and understanding.)

Now each time I come back to writing, something else seems to drag me away from my makeshift work surface, or I simply feel too tired or uninspired to write. Yet within the darkness of the open wounds is a flame, a little spark of light. Beautifully symbolised by the final personification that crept out of Pandora's terrifying box, hope can always be found in the dark gaping chasms of life. And this image of hope within excruciating pain, trauma, and brokenness is the central reason why the literal/mythic story of Jesus Christ still makes sense to me.

The most recognisable symbol for Jesus Christ is an instrument of torture—a huge, ugly wooden tool used in ancient Rome to publicly execute enemies of the state and criminals. Sometimes the symbol is simply a plain empty cross, but in many churches it also carries a naked bleeding human figure—a crucifix. I have to say that I personally know a number of Pagans who are thoroughly repulsed by this image. However this is usually quite simply because the most popular theological understanding of the cross is what might be termed substitutionary atonement, where Jesus as the Son of God somehow pays the price for human sin in blood. This means that humans can be forgiven their own divine punishment if they apply that blood sacrifice to themselves through faith. I admit it's a horrific belief, but it is not the only way Christians understand the cross. Indeed, throughout my ten years as a parish priest I never preached about Jesus Christ as a blood sacrifice in this way. For many, far from being a symbol of God's wrath and punishment, it is a declaration of divine love. The following is an extract from a short Easter talk I gave about ten years ago as a Church of England vicar:

> Holy Week is perhaps the most poignant eight days of the entire church year. In Lent we faced our own inner shadows and compulsions, just as Jesus faced his in that hot and barren wilderness. But now in Holy Week we face our human tendency to get things so badly wrong.
>
> Two thousand years ago a man rode into the Holy City and, only days later, was made a scapegoat by the masses. In fact he was scapegoated by both the religious and secular authorities—church and state. They were the very ones that ordinary folk ought to have been able to look up to, yet they got it so badly wrong.
>
> It was a dark day—a dark, dark day that saw the death of the Son of God. And, contrary to what so many folk still teach, he was not a sacrifice to an angry God who needed appeasing, but a gut-wrenching symbol of God's sacrificial love poured out for an angry humankind. It was not God's mind about humanity that needed changing, but our mind about God. The Cross is God saying, "Go ahead, kill me if you like; I still won't stop loving you."
>
> Then, oh yes then we can fully understand the power of Easter, for Easter cries out with bells and chimes and a thousand tons of spiritual gelignite, that God's love cannot be locked away in a tomb,

or a box, or a book, or an angry heart, or anything else. Those first-century religio-secular authorities got it so badly wrong, but even their terrifying mistake was turned into life for the whole world.

While I wouldn't use all of the above language now, I am still moved by the image of a God who loves us enough to die. And in a sense, part of God did die with Jesus on the cross, just as part of God dies with every death, and is born again with every birth. God (Source) is constantly dying and being re-born. Taking the idea from the previous section on Incarnation—that Jesus somehow embodied God metaphorically—the cross can be seen as a symbol of a God who mysteriously suffers with us.

I've always argued that the cross should be seen as the death of a toxic view of God. God does not punish Jesus for our sins. The cross is a symbol of a God who allows himself to experience the very darkest, most broken and most abandoned reality of what being human can involve. It is an image of a God who would literally love us to death. Though this may not be something that Pagans find helpful, I used to enjoy talking about the cross of Jesus as something that changes humanity's view of the Divine rather than (as the older substitutionary theories go) changing the Divine's view about humanity. In other words, it replaces a God of judgement and wrath with a God of compassion and love. In my book *The Path of the Blue Raven,* I put it this way:

> *Christ comes to show humans who they are, not what they are not. The sacrificial love displayed on the cross does not change God's mind about us (as the so-called objective views of the Atonement states). The spectacle of the cross changes us, not God! How? By displaying costly love rather than brutal judgment. If we see Jesus as a literal, perfect offering, a human blood sacrifice, then we have no choice but to view God as wrathful, and who needs his mind changing by having Jesus pay the price for our sins. He dies; we get let off the hook! But if we see the symbol of the god-man Jesus hanging on a tree as a selfless act of love, joining humankind at its ugliest,*

lowest, shittiest place, and not retaliating with any sense of hatred or revenge, then there is more chance of our own view of God being changed. We might even fall in love with such a loving God rather than being terrified of Him. Thus the Jesus-Tree can either perpetuate a toxic view of God or it can heal it.[89]

Forgiveness is also a key element here, and while one might argue that forgiveness in not a Pagan concept, I have come across some Pagans who've found themselves deeply moved by notions of forgiveness. For example, I have many Pagan personal friends who hold that their ideal is to always bless and never to curse, even when wronged by others. I know there are just as many who would not subscribe to this, but I do feel that the former group have a powerful teaching here deriving from the notion of the three-fold law of return, a quasi-karmic belief that is found within many modern forms of Pagan practice. In a nutshell, the threefold law says that whatever one sends out eventually returns to the sender with a stronger force. Jesus's teaching "bless your enemies and do good to those who hate you" holds within it a similar idea. It has to do with self-protection as much as it is about compassion. When you hold on to resentment and send out negative energy in revenge, it can seriously damage your own quality of life. Love breeds love, hate breeds hate.

In his book *Psychic Protection,* magician and spiritual teacher William Bloom highlights forgiveness as a way of actually removing the karmic connections between you and someone who has wronged you. He offers a healing technique from the Hawaiian spiritual tradition known as kahuna, which he sees as having close connections to Christian forgiveness and Buddhist compassion.[90]

In the story of the final hours of Jesus Christ (which is made up of both fact and interpretation), we see him forgiving the men who'd sanctioned his execution and even the ones who drove in the nails. In the book *Pagans and Christians: The Personal Spiritual Experience,* Gus DiZerega refers to an illuminating experience that happened to him when he climbed the Colorado Rockies and caught a glimpse of the usually hidden Mount of the Holy Cross. He tells of how he then climbed further up the track to get an even better view and when settling to gaze upon the place, how this prompted a genuine spiritual experience that (while a Wiccan) gave him a deep appreciation of the person of Jesus and his message:

Christianity's message, I realized, focused on love and forgiveness, but not so much on God's forgiveness of us as on our own capacity to forgive one another. God's son had walked, taught, and healed among men and women, and had been cruelly murdered. Even so, God's love for humankind had not weakened. "Forgive them, Father, for they know not what they do," is perhaps the most famous account of Jesus's last words, words He had spoken while in agony on the cross. The entire Christian message seemed to be summed up in the insight that as God could forgive the murder of His innocent son, so we were called upon to forgive the wrongs done to us. And if we truly forgave, we would be freed form the poisons of resentment and malice. Our hearts would be opened more fully to love and compassion, and so more fully to God. The central lesson of Christianity was a lesson about unconditional love. I finally understood that the Christian message was a true gospel, a genuine good news for human kind.[91]

With regard to Pagans is another connection to the cross and the image it presents of a wounded, suffering god. After all, it is a striking image and (I would hold) universal. As Carl Jung was reported to have said, "the naked man nailed to a cross is perhaps the deepest archetypal symbol in the Western psyche."

The death of Jesus Christ symbolically points to an experience that is worldwide, and has ever been so for members of the human family—that life always involves death, physically as well as spiritually/symbolically, and that woundedness is simply part of what it means to be human. Two of the most powerful spiritual experiences I've ever had were within the context of nature-based rituals that involved a certain amount of symbolic and emotional wounding and pain. I spoke about them both in an interview for a Pagan magazine I gave a few years ago. This is how I put it:

The sword's sharp end dug into my shoulder blade and jagged stones pierced my knees. The discomfort was intense and my heart pounded as I awaited the next instructions. I'd been warned that such rituals were demanding! But as I knelt in the dark wet cave I felt like I'd been plugged into an electric socket, such was the energy of the place.

All was silent, save for the occasional droplets of water that fell from above, splashing into the pool below. I raised my head and caught a few drops in my mouth. I wasn't thirsty; I just wanted to taste the enchantment of the moment. I wanted to suck the magic marrow out of the very "bones" of Gaia.

"You've entered the womb of the earth Mother," the Druid Chief whispered, "now prepare to be re-born into a magical new universe."

He gave a few more instructions and then left me.

I stayed for some time, knees sore and back aching, but it didn't matter. The pain was worth the experience. The Druids had pre-pared the place earlier, while I'd been sitting in solitude a little way down the hill. As I absorbed the breath-taking beauty of the Welsh mountain valley, so they transformed the cave into an exquisite grotto with candles, symbolic objects, and incense.

There I knelt, gazing at the animal skull, left as a symbol of the death of my old life, and illuminated by orange flickering light. Were it not for the physical discomfort I think I could have stayed there forever. I felt safe, held, loved, and at one with the heartbeat of the universe. But now I had to make my way out.

As I approached the light, the Druid Priestess greeted me and gave me symbolic gifts of the rite of passage. Her words were comfort-ing and she seemed to personify the Goddess herself.[92]

It was an awesome experience, my initiation into the Druid Order, and the more I think about it, the deeper the parallels become between it and other ceremonies of my past—of my *Christian* past.

Almost a decade earlier, while still working as a Priest of the Church of England, I underwent a magical and, at times, gruelling Vision Quest in the New Mexican desert. It was a male rite of passage, modelled on the tribal initiation rites of the world's various native cultures. It was Catholic yet Pagan and, like my Druidic Initiation it, was also a ritual of death and re-birth. Lasting for five long days and forcing me to dig deep into the hidden resources of my own soul, this process challenged body, mind, and spirit. Only recently have I begun to realise what it did for me.

The indigenous people of the world always have practised initiation rites, and, more often than not, they involve ritual wounding (usually real, sometimes symbolic). Anthropologists who've studied these rites suggest that they were designed to show pubescent adolescents (usually boys) that life always involved death and that the sooner they learned that lesson and surrendered to it, the sooner the fear of pain and death would lose its grip on them. It was like dying ahead of time. The fact that we in the modern West have no teenage puberty rites has left us poorer and often psychologically ill prepared for the enormous feelings of death and loss of childhood and the ambitions of youth that occur around midlife for many of us.

While studying the Bardic course material of the order of Bards, Ovates, and Druids (called Gwers, after the Welsh for "lesson") I learned that many modern-day Druids also practise these rites and certainly believe that their ancient Celtic forebears did. As is says in Gwers 14 of the course material: "In the old days, the mourning for the loss of childhood occurred at this time of transition [puberty], not twenty years later. And rather than the fear of old age and death being repressed, it was dramatised and set within a worldview which affirmed the value of elders, and the existence of the ancestors and life after death. All this was enacted at puberty, not at middle age—avoiding its manifestation in mid-life depression."[93]

But this amazing indigenous phenomenon not only points to the healthy psychology of those cultures who accept suffering and death, it also offers an insight into the meaning of the next stage in this mythic god-man Jesus Christ's story—his resurrection.

Rebirth/Resurrection

We naturally want to avoid suffering, so it can seem crazy to suggest that the path to enlightenment involves becoming more aware of our woundedness. But the fact that most traditional initiation ceremonies involve some sort of wounding, symbolic or actual, and the fact that mythology is full of stories about sacred wounding, suggests an acknowledgment of wounding as essential for our maturity and spiritual development.[94]

The above words come from the Bardic Gwers 14 and I have found this emphasis on the sacred wound to be the single most exciting link between the mythologies of the Pagan and the Christian worlds. As I said above, the "image of hope within excruciating pain, trauma, and brokenness is the central reason why the literal/mythic story of Jesus Christ still makes sense to me." And his story, like the many Pagan insights into sacred woundedness, does not remain in brokenness. He does not remain on the cross, or in the tomb. There is a resurrection. There is a rising back to life, but not life like it was before, a new life that is different, a glorified life. The story of the death and resurrection of Jesus Christ is thus another metaphor for all of our lives. It says "life is hard, death will always be part of life, and we will not escape the wounds—*but* the wounds are where the gold lies."

My first book was completely based on this truth that brokenness is often a more direct way to discover gold than any attempts at so-called perfection. In one chapter I use an object lesson which, in the book, is simply a series of photographs of a clay pot. In my retreats and quiet days when I use this chapter as a visual meditation, I use an actual pot. The pot I use contains a lit candle, but no one can see it. There is a big crack in the back of the pot, but that is concealed from the audience's viewpoint. Then I hold the pot up and use these words:

·····

"So, let me now show you the great mystery and miracle of *The Gospel of Falling Down*. We are beautifully and intricately designed clay jars, fashioned lovingly by a wonderful Creator. Yet, we are also fragile and poor. And from time to time life causes us to splinter and crack.

"Life may dish out something totally beyond our control, something we would have never asked for, something 'out of the blue.' *Or* it may be that we have walked for a while the road of the Pharisee and tried to make ourselves into little icons of religious perfection. Maybe we have fallen flat on our faces after the painful discovery that such a goal is impossible. Maybe our failure to achieve a goal has triggered a humiliating fall leading to the recognition of our limitations and weaknesses. This falling of the clay jar has wounded us and we have started to crack and splinter.

"These cracks and splinters—whichever way they came—are painful, horribly painful; even like death. Yet if only we knew how close we were in this state to the discovery of our lifetime.

"For when we fall and splinter and crack, we see our ego, our false self, our little-me for what it is, and sometimes—just sometimes—we are able to let go of it for a while. Then the most profound experience is waiting to hit us. You see, the crack, the fault, the brokenness exposes THE INNER TREASURE AT LAST!

[At this point I slowly turn round the clay jar to reveal a huge crack in the other side. And due to the fact that there is a hidden large burning candle inside the jar the light pours out through the crack for all to see.]

"And then we can truly say that we have met God, and have met Him not out there at the end of some great quest but within our very selves. The treasure that we were searching for *out there* is finally re-discovered.

"And know this; the treasure is not something that has been suddenly added to ourselves, for it was always there. Rather it is our perception that has changed, our 'inner eyesight.' That's why people often say spirituality is about 'seeing.'

"Of course this doesn't happen automatically. It may be months or even years after our fall that we see ourselves in our own God-given-glory. We may be so hurt by our fall that we grow bitter, and again close ourselves to our inner beauty and treasure.

"But make no mistake, such falls, and the cracks they produce, *can* indeed give us the sacred opportunity to catch a golden glimpse of the God-self."[95]

•••••

When it comes to the actual events of Jesus's death upon the cross and his burial in a tomb, I happen to think that something remarkable did happen, and it happened to the early followers of Jesus. For some reason they were turned from terrified hunted outlaws into fearless heralds of a new message. It's interesting that most of the (even very liberal) modern biblical scholars hold that the resurrection experience is likely to be authentic history.[96] This does not mean they believe that Jesus literally rose from the dead, but certainly that something of the spirit and energy of Jesus lived on and motivated others. So I cannot say whether the disciples' experience involved them literally seeing Jesus again, but I do believe it involved them sensing something powerful and new around and within them. This now leads us to the Cosmic Christ.

Seven

......

The Cosmic Christ

One basic datum underlies every religion under the sun, the principle of Incarnation. The Word or Logos, God's self-expression made manifest, has given the light of its divine spark to every mind/soul coming into the world. Christians call this the Christ or "Christ in us." Other faiths have different names or modes of expression for this same inner reality.

—Tom Harpur[97]

In an earlier chapter, I spoke of my discovery that there are three distinct Jesus personalities. Since making that discovery I have come across a number of writers and scholars who also recognise three Jesuses (or three Christs, depending on the writer concerned). Not all of them are Christian. Deepak Chopra, a Hindu, speaks of Jesus the human, Jesus the Son of God, and the Third Jesus, the latter of whom embraces all humanity with a universal significance. Janet Farrar and Gavin Bone, Wiccan teachers, talk of Jesus the human, Jesus Christ (of the Church), and the Astral Christ, again the latter corresponding to that universal/cosmic notion of

Christ. Within Christianity there are also advocates of these three distinct Jesus/Christ personas, especially from the more esoteric and mystical side of the Church. For example, when looking at some of the theological and spiritual writings of the so-called Independent Sacramental Movement, and in particular the Theosophically inclined Liberal Catholic Church, I discovered many clergy and teachers who advocate some sort of trinity of Christs. A well-known personality within the esoteric Christian tradition was Annie Besant, an early president of the Theosophical Society. Besant, in her book *Esoteric Christianity*, spoke of the three Christs. She called them the Historical Christ, the Mythic Christ, and the Mystic Christ. Part of her book was an attempt to separate them so that each aspect/persona could be seen and appreciated for what it represented. As she says:

> *What is needed ... is to disentangle the different threads in the story of the Christ, and to lay them side by side—the thread of history, the thread of legend, the thread of mysticism.*[98]

Notice how she happily refers to the second of her Christ personas (which roughly corresponds to what I've been calling the Church's Christ) as "the thread of legend."

Clearly, by using the terms Historical, Mythic, and Mystic for Christ, she agrees with the principle that there was a literal Jesus of history, a theologically constructed Jesus Christ of the Church, and a more cosmic (universal) Christ—a Christ beyond the Church's confines. A clue that she means precisely this is detected when she says that Christ has "been called by other names and worshipped under other forms."[99]

Another writer from the esoteric Christian tradition is Bishop Markus van Alphen from the Young Rite, a tradition within the Liberal Catholic Movement. In his paper *Jesus Christ and His True Disciples* he uses the same three titles I myself have tended to use: Jesus, Jesus Christ, and Christ. With reference to the last title, Christ, van Alphen says that it refers to that which is "indwelling within us" and later he seems to suggest that we might all, in our deepest selves, be a Christ: "Our way of looking at the human being is that each and every human is truly a monad, a spark of the divine from which it came. This life principle is a common factor held by all humans, nay, by everything in the universe and even the universe itself."[100]

This universal spark of deity in all things is what we mean by the term the Cosmic Christ, and once we've looked at some of its more recent advocates it will become clear how profound a link it is between the two vastly different worlds of Christianity and Neopaganism. The Cosmic Christ is a beautiful bridge spanning the gulf between them.

"Christ" is a term borrowed from the Greek Pagan world. It is a rough translation of the Hebrew term *messiah* meaning "anointed by the Spirit of God." Essentially that's what Christ means—anointed by God. Over the last few decades, a handful of daring theologians and teachers within established Christian traditions (especially Roman Catholicism) have been advocating a recovery of what they see to be the long lost tradition of the Cosmic Christ. Pre-eminent among these is Dr. Matthew Fox (now an Episcopalian).

Indeed within his monumental work *The Coming of the Cosmic Christ,* Fox speaks of the need for a shift away from the "quest for the Historical Jesus" to the "quest for the Cosmic Christ." He also suggests that, while the churches have lost sight of the Cosmic Christ, the native peoples (the indigenous Pagans of the various Aboriginal communities of the planet) never have. Using examples and quotations from just about every era of Christianity, as well as many from far outside the confines of the Church, Fox paints a picture of a living breathing cosmos, and a world under our feet that shimmers with the divine. A planet that hums with God's presence and which feels the pain when she (the earth) is abused, neglected, raped, or fought over.

The problem is that the Cosmic Christ has been a most neglected area of theological study. As the great Jesuit spiritual master Teilhard de Chardin said, "This third nature of Christ (neither human nor divine, but cosmic) has not noticeably attracted the explicit attention of the faithful or of theologians." But that's not to say it was always thus, as Fox demonstrates with an array of pre-Enlightenment examples of Christian mystics and teachers. For example:

Without the Word of God no creature has meaning.
God's Word is in all creation, visible and invisible.
The Word is living, being, spirit, all verdant greening,
all creativity.
This Word manifests in every creature.
Now this is how the spirit is in the flesh—the Word is
indivisible from God

—Hildegard of Bingen[101]

Of course, the most famous and beloved of all the saints (after the Blessed Virgin Mary) is St. Francis of Assisi, whom Fox sees as almost Pagan in his extravagant vision of divinely infused creation. Sadly, St. Francis has largely been denigrated to birdbath sentimentalism, but the real Francis was a true radical, a revolutionary who saw God's presence in the most unexpected places. Within his famous Canticle of the Sun, he gives praise to the cosmos and the earth and her creatures but never mentions the name of Jesus once. In some churches today he'd be cast out as a non-Christian! However, though his poem had no mention of Jesus, it shimmered implicitly with the Cosmic Christ:

Be praised, my Lord, through all your creatures, especially through
my lord Brother Sun, who brings the day; and you give light
through him. And he is beautiful and radiant in all his splendor!
Of you, Most High, he bears the likeness.
Be praised, my Lord, through Sister Moon and the stars; in the
heavens you have made them, precious and beautiful.
Be praised, my Lord, through Brothers Wind and Air, and
clouds and storms, and all the weather, through which you give your
creatures sustenance.

Be praised, My Lord, through Sister Water; she is very useful,
and humble, and precious, and pure.

Be praised, my Lord, through Brother Fire, through whom
you brighten the night. He is beautiful and cheerful, and powerful
and strong.

Be praised, my Lord, through our sister Mother Earth, who
feeds us and rules us, and produces various fruits with colored flow-
ers and herbs.[102]

The medieval Christian mystic Fox most admires is Meister Eckhart, who applied Word of God (Logos) language to all people and even to animals. Meister Eckhart's work had been buried among the medieval theologians for centuries, and Fox has been one of the major players in his excavation and re-presentation to the Christian world. Eckhart preached on the notion of the presence within us all of the "divine spark" that is God. He trained as a Dominican friar and, stemming from his affirmation of the divinity or god-spark in all human souls, taught that man could become God's son just as Christ was. There was a subtle difference between Eckhart's vision of the spiritual quest and the more orthodox of his day. Whereas some contemporary mystics looked outside themselves to achieve mystical union, Eckhart and his followers looked to the center of consciousness within every human heart.

Another priest who is currently lecturing (globally) on the theme of the Cosmic Christ is Fr. Richard Rohr. I had the privilege of hearing him recently when I was invited to perform my soulful magic at an event where he was speaking. Fr. Rohr has spoken and written many times on the Cosmic Christ. While still operating within a fully Catholic and Orthodox context, he beautifully presents a viewpoint on the Cosmic Christ that connects all spiritual paths and which would make much sense to the Pagan world. To Rohr the Cosmic Christ is the living Christ which includes within it all of creation. As he says, "it includes you and I and all of the material world ... for whenever the material and the spiritual coexist you have the Christ."[103]

Both Fox and Rohr see the fully human Jesus of history and the eternal Cosmic Christ as of equal importance, but they take us on a stage further than where the Jesus Quest scholarship ends; i.e., with a man who's just a man. However, they do not simply give us the repackaged version of the literalized Jesus Christ of the Church. As Rohr says, "we made Jesus into the supreme being, and that's theism."[104] The mystery of incarnation is the primary revelation of Christianity, which is the belief that the physical and the spiritual coexist. Panentheism is what Jesus and the Christ tradition point to, not theism (belief in a supreme being). God (at Christmas) has revealed that he's already here. The Cosmic Christ is the incarnate spark of God hidden within all things. Says Rohr, "We've spent nearly two thousand years worshipping it in Jesus instead of discovering it in ourselves."[105]

For Fox there is on the one hand the historical Jesus, and on the other the cosmic Christ. They are connected, of course, but the latter refers in an infinite way to what was finite in Jesus the human who embodied something of God. For Rohr Jesus is the microcosm and Christ is the macrocosm. There is a similarity with the Buddha. There was the historical person who lived a little over eighty years about 2,500 years ago in India. And there is the Living Buddha which is the spirit of the Buddha alive in everyone, the Buddha nature. In a lecture on this very subject, Fox picks up this theme beautifully and helps his audience to see that the Christ can come in many forms like, as we've seen, Old Testament wisdom and the Buddha nature or the Jewish notion of Tekamah, but one does not have to become a Buddhist or a Jew to gain from these insights. Once we are able to truly see the Buddha nature within a leaf or a human face or the stars above our head, we will also see the Cosmic Christ in those places.

Rohr goes to great pains to stress that this is not some twenty-first century New Age teaching out of New Mexico. He (like Fox) uses Church history and the Judeo-Christian scriptures themselves to prove the authenticity and orthodoxy of the notion of the Cosmic Christ. For example, the Cosmic Christ, God's presence in all things, is clearly a Biblical tradition, the earliest hint of which appears in the very first book of the Bible, Genesis. In the first chapter of Genesis, humanity was created "in the image and likeness of God."[106]

......

The next scriptural hint appears in proverbs and what we call the wisdom literature of the Old Testament. In the books of Proverbs and the apocryphal book of Wisdom, God's pre-existent wisdom is personified by a feminine image of a woman calling out in the streets. The word used here for wisdom is the name Sophia.

I had a strange experience of synchronicity when researching this notion of the personification of wisdom. I was leading a retreat on my book *The Gospel of Falling Down*. There was an evening when I had to lead the nighttime prayers and choose a passage from the Judeo-Christian scriptures. I was reading a Richard Rohr book at that time, and, as it was with me in the chapel, I made use of it for a quote. Turning a few pages I came across a beautiful passage from the apocryphal book of Wisdom. As I was reading it I wondered which particular translation it was, and ended up introducing it by saying, "I don't know where Rohr got this translation, maybe it was his own." It sounded too incredible, too profound, too nature based to have been a regular Bible translation.

The next morning I was asked to select and read another passage and was given a big Bible. I sat there with it on my lap and noticed that it was the New Revised Standard Version (NRSV), which wouldn't normally include the apocrypha. I opened it, and amazingly, it fell open on the book of Wisdom (it did indeed have an apocrypha). On looking closer, it was indeed the chapter of the passage I'd read the night before. Even more incredibly, I noticed it was the same translation! Amazing, I thought, these words were profound. They spoke with beauty and elegance about the feminine personification of divine wisdom. There are only two books in the Bible where this is spoken of in this way—Proverbs and Wisdom. I wanted to take the Bible to my room so I could find some more quotes but didn't because it belonged to the guy who'd loaned it me. So I looked on the book shelves for another Bible with the apocrypha. I saw a Jerusalem Bible (the Catholic Bible) and reached to grab it. When it was in my hands, I opened it and it fell open within the book of Proverbs, and I saw the big bold type heading facing up at me—**The Personification of Wisdom**. Incredible.

Because this book is by an ex-Christian vicar (still priest) writing primarily for Pagans, I've deliberately avoided lots of the Bible quotations as one finds in more standard Christian books. However, this is a case where I feel it would be both pleasantly surprising and hugely edifying to quote from a little of the Bible's Wisdom literature. It is a beautiful, mystical, and wonderfully feminine portrayal of God's essence in creation. The quote I used from Wisdom for those evening prayers was this:

> *Wisdom (Sophia) is radiant and unfading, and she is easily discerned by those who love her, and is found by those who seek her*[107] *... she goes about seeking those worthy of her, and she graciously appears to them in their paths, and meets them in every single thought*[108] *... There is in her a spirit that is intelligent, holy, unique, manifold, subtle, mobile, clear, unpolluted, distinct, invulnerable, loving the good, keen, irresistible, beneficent, humane, steadfast, sure, free from anxiety, all-powerful, overseeing all, and penetrating through all spirits that are intelligent, pure, and altogether subtle.*
>
> *For wisdom is more mobile than any motion; because of her pureness she pervades and penetrates all things.*
>
> *For she is a breath of the power of God, and a pure emanation of the glory of the Almighty*[109] *... Although she is but one, she can do all things, and while remaining in herself, she renews all things; in every generation she passes into holy souls and makes them friends of God, and prophets.*"[110]

The passages in the book of Proverbs are equally (if not even more) astonishing, for here "Lady Wisdom" speaks of her own pre-existence, that she was the first creation of God, a divine force (goddess) through which all created things emanated:[111]

> *When he established the heavens I was there, when he drew a circle on the face of the deep, when he made firm the skies above, when he established the foundations of the deep, when he assigned to the sea its limit, so that the waters might not transgress his command, when he marked out the foundations of the earth, then I was beside him, like a master worker, and I was daily his delight, rejoicing before him always, rejoicing in his inhabited world and delighting in the human race.[112]*

Many modern biblical scholars hold that the Wisdom literature notion of the personification of divine Wisdom was the inspiration behind the New Testament Logos language in the prologue to John's Gospel, which also carries the theme of pre-existence. We will come to that in a moment.

The third hint of the Cosmic Christ in scripture is the apocalyptic term "the son of man," a prototypal figure who sums up what's happening everywhere else. It's found in the Old Testament book of Daniel and other apocalyptic works. Jesus uses this term for himself. In fact, it is his most common term of self-description. In essence he's saying, "I am the son of the human, the everyman, the archetypal human." The son of man is a human title, but one which is representative. Jesus thus represents and includes all of humanity. What's true for him is true for all of us, in fact for all things. The symbolic meaning of the resurrection stories means that Jesus's identity is translated to everything else. Jesus becomes the Christ, he moves from the physical/historical to the non-physical/eternal.

Then we come to Saul of Tarsus, later called Paul, who becomes the man oft credited as the second founder of Christianity. One of Paul's most frequently used phrases is "In Christ." However, he never bothers with the historical Jesus. He hardly (if ever) quotes him at all. Why? Because he never met him. Paul's conversion occurred when he had an experience of the outside-of-time-and-space Christ—the universal Christ. Paul's Christ is cosmic, not historical. Many modern-day liberals write off Paul as a misogynistic control freak and dogmatist. In reality, he was a true mystic. Who but one in touch with the mystical Cosmic Christ could have written such a passage as this?

> It is necessary to boast; nothing is to be gained by it, but I will go on to visions and revelations of the Lord. I know a person in Christ who fourteen years ago was caught up to the third heaven—whether in the body or out of the body I do not know; God knows. And I know that such a person—whether in the body or out of the body I do not know; God knows was caught up into Paradise and heard things that are not to be told, that no mortal is permitted to repeat. On behalf of such a one I will boast, but on my own behalf I will not boast, except of my weaknesses. But if I wish to boast, I will not be a fool, for I will be speaking the truth. But I refrain from it, so that no one may think better of me than what is seen in me or heard from me, even considering the exceptional character of the revelations. Therefore, to keep me from being too elated, a thorn was given me in the flesh, a messenger of Satan to torment me, to keep me from being too elated. Three times I appealed to the Lord about this, that it would leave me, but he said to me, "My grace is sufficient for you, for power is made perfect in weakness." So, I will boast all the more gladly of my weaknesses, so that the power of Christ may dwell in me. Therefore I am content with weaknesses, insults, hardships, persecutions, and calamities for the sake of Christ; for whenever I am weak, then I am strong.
>
> —Paul of Tarsus[113]

Perhaps the most bold and unquestionable reference to a "Cosmic" portrayal of Christ in the whole Bible comes with the fourth Gospel, John. John's famous prologue—"In the beginning was the Word, and the Word was with God, and the Word was God"[114]—identifies Jesus Christ as the eternal Word (the Logos) of God. So the author asserts that Christ was there at the very beginning of creation. It is believed that the author is adapting the doctrine of the Logos, God's creative principle, from Philo, a first-century Hellenized (Greek-influenced) Jew. Philo's term "Logos" was borrowed from Greek philosophy, and he used it in place of the Hebrew concept of the personification of Wisdom (Sophia). As John says, "Through him all things were made; without him nothing was made that has been made. In him was life, and that life was the light of men [humankind]"[115] so if we get it in him, we'll get it in ourselves. Yes the Cosmic Christ is no new invention. It was there at the very beginning.

•••••

For Matthew Fox, authentic Christianity runs on two wings, like a big bird. One of them is the Historical Jesus and the other is the Cosmic Christ. And, as he says in a CD series, "if either one is not relished, you won't have a healthy spirituality."[116] He goes on to mention the work of the Jesus Quest and sees the culmination of these two hundred years of scholarship as one of the wings. The other wing is the mystical tradition of the Cosmic Christ. He sees one of the great insights given us by the Jesus Quest as the discovery that only about fifteen percent of the words of Jesus in the New Testament actually came from him. The rest was made up by the community. But Fox does not see why this should be a problem. On the contrary, it should raise the question, "Where has all that creativity gone? People were so overwhelmed by the spirit Jesus released that they didn't hesitate to put all these good words into the mouth of Jesus."[117] Fox asks why we're not writing new gospels today and points out how the Celtic church did just that, constructing their own "I am" sayings and equating Jesus to images relevant within their worldview like "I am the wild boar fighting," or "I am the salmon of wisdom."

We clearly need the Cosmic Christ as well as the Historical Jesus because it makes sense of the 85 percent of New Testament quotes that were clearly not from Jesus. We can still read those texts as meaningful but not because they were literally the words of Jesus. Rather the in-dwelling Christ spirit unleashed creativity within the authors. They wrote holy myth. As I've suggested, however, this "holy myth" was then literalised in a way that other (Pagan) dying/rising god stories never were. We need the man Jesus who shook the religious and political world and we need the Christ which is non-historical, not bound by time or space but is in all things. But we need to see each of them for what they truly are.

Fox sees the literal meshing together of Jesus and Christ into one persona (Jesus Christ) as the death of the message. He values Quest scholarship because it helps us to recognise what is Jesus and what is Christ in scripture. 95 percent of John's Gospel is not Jesus talking at all; it's Christ. Jesus didn't literally use terms like "I am the way, the truth, and the life"—they were the Christ's words, so in a sense they are our words. Fox encourages his audiences to ask themselves how are they the way, how are they the light, how are they the door, etc. When we really get this, the whole thing opens up to a new level of relevance. In the other three Gospels we can see the same and not just with the so-called Jesus words but with the actual stories, too. For example, the Bethlehem scene is a Christ story, not a literal Jesus story. Some of the super-left-brain-dominated rational scholars may tell us to throw these stories out altogether because they are not true literally, but they've missed the point. We can't throw these stories out because they are just too powerful on a mythic, archetypal level. The story of the one who is born into the human mess and poverty of the stable or animal cave is a universal story of hope for a broken humanity. The story of the one who is discovered by the lowly shepherds, who has homeless parents, and whose birth is first witnessed by an ox, an ass, and probably a rat or two is a mythic story that touches the soul deeply in a symbolic way.

Of course, the essence of both the Jesus story and the Christ myth is this: "There is no division/no separation between the divine and everything else. The Incarnation of God in Jesus is the symbol of what's true, of what has always been true, for everything."

Much of Rohr's rhetoric is against what he calls the performance principle of most Christian religion—people trying to achieve some sort of goodness or holiness by good works or believing the right things. On the other hand the Cosmic Christ—the incarnate God in all things—shows us that earth and spirit are already totally interconnected, which includes all humans. As he boldly says, "We use that phrase now, the Cosmic Christ, to remind us that what we believe in includes everything."[118] And

> The Christ comes again whenever you're able to see the spiritual and the material coexisting, in any moment in any event in any person.[119]

Finally, perhaps his most radical statement on this notion is this:

> You're doing God and the gospel no favour to project all of this power onto Jesus, and therefore suck it out of the rest of the universe. That was not the meaning of salvation, and it's got us into the state we're into today where we hate the earth, we hate other races, we hate other religions, we even hate ourselves ... Jesus is the blueprint of what God is doing everywhere all the time and we chose to worship the blueprint instead of seeing where the blueprint was pointing us. The Cosmic Christ is God hiding inside his creation. He always has done this and the Jesus event was a symbol/blueprint of this.[120]

One of the most inspiring metaphors I've ever heard for the relationship between Jesus and the Christ comes from the world of physics. The first chapter of John's Gospel refers to Christ as the light within all beings. Light is a very prevalent symbol for divinity and in fact is one of the oldest universal images for God's presence. Modern science has established that light does indeed penetrate all things. Light particles (photons) exist in every atom in the universe. On top of this, over the last few hundred years there has been a debate among physicists over whether light is a particle or a wave. To cut a very long story short, the consensus is that it has properties of both a wave and a particle. This was an amazing discovery, far outside the realm of how we normally perceive things to be. The difference between the behavior of particles and waves is similar to the difference between billiard balls and oceans. Photons act as both a wave and a particle all the time.

Matthew Fox sees this as a marvellous creation-centred symbol for what's going on in Christology. Jesus is the particle, the frozen incarnation of deity in time and space, and Christ is the wave, the limitless and timeless presence of deity in and through all things. But the wave—the Cosmic Christ—is also in Jesus and is also in each one of us.

We should not, therefore, bow down and worship the Christ spark in Jesus alone, but follow the historical Jesus through his journey into the Christ, for it is our journey too. The problem (for us, of course) is that part of Jesus's journey was suffering and the carrying of his cross. It was also death, but a death that led to resurrection. This is the hinge in the story— the place where the historical Jesus gives birth to the mythic Christ. Rohr sees Jesus as morphing into Christ (at the resurrection), which is the journey he feels each of us should take. As Fr. Sean O'Laoire puts it, "I invite you to emulate what Jesus did in his movement from being Jesus the Carpenter of Nazareth to being the Christ. Every one of us is meant to go from who we are into carriers of Christ consciousness."[121]

Part Two
Jesus Through Pagan Eyes:
A Selection of Stories and Essays by Respected Pagan Elders

⊛ † ⍟ ∝ ⊛ ✳ ⳨ ✝

A bodhisattva is a perfected Individuality which no longer needs to reincarnate but chooses to do so of its own free will in order to help and guide less-developed mortals. One may reasonably infer, for example, that Jesus and the Buddha were bodhisattvas; and human nature being what it is, the impact of such entities on the people of their time often led to their deification in later memory.

—Janet and Stewart Farrar[122]

Introduction

......

You are now going to take a step even further into the adventure of *Jesus Through Pagan Eyes*. I am about to introduce you to a collection of truly spell-binding accounts from some of the most fascinating men and women I've ever met, men and women who represent a world usually at logger heads with the followers of Jesus. Yet here we meet Pagan teachers, priests, and priestesses of Druid, Wiccan, and Heathen paths describing Jesus in ways that have rarely, if ever, been done before.

There are fifteen pieces in total, and they vary from being more personal/anecdotal stories to more theoretical essays. Each piece will close with an author biography. Enjoy!

Eight

......

Jesus: A View
from the Earth

by Emma Restall Orr

Much of my early childhood was spent in Madrid. Far from the colorful vibrant city of today, the capital I knew was cowered, dusty, and grey, tight in Franco's dictatorial grip, its face still shrouded with the guilt and recriminations that lingered like a smog of the civil war. It was there that first I came across Jesus.

The name was as common as John is in English. Everywhere you turned there was a Jesus *(He-soos):* amongst my classmates, the neighborhood kids, adults in their adult worlds, and perhaps as a result the stories told to me didn't seem to refer to anyone special. However, one Sunday at the Protestant church my parents attended now and then, a guest minister came to speak. He was a travelling evangelical who spat thunder and rage with his words, slamming his fist down on the pulpit again and again, and I remember staring up at him realizing that, perhaps, I had got it badly wrong: one of these many Jesus fellows was clearly an exceedingly tricky and dangerous character. The memories of that Sunday morning remained as a nausea in my belly for many weeks, until once more the comfort of his insignificance returned.

The second moment that his presence hit me was in my pubescence. With my sexuality emerging, I found myself in some vast cathedral transfixed by the beauty of his thighs: raised life-size above me upon the cross, head bowed, and naked but for the tatters of his sparse loincloth, the smooth curves of those polished muscular thighs shone in the candlelight, velvet in the dark richness of the wood from which he'd been carved. I don't mean to offend by admitting such an experience, but it was unforgettable. I have no doubt that other girls and boys have felt the same.

A third memory I would share here is quite a different one but equally pertinent amongst my encounters with Jesus. My son and I were being shown around the little church where a friend lived in the rural Cotswolds. An intelligent home-educated lad of around ten at the time, he wandered off to explore by himself, sneaking behind the curtains into the bell tower. When we asked what he'd found, he shrugged and told us about the bells and various odds and ends, adding, "oh, and the usual dead bloke." Unusually for an Anglican church, tucked away for special occasions there was indeed a large crucifix. His dismissive irreverence shocked me, revealing just how I had brought him up, not to be rude about others' faiths, but not to diminish the value of stories with superstition.

Brought up within an animistic Druidic family saturated in folktales and mythologies, he had read the Bible's stories, along with those of many other cultures, from our own British to the Maori, Hindu, Japanese, and Native American. He had noted that, although a small proportion of Jesus's tales were about his death, churches seemed fixatedly to focus upon it, and as a result, Christianity appeared to him to be a death cult. While it did seem to me wrapped up in the primal notion of sacrifice, concerned that I had left a gap in his education I spent time showing him what I could of the broader aspects of the faith, but nothing shifted his impression: as so often our children do, he had shown me a mirror within which I saw my own impressions and what had formed them.

Pondering words for this essay, I sat in the meadows, watching the swallows and sky larks diving as they caught tiny flies, playing in the breeze, the whispers of clouds high above moving upon invisible currents, the sunshine softly warm on my skin, a perfect English summer's day, and I was filled with the exquisite gratitude that comes when I pause to acknowledge the presence of my gods and ancestors. The ridge and furrow of earlier farmers' ploughs still visible beneath the grass, the hay just cut in adjoining fields, I could hear through the humming of the bees, the fiddles playing, the laughter, of lives lived upon that land before me. I knew the breath that filled me had been breathed before. I knew the stories of love and loss, struggle and success had all been lived before. And I closed my eyes, lying back in the long grass.

In Druidry, as in many old traditions, there is no necessity to separate fact from fiction, indeed the distinction itself is considered irrelevant, for life is crafted instead wholly of *stories:* individuals are able only to perceive and experience their own lives, and as we each walk in our own shoes we each relate tales from our own perspective. This was how I was brought up, and in part why Druidry made so much sense to me. The Biblical Jesus was, consequently, to me only ever a character (or a series of characters) in a scattering of stories written by a scattering of people. Perhaps most influential to me, none of those stories had him leaving footsteps in the landscape where I lived. His breath was not breath that I was now breathing. That didn't make his tales irrelevant to me, for we share a human nature, but it made him a stranger: the songs he sang were in another tongue.

Of course, human literature from all over the world—fairytales, plays, movies, news reports, even some product advertising—are all based upon the same foundational yarns: the adventures of a hero who, facing overwhelming odds, somehow wins though. The stories that persist, those told generation to generation, are fascinating to explore, for the qualities they possess that inspire are somehow more profound. Some would say that they survive because they are based upon truth, meaning historical fact: indeed, many need the stories of Jesus to be true—to be proved to be historical truth—because by being true the stories make sense of one's own life and of one's own death. Such truths take away the fear of death, replacing it with the promise of eternal life, the welcoming ease that is "heaven." Yet from a Druidic perspective, all that is ever really true is that a tale's words have touched the strings of the human soul: hearing such music, we pause to listen to the songs of human nature, those ancient songs of our ancestors we too can't help but sing.

Some heroes are giants or magicians, or people of political power, an uncle we wish we had who would always protect us, such as Bran in the British tradition, Myrddin, Arthur, Gwyddion, and so on. In many, however, it is only in facing adversity that the character discovers he has extraordinary powers, given him by the gods (or God), the ancestors, spirits of nature, or some brewer of mysterious potions; here we find Batman, Asterix and other comic book superheroes, the global superstar that is Harry Potter, and Jesus.

Tales of the ordinary person, forced by some extraordinary circumstance to find resources within himself that it is hard to imagine having the courage to find within our own soul, are richly inspiring. But it is that lack of belief that we would indeed manage to overcome; the odds that makes the *superhero* so very appealing. His resources are magical, mysterious, miraculous, perhaps given by the gods (or God), allowing him an advantage that makes the tale so thrilling. Of course, being now above the level of ordinary society, a part of the tale is also tragic, for the price of being so special is the necessity to make an extraordinary sacrifice. He pays, with the anguish of loneliness, so often misunderstood, and targeted as a trouble-maker; he may even need to forfeit his sanity or his life.

From the tales of Jesus I was told or read as a child the impression I gained was of a young man, indeed a number of different young men, some portrayed as Gandhi-type figures, exquisitely peaceful, ascetic, and altruistic, others more radically political. In my teens and early adulthood, as I sought out and read spiritual and philosophical texts, I found Gnostic Gospels, texts discarded by those creating the definitive, "authorized" Christian scriptures, within which Jesus was a character more fundamentally influenced by Near-Eastern thought. I read books that spoke of him as a resistance fighter, inspiring my adolescent and ill-informed idealism about other populist heroes like Che Guevara, images fuelled by those beautiful sculpted thighs revealed in his ultimate sacrificial pose.

As I grew in my spiritual exploration, it was clear to me that there was no single man, no one historical or mythical Jesus. Yet the value of his tales is far from diminished by that plurality, as long as each tale is taken as a story in its own right, a tale of an ancient hero facing adversities that we ourselves would likely fail to face as honorably. So can he teach us of courage, grace, and wisdom as human beings.

For myself, however, as my spirituality became thoroughly rooted within Britain, its heritage and ancestry, Jesus's stories continued to feel foreign to me. At the same time, though the English church in some ways adapted to these lands and their people, it lost the potency of any spiritual teachings by becoming a political and economic power, asserting authority together with a claim on universal truth. Christianity and its many faces of Jesus has certainly been a part of British history over the last thousand years and more, but for me it has never been a British *religion*.

The heroes which I feel most powerfully are those whose stories take place within these islands of Britain, islands that are my home, that were the home of my ancestors. For we share not simply common humanity, but the experience of the honeysuckle breaking into leaf in the late winter woodland, the scent of the elderflowers blooming in the hedgerows, the push of Lammas growth in the ancient oaks, the song of the sky larks and the humming of the bees: lying in the green meadows as the hay is brought in.

In presenting this perspective, asked as I was to express my personal experience of Jesus rather than an academic or theological survey, I am acutely aware of just how wide is the gap between my Druidic view and that of a practicing or cultural Christian. To someone for whom Jesus is divine, his teachings sacrosanct, my words may seem an incomprehensible attempt to normalize that which is beyond human influence. That gap is an important one to reveal, however, for I do indeed perceive a single level of life, with no transcendent or *super*natural force or deity:

human beings are an integral part of nature as are our gods—and our heroes. So may it be.

ABOUT THE AUTHOR

Emma Restall Orr is an animist, philosopher, poet, and priest within the British Druid tradition. Joint Chief of The British Druid Order for nine years, she left to found The Druid Network in 2002, her focus now being mainly on the work of Honoring the Ancient Dead, an advocacy group for the remains of ancient British human remains, and the natural burial ground and nature reserve she runs in Warwickshire. Her recently published books include *Kissing the Hag: The Dark Goddess and the Unacceptable Nature of Being* (O-Books, 2008), *Living with Honour: A Pagan Ethics* (O-Books, 2008), *The Apple and the Thorn* (Thoth, 2007), and *Living Druidry: Magical Spirituality for the Wild Soul* (Piatkus, 2004).

Nine

······

A Witch's
Tale of Christmas

by Reni at "Spells and Witchcraft"

Note: There are many Wiccan websites that offer all sorts of information for those interested in the Craft. One of the most beautiful that I came across during my research was www.spells-witchcraft.org. I found its artistic style and background music to be calming and inviting. I also discovered that Reni, one of the main contributors to the site's information, had obviously worked hard at formulating her own opinions about Jesus. Amongst her articles were many references to him, some of them profoundly insightful, so I decided to invite her to contribute a piece for this book. I was delighted when she agreed, and over-awed by what she finally sent.

Last Christmas, after I had hosted our annual Yule Dinner and Celebration, I spent a Christian Christmas with my biological family. There we attended Midnight Mass, a short walk away on snow-covered sidewalks, up the wide stone steps beneath the ruby, sapphire, topaz, and emerald stained glass glowing as if from the fervor of the congregation inside. The nostalgia value alone of this cherished tableau was worth the trip, but the best part came later in the mass when my sister gave out communion. It is her I think of when I think of goodness.

I almost wished I could accept this sacred gift from her but one does not commit sacrilege in the temple of another, especially my family's church where I had been baptized—although I understand I screamed as if I were being waterboarded. Should have told them something. After all, "Thou shalt not suffer a witch to live" (good old Exodus 22:18, the revealed word of God).

But my sister, she well deserved the honor of giving the host, having worked tirelessly to restore this, her church. And it had never looked more glorious in its soaring columns, marble and gold glowing in candlelight; frankincense and celestial music filling the air. Here is where she and her fellow parishioners attend the needs of the flock as good Christians had for each other since the time of Jesus. Next morning there would be turkeys and stuffing to take to the homeless.

I was born into this devout Roman Catholic Church but never took to the religion. While this was a source of contention with the family, I've always known that I had to be who I am, an authentic person, no one else. I believe that the family eventually understood this on some level and did not perhaps blame themselves for raising a witch. We all get along famously now.

Back then, however, I even refused to attend mass every morning with all the other parochial school children. Looking back, I have to say, that took chutzpa, the nuns fervently trying to whip the devil out of me every chance they got.

After mass and many years later I said to my sister, "Wow, that was amazing. A woman giving communion in the Catholic Church and the woman being you. Who would have thought we would both end up clerics. But no surprise that I'd end up on the Pagan side, huh?"

I ask myself: How had two closely raised siblings taken roads so divergent toward the same God/dess?

My problems with the Church were many but mostly with the ideas of a sect that revered a God who had a taste for bloody human sacrifice from Isaac to His only son to pay for some apple of knowledge that was supposedly stolen in the Garden of Paradise a very long time ago. I also had a problem with their condemnation of sex, even with myself.

Not only that, but Jesus, to tell the truth, didn't seem like much of a God to me. Now Diana or Isis or Epona (the Horse Goddess and a personal favorite at the time) now *those* were Goddesses. *And* Jesus got at least two things dead wrong. I couldn't avoid these truths even at age nine.

First, he said the Kingdom of Heaven was to come in his or the next generation, depending on who you read: it didn't. We're still waiting. Second, he said he would return from the dead: we're still waiting on that one too. But what really got me was what we were brainwashed with in catechism class about the ultimate truth of God:

1. God is all good

2. God is all powerful

3. God is all knowing

The other fundamental belief was that our lives are a test to see if we are worthy of eternal reward or deserving of eternal agony in the fires of hell. Sure, our teachers need to give test to ascertain what we know and don't know. God already knows.

Then how can an all-good god who knows the outcome of every life, every action, every second, every thought, create that person who must irrevocably go to hell. Anything else would make God wrong, right?

Something I don't understand here, Father. I am who I am
because God made me that way. Right? Every twitch, every good
or bad thing is known beforehand—especially the part where
Saint Peter checks my stats at the Pearly Gates to see if it's heaven
or hell for me? Right?

The answer I would always get was "We have free will. God doesn't make us sin." No, He doesn't have to, since He already knows what we'll do. Finally, predictably, the questions, the paradoxes, would be settled irrevocably by a self-satisfied, "It's a mystery." Or, "Faith is believing what we know cannot be true." No, believing what we know is not true is insanity!

My views have softened since, and I have found much better uses for the name of Jesus Christ than as an all-purpose expletive. But to this day, logic and reason still guide my quest. I believe that these great gifts were not stolen from the Tree of Knowledge but are the supreme blessings given to us by our Creator in His own likeness—not physical but awareness, consciousness.

This revelation first dawned for me on the roof of St. Peter's in Rome: *separate the teachings of Jesus from what the Church hierarchy has wrought upon the world ever since.* Certainly, absolute power had corrupted absolutely. From the savage inhumanity of the Roman Emperor Constantine who demanded to be called "god" and "master," rebranding Christianity into a predatory religion Jesus would never recognize, to the Crusades, the Inquisition, the Witch burning times, Nazi collaboration, to the present pedophile ignominy and the usurping of the American military by right-wing Christian fundamentalists who espouse the end of days in their lifetime—even if they have to precipitate it themselves (for anyone thinking these are only Roman Catholic atrocities). But don't get me started. Oops, too late.

All that was the Church and had nothing whatsoever to do with Jesus or his teachings. Yes, I still saw him as a mortal man but a highly exceptional man who had attained a magnificent connection with the Divine. While many try to attain enlightenment, Jesus succeeded.

To us he gave the gift of his divine awakening to the most essential of human virtues: Do unto others, the Golden Rule, love they neighbor, my neighbor's sorrow is my own, even the only doctrine in Wicca: Do what you will shall be the whole of the law *save in harm none.* All spiritual teachers have been urging just those qualities through the ages.

The other way, the dark path, is the law of the jungle, survival of the fittest, nice girls finish last. All's well and good if we want to stay in the jungle. There's nothing particularly new in these opposing positions, just the age-old struggle of good versus evil, the quest for justice so that evil does not always triumph over the good.

What Jesus did that was new was to extend his grace to women at a time and place where women were one step above pariah. (Of course, the Church quickly rescinded a woman's God/dess given-divinity and revered only virgins.)

Then there are the miracles. Did Jesus actually perform these apparent scientific impossibilities? I believe his apostles truly believed he did, and so Christianity at its source was pure and true in the Divine Spirit.

Those men and women, early Christians, willingly laid down their lives for God. Nobody is martyred for a scam, nobody. Rather, their ultimate sacrifice is an affirmation of the courage Jesus himself engendered in his triumph of the spirit over the flesh in attaining the Divine. This then was his—and our—victory over death in the only way that it is granted in the thoughts and deeds we leave the children of the ages.

Then too, the apostles performed numerous miracles after his death. To me, this says that the miracles, *magic,* Jesus performed, especially healing, are feats attainable by mere mortals. Just how he did them remains something of a mystery but one we are unraveling slowly, day by day, year after year.

Nevertheless, what is within reach now are Jesus's teachings of compassion and love. While this might seem to make anyone more vulnerable to those who would exploit such idealists as hopelessly naïve, what actually happens when we take the path of Jesus in truth and oneness is that we walk with God/dess on our side. This makes us incredibly strong as individuals and as a people.

We simply dedicate ourselves to the ultimate good and heed the Divine Voice of Reason, Logos, Truth, and God/dess within and without, our semi-divine selves ever expanding upward and outward in awareness and love. Okay, it's not so simple but well worth every effort possible. Nothing else in existence is as essential.

The irony is that Catholicism had provided just such blessings for my sister and our family without all the fuss. For her, an off-the-rack religion (with a few brilliant alterations of her own) serves the same purpose as my synthesized, highly eclectic, ever-questioned cosmology. Oh well. It is my journey, after all.

Here now at the shining holiday table, four generations join hands from great-grandmothers to newborns. I bow my head and take the hand of my niece and nephew and feel the grace of God/dess as surely as any Wiccan sabbat gathering beneath the full moon. We are most certainly all God/dess's children. God bless us, every one. And S/He has.

ABOUT THE AUTHOR

Reni is a witch, ordained Pagan minister, and the webmaster of www. spells-witchcraft.org, where Wicca is taught at the neophyte to adept levels to a worldwide virtual congregation, in addition to local New York followers of the Old Ways of peace and harmony with nature and the divine.

Ten

······

A Confession

By Adele Nozedar

My name is Adele. I have two shops in Hay on Wye, one called Nepal Bazaar, which sells fair-trade clothes and crafts primarily from Nepal and Tibet, and another called Spellbound which sells occult books and magical supplies. I also run a recording studio up in the mountains of Wales. I like taking photographs, and I'm lucky enough that from time to time people pay me money to do this. I write books, too. I like doing all of these diverse things.

Although I was flattered to be included in this book, I wasn't exactly sure if I was a Pagan, so I looked at two different dictionaries to define exactly what it means. First, I looked it up in the *Student's English Dictionary* by Ogilvie and Annandale, published by Blackie and Son, dated 1913:

> **pagan**, pa/gan, n. (L. paganus, a peasant; fr. pagus, a village or country district, same root as Gr. Pegnymi; comp. origin of heathen. Akin peasant, page) A worshipper of false gods; one who is neither a Christian, a Jew, nor a Mohammedan; a heathen;

an idolater—a. Pertaining to pagans or heathens; heathenish; idolatrous.

Then, as a check to see if definitions might have changed after two world wars, I looked it up in the Concise Oxford Dictionary, ninth edition, published in 1996 (I really must get an updated version). Here's what it says:

pagan/ peigen/ *n & adj.* n; a person not subscribing to any of the main religions of the world, esp. formerly regarded by Christians as unenlightened or heathen. *adj;* 1a of or relating to or associated with pagans. b. Irreligious 2 identifying divinity or spirituality in nature; pantheistic. paganish *adj.* paganism *n.* paganise (middle English from Latin *paganus* villager, rustic from *pagus* country district; in Christian Latin = civilian, heathen)

Now, this is all very interesting. It's good to see that the definition has shifted a little bit and is a little less harsh than it was previously. After all, it's a well-known fact that the Christian church was responsible for the persecution and torture of non-Christians (the very Pagans we're talking about here), but it's worth bearing in mind, too, that the Romans threw the early Christians to their deaths in arenas full of ravening lions.

Am I a Pagan, though? No. Am I a Christian? No. I like the term "heathen" because it sounds a bit racy, but I'm not one of them, either. I'm interested in all expressions of belief and spirituality, but I don't like to categorize myself as one thing or another; to me it's just another form of territorialism the world can well do without.

Maybe it's time to stop all this "out with the old, in with the new." Maybe it's time for us to understand and tolerate ideas that are not ours; there may be Christians out there who are afraid of Pagan communities, but there are also Pagan communities that will vociferously denounce Christians, too. In fact, wasn't it Christ who told us to turn the other cheek? I think he also said something about considering lilies, how they don't appear to do anything except exist, and yet they have everything they need. This sounds to me to be quite a Pagan and irreligious sort of a concept.

Now I'm going to tell you a story. I'll say again that I am not a Christian, but I believe that I have a strong understanding of the thing that people call the "Christ Spirit." I went through what many people might perceive as a very strange period in my life, about twenty years ago. In fact, the whole thing was *so* intense that some of my friends thought I was going mad or having a breakdown, or something. To me, it was more of a break*through*.

The events leading up to this epic part of my life weren't great. I had split from my partner after ten years. This was painful and protracted; we'd been together since our teens. Years later, by the way, we are still good friends, but during the course of the separation I found the REAL version of the truth and started to express how I was really feeling inside. I needed to express myself, and my immediate surroundings became the object of that expression.

The more I worked out my own feelings, the more empowered I became. Sometimes I felt as though I could rule the world. I knew that I was a part of the Universe, that all the distressing and disempowering things that had happened with my partner were a sort of bow designed to pull me back so that once I could release myself from the confines of that bow, then, like an arrow, I'd fly really high!

I started to feel things about people; I knew what was wrong with them physically and knew that I could help them with the energies that were flowing through me. I had no self-consciousness about going up to people and telling them where their pain was, and asking permission to take it away. I just let it all flow. At work, if people were arguing, I found that if I just let the energy flow through me, then they would gradually grind to a halt and the argument would stop; like a juggernaut going into reverse, the energy that was flowing through me would turn any arguments back the other way and the nasty, discordant atmosphere would be replaced with one of harmony and concord. But I could never call myself a "healer"—none of this was my doing.

I felt so free, so alive; I would stop and talk to tramps in the street, sit with them, buy sandwiches and things for them. I spent a lot of time with a fabulous tramp lady called Rosie England, who was one of the wisest people I had ever met. Like me, she had "woken up" but found the everyday world hard to cope with in such a state. She had made a conscious decision to become a tramp, to help the many disturbed and often schizophrenic people that end up on the streets. I met one old Jamaican guy who stopped me in the street, crying; he told me that the energy of Christ was all around me, and asked me to look after his seven daughters who were all overseas. Another day, I was sitting in the sunshine outside a cafe with a friend when another old man came up, knelt at my feet, handed me a flower with shaking hands, and, in front of my astonished friend, told me that I was Fatima. He was weeping in the gutter and I really didn't know what to do, so I just laughed, pulled him up and sent him on his way. I know all this sounds vainglorious, but I'm just telling you how it was.

At this time I had an experience which showed me what had really happened when Christ had turned the water into wine in the miracle of the Wedding at Cana. When celestial energy flows through you, then it flows through everything you handle. I was pouring water from a jug for friends at a dinner when I suddenly realized was happening; it wasn't just water that they were receiving, but the Holy Spirit. The water was transformed by coming into contact with the Divine. I still feel silly calling it the "Holy Spirit," because I'm not religious and it reminds me of all those tedious RE lessons at school—but it's the most obvious explanation and the most immediate description. It's the same energy that people call "healing" energy, the same source that people call on to create music, art, or anything at all that is done in a creative, ego-free way.

I couldn't stop this energy flowing; I didn't want to. I gave everything away (apart from the flat, half of which actually belonged to my ex). If it had been mine to give, I would have done so. Giving things away, freely, is a heady experience. Friends came round and took crockery, furniture, the TV, books, records; everything. I kept a telephone answering machine with a cassette that I used for music, some clothes, a toothbrush, but very little else. The pleasure in seeing all these things go was intense. The delivery driver who came to fetch my bed to take it to an orphanage turned out to be a spiritual medium. As we were moving the bed I heard laughter in the next room although there was no one there. The medium heard it too; we stopped what we were doing, and he told me that the laughter was from a sister that I had never known about, who had died before she was born, and who was now an angel. He took my hands and showed me how to touch her; I felt something invisible but hot, and something soft and very like feathers, and I cried and cried. Later I spoke to my mother about the loss that she had never mentioned to anyone, not even my father.

One day, I got on the bus with a bag of biscuits. As I stepped on, I could see everyone's souls shining out of their eyes. It was overwhelming, but also so beautiful, seeing this union, that the same spirit was shared by everyone. I went the length of the bus offering everyone a biscuit from the bag, knowing that the same energy that had flowed through me and into the water would happen with the biscuits. Everyone took them, happy and smiling, except one person, who was afraid of me and looked away. Even the driver was happy. And I suddenly understood the meaning of the word "communion."

All through this time, believe it or not, I was managing to hold down a very important and well-paid job; I was effectively my own boss, although I did have employees to look after. I had freedom so long as I managed to get my work done.

A couple of days after the incident on the bus, someone came into my office and told me a story a friend of a friend had told her. Someone had been on the 72 bus a couple of days earlier when a woman had boarded, whom everyone had seen as an otherworldly being, an angel; she was apparently very bright and difficult to look at directly, haloed in blue light, and blessed everyone by offering them an ordinary biscuit from a bag. This vision had been shared by everyone on the bus.

How amazing, I thought, and then realized that this supposed angelic being must have been me.

That was REALLY weird. It made me think a lot, and I'm currently writing a book about angels. I'm not sure if this story will be in it.

Since then, I learned to control the flow of this energy; I studied massage and healing techniques, and rarely talk about that intense time that lasted for about three months. I don't even think about it that often. I am no angel—that's one thing I know for sure! But the incident on the bus really made me think about the nature of the divine; perhaps we are all sparks of that divine light, waiting for a match of some kind to light the touch paper that will make that spark burn. I see that light in people, in trees, in animals, in plants, in cloud formations. I am not a Pagan, I am not a Christian, and I don't like definitions per se.

I know now why some people call madness "divine," and would never question any of those things that we read about, that happened in the Bible or elsewhere, as fanciful or invented. I experienced those same things. I know what the spirit of Christ is, because I have felt it and experienced it; but I am not a Christian. I didn't look for these experiences, and they didn't result in me becoming "religious" or going to church, or anything like that. I wrote everything down as it was unfolding, but I've never shared this before. Now feels like the right time to tell this story. There's more, but this will do for now.

My experience can't be unique. Can it?

Maybe it's time to re-write the dictionary.

ABOUT THE AUTHOR

Adele Nozedar is an author, photographer, and dealer in fair trade goods. In a previous life she ran major and independent record labels. Her first book was the groundbreaking *Secret Language of Birds,* which has also been developed into a tarot deck of the same name. Her other books include *The Element Encyclopedia of Secret Signs and Symbols, The Signs and Symbols Sourcebook, The Magic of Angels, Fairies!,* and *The Book of Hedgerow Recipes.* Adele lives in the wild mountains of Wales and frequently travels in the East.

Eleven

......

The Gift of Jesus to Pagans and Christians

by Joyce Higginbotham

I was raised in a sect of Mormonism in a devout home that went to church twice on Sunday, and several times throughout the week for prayer service and meetings of various kinds. People unfamiliar with Mormonism may think it is not a "Christian" religion, but Mormonism shares many beliefs with Catholics and Protestants concerning the mission, death, and resurrection of Jesus. In our church he was viewed as a human being who was exalted by God because of certain choices he made in heaven, but he did not share an identity with God as divine. Because of his choices Jesus earned the adoptive status of "son" of God, a status I was taught we could all achieve. I attended other Protestant churches now and then in my youth, with family or friends, and found myself uncomfortable with the way Jesus was emphasized in their services. He was treated as a type of superman who waved a magic wand and saved you no matter what you did thereafter. These folks actually *worshipped* Jesus, as though he were himself God, a concept that was distasteful and foreign to me. So while the figure of Jesus was certainly prominent in my upbringing, the role he played in my church was different from that in other Christian denominations. Even so, we were taught to end every prayer with the words "in Jesus's name," and it was okay to pray to Jesus as well as God, since he was a spirit in heaven and could hear us. He felt important to me in my youth because I was told he was important, and he clearly played an important role in the religious story, but I never had any spiritual experiences with him.

Throughout my youth and young adulthood I believed that Jesus was a real historical person. I was told he was and so I believed he was. I believed the entire religious story was literally and historically true. As I got older and encountered other denominations, my literal view of the religious story began to be challenged. How could everyone be correct? What if other versions of Christianity were also valid? What if it wasn't true that my church was the one and only right church? Very gradually, over a period of ten or fifteen years, my spiritual horizon began to grow and it expanded first toward Catholicism. I liked the liturgy and ritual and even the "idolatrous" trappings I had been warned against. I learned that Catholics didn't actually "worship" statues or candles or any other physical thing, but used them as reminders of spiritual realities. Catholics prayed to a much larger assortment of spirit beings, but if as a Mormon I could address my thoughts to Jesus as a spirit in heaven, why couldn't I address myself to other spirits in heaven? From about the age of fifteen I was particularly attracted to the Catholic ideal of religious life, the chanting of the Hours, and adoration of the Sacrament. I would eventually live in a convent for a year as I sorted out these feelings.

Opening to Catholicism required a big expansion on my part, as there was a strong anti-Catholic bias in my faith of origin. A Catholic church was considered the home of the devil, filled with idols, and to associate with Catholics was to put myself directly into Satan's power. My mind rejected this as absurd, but it still took a great deal of courage for me to go to a Catholic church and associate with Catholics. I had been raised to believe that ours was the only true church and everyone else's was an instrument of the devil. My experience argued against that belief, however, and the more I interacted with other spiritual paths, the more I knew the belief to be false. Over time my reason and my conscience demanded that I abandon this belief, and so I did.

In my twenties I encountered Neopaganism for the first time and was attracted to it. I began to incorporate it into my mixed bag of Mormonism and Catholicism. Paganism may seem like a big leap from a Mormon-Catholic background, but it really was just an extension of my Mormon upbringing. All Mormon sects use the Book of Mormon as a scriptural text. This book claims to be a record of what happened to the lost tribes of Israel, who it says sailed to the New World, settled in Latin America, and eventually became the precursors to the Mayans and some Native Americans. Our church had an entire department devoted to Native Americans it called (in the days before political correctness) Indian Ministries. This ministry regularly hosted conferences and worship services that were open to the general membership. When I attended these services I found that I got more out of them than the usual Sunday service. I liked the drumming and the dancing and the more generic references to God as Great Spirit. I liked their reverence for the earth and animals, and the inclusion of them into the spirituality, as though the earth and its creatures had a consciousness or spiritual reality of their own. So by the time I encountered Paganism in the 1980s, I felt at home in it.

The gift Paganism gave me then was the freedom and permission to explore the full range of religious story. Every mythology was mine to study. No time period was off limits, no belief system was forbidden. Every pantheon of deities could be explored and treated as valid. I was enjoying a global feast, one that opened up to me the entire realm of human religious experience. The more I studied, however, the more I found myself moving away from a literal view of any mythology. I began to see every religious mythos as a metaphor for deep realities of the human experience. I did not believe, for example, that the constellations were really formed by Zeus turning people into stars. I did not believe that Turtle really and truly carries the earth on his back, or that somewhere still lies the empty box that Pandora opened. Do any of us really? But eventually the day came when my mind posed the inescapable question. If I understood everyone else's mythology to be a metaphor, why would I believe the Christian story to be literally and historically true?

This was a question that I left alone for twenty years. It was enough for me to grapple with mythology as metaphor generally, especially in the context of a Pagan community that for the most part still sees myth in literal terms. But as my husband and I were writing our third book, *ChristoPaganism,* I was forced to look the question of Jesus's historicity squarely in the eye. I went into the writing of that book with my assumptions of Jesus as a real and historical person intact, and came out of the writing of it with my assumptions in tatters. Most surprising to me was how angry this made me.

I was angry for months, in fact. I was angry at the church for having lied to me. I was angry with the early historians who forged and interpolated as it suited them, the priests and bishops who burned up all the records that contradicted them. I was even angry at my training as an attorney that forced me to see the evidence dispassionately and draw conclusions I didn't like. On the other side of my anger and grief, however, a realization began taking shape. I can illustrate this realization with a story.

A friend of mine went to study with some Native Americans who taught her to listen and record her dreams. So she dreamed one night that she was a bird. And as this bird, she flew to a branch and landed on it. She picked up a beetle in her beak, but dropped it onto the ground, and from her perch watched the beetle run away. She told this dream to her Native American teachers, and they said to her: "you are every piece of this dream." And so she told the story of her dream again, and as she did she identified herself with each part of it. Like this: "the bird part of me and the flying part of me came to the branch part of me, where the picked part of me took the beetle part of me in the beak part of me, when the dropping part of me and the grounded part of me and the watching part of me saw the running away part of me."

The beauty of our personal dreams, and of our collective dreams that we call religious story, lies in the reality that we are each of us the story that we tell. Out of my grief at the loss of one understanding of Jesus—a temporal, historically-bound Jesus—came a different understanding of him—an eternally-experienced Jesus that was never true but is always true. With this perspective I am able to touch more deeply the virgin-born part of me, the tempted part of me, the misunderstood part of me, and the triumphant part of me. And I can also really touch the persecuted part of you, and the miracle-working part of you, the abandoned part of you, and the redemptive part of you. For you see, Jesus is not a character in a story external to you, he is the reality of you.

This, then, is what I see the gift of Jesus to be—both to Pagans and Christians—because I see it as the gift of all religious story. It is too late to wonder whether one can be both Pagan and Christian, since we are already Christ within, and Zeus within, and Turtle within, and Pandora within. When we treat religious story as a *temporal* truth we are more easily drawn into arguments and schisms, even violence. But when we treat religious story as an eternal truth, then we can see immediately how much religions have to offer each other, for the *eternal* aspects of our mythologies are really inexhaustible.

About the Author

Joyce Higginbotham makes her home in the Midwest, where she and her husband River Higginbotham are active in networking on both the local and the national level. She has been a noted teacher for nearly two decades and has helped plan and host several hundred public Pagan and earth-centered events in the Midwest. Together with her husband she has authored *Paganism: An Introduction to Earth-Centered Religions*, *Pagan Spirituality: A Guide to Personal Transformation*, and *ChristoPaganism: An Inclusive Path*, all published by Llewellyn. The Unitarian church has adopted their introductory book as a text for an adult religious education course on earth religions, and several universities use their books as a text or required reading for both graduate and undergraduate religious studies classes. For more information, visit their website at www.riverandjoyce.com or visit their Facebook page.

Twelve

......

Jesus Through the Eyes of a Witch

by Christopher Penczak

I t's funny that I have a better relationship and understanding of Jesus
now that I'm a High Priest in the tradition of Witchcraft than I ever
did as a Catholic. I really didn't have any particular love or understanding
of Jesus back at the Central Catholic High School for Boys. I didn't really
understand him. The voluntary sacrifice made no sense to me. I didn't
understand the point of it all.

What I did like was some aspects of the rituals. I liked the candles, and
on the special occasions when it was lit, the incense. I liked some of the
singing, but as I grew to have a more critical ear, I found that the Catholic
Church was probably not the best place for good religious music. I like the
vestments of the priests and deacon, though I never desired to be an altar
boy because I didn't like the idea of taking orders. I like the altar and the
statues, and all the things to look at and be absorbed into the details of
their craftsmanship. At heart I was really a Pagan waiting to happen, but I
think a lot of Catholics are.

The theology of original sin and the need to be saved and redeemed didn't sit too well with me. I didn't understand why Jesus needed to sacrifice himself to save us. I thought if I understood this was all rather silly, and probably made up by religion, not God, then why didn't he? It never occurred to me that perhaps there was a difference between the historical Jesus and the one painted in the scriptures, assuming such a person existed as flesh and blood in the first place. I assumed if there was another view of Jesus, then of course, to be fair, the Church would present that. Looking back, I thought myself so jaded and worldly, but I was really still innocent and naïve.

It was only through the study of witchcraft that I got a new view on Jesus, quite unexpectedly. When the topic first came up in conversation with a teacher, she said, "Well, we think he's one of us, not one of them." I was perplexed. What did she mean? "Well, he's a witch, a magician, an initiate of the old ways. Think about it: a man who went around with twelve other men like a coven, wandering place to place in nature, performing magic. He respected and honored women. He spoke with prostitutes. He gave wisdom and advice. He's a lot closer to us than to Christians today." I didn't quite believe it until I started to think about it, and I had to agree. Perhaps Jesus was some kind of witch or magician of the old ways.

Through the mysteries of initiation, I saw the parallels of Jesus's ordeal in my own training, the descent to the underworld and the resurrection to the stellar (or heavenly) consciousness. I saw that it was not just Jesus's story, but the story of many initiates on the path. Through historical research, I saw the influence of the ancient mystery schools upon the early Gnostic Christians. The Egyptian iconography of Isis, Osiris, and Horus influenced Catholic artwork in depictions of Madonna and Child, and there was some influence upon the story. The Mystery Schools of the Greeks, looking to Dionysus and Orpheus as models of descent, also influenced the Christian vision. Jesus and Dionysus were both associated with wine and miracles. And of course one cannot discount the Sun god Mithras in the evolution of Christianity. All of those traditions, images, and icons have also influenced modern witchcraft traditions. I saw the mystery of Jesus in terms of the agricultural and solar cycle, the returning and triumphant Sun of God if not the Son of God. He is the Child of Light, Hope, and Promise.

As I learned more about magick, particularly studying the influence of Hermetic and Qabalistic influences upon modern witchcraft, I got to understand more about the principle of Christ beyond the personality of Jesus. For the Christian alchemist, Jesus can be seen as the philosophical gold, the perfected man who has found the secret of the Philosopher's Stone. He has been elevated from the lead of the world into the gold of heaven. To the Qabalist, he is the heart of the Tree of Life. He is Tiphereth, solar harmony who grants the Vision of Sacrifice and the Vision of Harmony. He is an expression of all the sacrificed gods, not just sacrificed for religion, or agriculture, but of the selflessness of doing for others without thought or return for the self. It is the vision to be willing to give up everything to be the solar light for others. And in that realization, one truly gives up nothing, for all is gained. You pass through the veil of illusion and enter a new level of spiritual initiation, a new path with other challenges and blessings.

Rather than blind belief, in these ceremonial traditions one must be Christ-like in action, and through the arts of alchemy and magick, attain this perfected state. The body and consciousness is the laboratory as well as the more traditional workspace of tools, herbs, and metals. Ideally, through this path of magick, one reaches enlightenment. There it was again, Jesus as magician. In this sense, he didn't seem so bad. I could almost like the guy if not for those who supposedly followed his teaching and named themselves after him.

But not until I met and studied with those who inherited the Theosophical traditions, today known as light workers and ascension practitioners, did I experience Jesus in a new light. To divorce him from the teachings of the Christian church, some practitioners believe that Master Jesus is an ascended being, one of many who attain this level of "Christ Consciousness." These ascended masters come from all religions, races, traditions, and time periods. They believe his name on the "inner planes" is Sananda, and I was okay calling upon Master Sananda rather than Jesus Christ. He is the Cohen, or master, of the sixth ray, the ray of devotion, religion, and philosophy, which is giving way to the seven ray in the new age, the violet ray of magick and ceremonial order. One of the assignments in a particular ascension course was to make peace with your birth religion. Done! I had no problem with Catholicism. It wasn't for me, but I wasn't at war with it. Or was I? I had to admit upon meditation that I had a lot more resentment than I realized, but I also had a lot of resistance to this particular task, as I had no idea how to go forward with it.

Then something happened in meditation that was like a dream, surreal in the way that dreams can be. I had a vision of Jesus making his way through a crowd of other deities, spirits, and allies with whom I had more familiar relationships. He came in to my meditation rather politely and though much of the salient details were lost in the dream-like state, he basically wanted to make peace with me. He was not my guide. He was not meant to be my guide, but he was not my enemy and he didn't endorse all the actions done in his name. But he gave the world a view on the mysteries, a new particular slant that will be the Christian mysteries. They had a purpose. They are part of the greater whole and can be valued without getting into politics. Then he disappeared back into the crowd.

After that vision, I was much more at peace with the figure of Jesus Christ and those who profess to be Christians. I stopped looking at myself as a persecuted person, as a modern Pagan, a witch, a gay man, a non-Christian in a Christian-dominated world. I realize now that if I truly believe everything happens for a reason, that everything and everyone serves the Goddess, whether consciously realized or not, then so does Christianity serve the Goddess. I'm not sure how, but it has had a purpose in the evolution of our society. Like the Theosophists, I also believe its time of dominance is over. A plurality of voices in the age of magick, of the violet ray, will rise. It has set the stage for what comes next, to transition from the Age of Pisces to the Age of Aquarius, and must now be one of many voices, one of many viewpoints on the mysteries, along with witchcraft and all the Pagan traditions, along with all the world religions, East and West.

ABOUT THE AUTHOR

Christopher Penczak is a modern Witch, teacher, and award-winning author. His books include the *Temple of Witchcraft* series, as well as *Magick of Reiki* and *The Three Rays of Witchcraft*. His aim is the synthesis of magickal, philosophical, and healing traditions through the lens of Witchcraft and magickal spirituality. He is co-founder of The Temple of Witchcraft, a nonprofit religious organization devoted to education and service, and co-owner of Copper Cauldron Publishing, a company devoted to the creation of books and tools for spiritual development.

Thirteen

......

The Lily Cross
and the Green Man

by Maria Ede-Weaving

As a Pagan Druid, Easter still holds meaning for me. It is hard not to make the rather obvious connection between the resurrection of Christ and the renewing of the natural world in spring; after all, this process is a living reality all around us, a joyous transformation that vividly articulates the mysteries of regeneration and hope.

It does not take a massive leap of the imagination to consider Christ as a kind of Green Man. Many Pagans—and a few Christians too—have already made the link, and here on the Isle of Wight, we have a beautiful mediaeval church mural that seems to express something of this notion. Of course, the mural's original symbolism would—I suspect—have been very different to that of my modern Pagan perspective, but no less meaningful.

The mural is in the beautiful village church of Godshill. Godshill is the Island's chocolate-box tourist attraction, with many quaint little thatched cottages, gift shops, and cafes. All Saints Church is the most photographed on the island, perched high above the village on the hill that gives this place its name.

There is a legend attached to the building of the church, one which is identical to that of Alfriston Church in East Sussex. Both are built on distinctive mounds and are believed to have originally been home to pre-Christian sites of worship. The name Godshill is thought to mean "hill of the idol," the said hill standing rather incongruously above the flat village. The view from its summit of the surrounding downland is stunningly beautiful; it's a place that feels ancient and curiously separate from the constant stream of tourists down in the village.

The legend goes that the Christian missionaries who built the church began its foundations on a level piece of land a mile or so south of the present position. On three successive nights, the stones were uprooted and moved to the hill by mysterious forces. The builders would take the stones back to their chosen site, only to find them relocated to the hill the following morning. After the third time, they took the hint and built the church on the hill, believing this to be God's choice. The more likely scenario is that Christians used the Pagan site, just as they had in other places as a means of conversion. The island itself strongly resisted Christianity, being the last Pagan stronghold in England. This link between Pagan and Christian religious worship at this extraordinary place gives the mural an added depth for me.

The mural shows Christ crucified on a flowering lily. The lily has three main branches, a further three shooting off from each of these. From a Pagan sensibility, it is clear that Christ's sacrifice reflects that of the Green Man's and this image seems to express the mythic qualities of both. As vegetation god, the Green Man offers his own body that others may live and flourish; he is grown up, cut down, and reborn in the yearly cycle of his living and dying, and the deeper mysteries of his sacrifice bring hope and the possibility of renewal for all beings. Like Christ's story, we find in the Green Man's cycle our own cyclical and eternal natures.

Historically, the structure of these layers of belief might be erroneously viewed as a separate Pagan stratum beneath that of the Christian surface. If we dig a little deeper, we find that—like the mulch in a forest, whose distinct layers are churned up and mixed in by the creatures that draw nourishment from it—there is a great deal of syncretic merging between that of the Pagan and that of the Christian. This is not only felt at the original point of contact but can resonate still, in subtle ways, hundreds of years later. This happens because our spiritual beliefs are not born in a vacuum; spiritualities are constantly being influenced and changed over time by "outside" ideas. There is no such thing as a pure belief, and as a Pagan who was once a Christian and who is now also influenced by Eastern traditions, this becomes all the more apparent to me. There are threads of my old faith, plus other philosophies that I am discovering along the way, that quite naturally interweave themselves into the main fabric of my current spiritual life. With regard to my Christian experience, I feel that I have been able to release what no longer has relevance to me, whilst holding on to the many valuable lessons and values it blessed me with.

Leaving behind Christianity was far easier than actually leaving behind the figure of Christ. The powerful impact that he had on my childhood has ultimately meant that many of his qualities continue to inform my understanding of the Divine Masculine. There is a great deal of Christ lurking in my understanding of the Pagan Horned God. To clarify, writing of the Horned God in the singular is rather misleading because, for me, he is a mixture of several different god forms—one of which is popularly referred to as the "Green Man." All of these expressions of the Divine intimately link with the natural world and its wisdom.

The beauty of a Pagan perspective on the Divine is that we are each free to honor it in whatever form feels most pertinent to us, without any rigidly prescribed notions directing our approach. For me, the Horned God is a nature God in its most expansive and deepest sense. I feel him working not only in the natural environments most familiar to me but in the mysteries of the atom, the spiraling of galaxies, the birth and death of stars, and the body and spirit of my own being. Many Pagans see him as a guardian of nature's balance. He is a God of fertility, vitality, sexuality, and abundance, but he is also a God of sacrifice for the greater good and in this aspect in particular, the Christ of my childhood faith bleeds into and merges with that of my present spirituality.

Like Christ, the Green Man's shadowed face is not one of destruction for its own sake; rather it is a compassionate expression of death that life may flourish. He is often referred to as both hunter and hunted, for as we are all subject to his "culling"—in order for life to continue and the balance to be kept—he is also himself cut down in the harvest of our food (be it animal or vegetable): he knows what it means to die and is seen as a guide and protector on the journey through and beyond death. He contains within his nature the paradox of "life in death and death in life," and we experience this most obviously through the seasonal journey he embodies and the cycle of our own lives.

Christ's journey contains this same paradox. As the Green Man's sacrifice maintains the integrity of the natural world through the cycles of life, death, and rebirth, Christ's maintains the integrity of the spirit through these very same cycles. Both have taught me to honor and trust in this process of shedding; of releasing and transcending my old self that the life in me might be reborn; that I might become more authentically myself. In the process of this sacrifice we learn about compassion, for ourselves and all life forms. Out of that compassion—born of the experiences of living—something verdant springs to life. What is so powerful about the image of Christ crucified on a living lily—as opposed to the "dead wood" of the cross—is that it speaks to us of this unending potential for the greening of our souls. It reassures us that despite the reality that life will bring us the toughest of challenges and the deepest of pain, living is essentially a thing of profound mysticism, beauty, and hope. What is striking about the image of the Lily Cross is that it articulates so directly the renewal at the core of loss; the regeneration from dissolution that both Christ and the Green Man embody.

I have long left behind the theology of the faith I was born into, and this has given me the freedom to explore a Christ unbound by the restrictions of dogma. Because of this, the Christ of my current understanding expresses a greater earthiness. The Green Christ and the Green Man are both the joyous life-force that bursts forth in bud, leaf and fruit: life's wild abundance. They are also the golden life-giving sun whose warmth and light fertilizes not only the earth but our own bodies, minds, hearts, and spirits. They are both the vital spark of life that brings us happiness and pleasure and the sacrifice of the harvest that feeds us. In their dissolution we find the mulch and leaf mould that rots into the Earth Mother's body, nourishing new life; we find also the remains of our ill-fitting lives transformed into the wisdom and guidance that will move us forward, guiding us to tackle the changes with trust and optimism. In embodying both the intense struggle and the deep peace of death, the challenge of endings and the promise of renewal, they enable us to embrace paradox. In learning to hold seemingly opposing energies within our understanding of the Divine (and therefore of life itself) there is the potential for a greater tolerance, compassion, and understanding, not only for ourselves and other humans but for all creation.

The Christ that has merged with and continues to inform my understanding of the Divine has regained his life-giving phallus and with it a joyous sexuality that honors the sacred connection between sex, life, death, and rebirth. His word is never carved in stone; it sings from the blackbird; and is heard in the rustle of leaves and the silent glory of the stars. It is the pain of letting go; the urgency and desire of a lover's touch. The Jesus of my childhood has resurrected in my consciousness as the Green Christ: the joy, hope, and poignancy of living. He is a vital part of my worship of the Divine Masculine. When I open to him, I open to the wonder and blessings of life; I see the wisdom and meaning of all life's experiences—both the happiness and the tragedy. When I reach for his empathetic understanding, I am infused with his strength and bolstered by his protection. In his sharing of the wisdom of seed and flower, of fruit and falling leaf, the turning tides of my life become a little easier to navigate; the joy at the heart of creation more apparent, more intensely felt.

About the Author

Maria Ede-Weaving is a musician and writer. A longtime member of the Order of Bards, Ovates, and Druids, she has had articles published in a range of journals, including *SageWoman* and *Pagan Dawn*. Maria explores the personal challenges and joys of following an earth-based spirituality in her blog, A Druid Thurible: luckyloom1.wordpress.com/.

Fourteen

......

A Goddess Advocate
Talks about Jesus

by Karen Tate

Author's note: In hindsight, it is probably rather telling that I gave little thought to Jesus until I was no longer Catholic. Growing up in the Bible Belt of New Orleans, a conservative Christian region of the southern United States, one was not encouraged to question religious authority, much less express dissent, but instead accept as fact whatever was preached from the pulpit on Sundays. When I actually identified with a spirituality that inspired my sincere mind and heart connection with the Divine, it was Goddess Spirituality that called me, and it was as a Goddess Advocate that I began to really think about Jesus, Christianity, and the institution I'll loosely call the Church.

Thinking back, Jesus was little more than that sad and suffering figure on the cross at the front of the church, or that little baby in the manger at Christmas time, while the sacrifice of his life to his father, our god, for our sins never made much sense to me. I felt that sacrifice, whether accepted or required, spoke volumes more about Jesus's heavenly father—a deity I cared little to claim as my god—and prayed I might escape his notice lest I might incur his wrath. There was something about a god who condoned suffering and accepted the sacrifice of sons that seemed too remote from the wise and loving deity, archetype, or ideal I could lovingly and readily embrace as Divine. I'm not sure when I actually put it into words, but I believe intuitively I rejected the Christian ideas of suffering and sacrifice. I wondered why a female face of divinity was so lacking. I think on some level, I wondered but could not actually put into words why life-affirming ideas seemed so lacking within this religion I was born into, because no one was talking about it. Everyone just accepted the dogma. You see, we lived in a bubble. We only met other Christians. There just was little to no opportunity or encouragement to question the programming. Everyone I knew was a Catholic or Baptist and they all seemed to toe the party line, or if they did not, they were not openly talking about it. We seemed to revel in and never question singing lyrics in church on Sunday like "Onward Christian soldiers, marching as to war." Or how bad deeds could be practiced all week, but on Sunday, in confession you got a "get out of jail free" card by saying a few Hail Mary prayers. But when I opened my eyes and took responsibility for my own education and gave myself permission to question, I began to see the Church dogma as giving license to a select few to control the masses and to the powerful to commit far too many sins—none of which seemed in alignment with the teachings of Jesus.

Reconciling Jesus within Her Spiritual Paradigm

When I first uncovered Goddess herstory from the sands of time and patriarchal lies and subterfuge, I'm not ashamed to say I was livid. I was metaphorically on fire that I had been duped for the first thirty years of my life. And when I found out the role of the Church in the subjugation of women and destruction of other cultures, I was filled with utter disdain. I'm having trouble even finding the words for the toxic emotion inspired by these realizations. At first, I hated anything related to the Church, including Mary and Mary Magdalene, Pope John Paul II (who loved Mary), and the nuns who taught me. I was ready to discard even these female faces, who had once been the only figures within Christianity that provided any solace or sense of heartfelt connection to this religion I'd come to see as despicable. Although this does not describe all Christians, when I saw how the religious right was using Christianity as a weapon to steer government in the United States, and as a wedge issue to fan the flames of fear and hate to divide people, I was disgusted even more.

Don't even get me started on the hypocrisy. Many of the vocal and self-righteous Christians who were always telling everyone else the right way to live were the ones getting caught starting bogus wars, having affairs, soliciting prostitutes, telling lies, stealing, abusing their power—all the while they failed to really live by the teachings of Jesus. Sure they would shout out at us from our television screens or from their multi-million-dollar pulpits about *finding Jesus* and by the way, don't forget to increase offertory giving and mail them a check—but the teachings of Jesus were hardly what these church leaders and many Christians were practicing. They stood for taking reproductive rights away from women, denying gay people equal rights, teaching abstinence instead of sex education, then failing to commit funds to poor people who could not afford to feed their children. It seemed their god was power, control, and the mighty dollar.

When this veil was lifted from my mind and eyes, it was difficult at first to return to anything remotely related to the Church—even Jesus, who was being used as their poster guy to legitimize suffering, sin, and abuse of the masses. Church leaders seemed to count on their belief no one was opening a book or discussing ideas on the Internet. They counted on everyone continuing to take their word as gospel and not question or give themselves permission to see history and spirituality through a fresh lens. And that is how I began to reclaim Jesus within my spiritual paradigm as a Goddess Advocate. In fact, I came to believe that if Jesus would ever appear back on Earth, his heart would be broken by the deeds perpetrated in his name. I remembered that Jesus was not part of the status quo. In fact, in his day he would have been a heretic; certainly not a sheeple or one of the voices perpetrating suffering among the many for the benefit of the few. In his day he railed against the abuse caused by Temple elders, as he would surely today. Forever seared in my memory are scenes from the *Jesus Christ Superstar* movie when he overturns the tables of the money-changers, walks with the poor, and treats women as his equals. The figure of Jesus began to become rehabilitated in my mind—and he had nothing to do with the institution that is the Church.

Jesus—The Sacred Masculine

I began to see Jesus in many new ways. I saw him and his mother Mary as the last figures in the long line of Pagan Goddesses and their consorts, with Jesus the dying and rising lord or king. Just as several of the Goddesses such as Isis and Artemis passed their baton on to Mary, Jesus was the Green Man, Attis, Tammuz, and Osiris. In fact during the season of Ostara, near the Christian holy day of Easter, I have a meditation I traditionally read to our group where we see in our mind's eye the face of the consort of the Goddess morphing from one god to another, finally ending with that of Jesus. And now Christmas time becomes an opportunity instead of a farce—I use my radio show and platforms to publish articles or open discussions to remind Christians of their Pagan roots. December 25 has associations not just with Jesus's birthday, but with Pagan traditions, Winter Solstice, and the god Mithras.

With my newfound relationship to Jesus, Mary, and Mary Magdalene, I also feel less hesitant to walk into a Christian church. I go in and look for the female faces of deity: Mary, Mary Magdalene, Guadalupe, and Black Madonnas. And when I see Jesus sitting in the lap of Mary, I see not only the consort of Goddess, but I also see Horus in the lap of Isis. And finally, I see in Jesus, the Sacred Masculine. He is the Sacred Bridegroom of Mary Magdalene, herself an aspect of Goddess, and in their pairing is the balance of the Divine Couple—Divine Feminine and Sacred Masculine, our sacred life force, in wholeness, in balance, in equality, as it always should have been. I see in this Divine Duo the common ground where Pagans and progressive Christians can come together outside of the confines and dogma of the Church to build a new and healthy society, culture, and spirituality that serves the many and not just the few.

ABOUT THE AUTHOR

Karen Tate is a teacher, speaker, ritualist, radio show host, sacred tour leader, and author. Her first book, *Sacred Places of Goddess: 108 Destinations,* has garnered prestigious endorsements and *Walking An Ancient Path: Rebirthing Goddess on Planet Earth* was a finalist in the USA National Best Books Awards. *Voices of the Sacred Feminine*, her long-running radio show, has been called a treasure trove of wisdom for our age. Karen's work has segued into writing, producing, and consulting on documentaries and film, and she still leads and organizes sacred tours that circle the globe. For more information, visit www.karentate.com.

Fifteen

······

The Shamanic Christ

by James Carrington

Though as a Pagan I have moved away from the Christianity within which I was raised, I still make room for the personality we call Christ and the stories surrounding him.

My path is based in shamanism and the animistic traditions of various tribal cultures. Both the subjects of tribal cultures and beliefs systems fascinate me, and over the last twenty-one years I've studied ancient stories and practices from cultures as far removed as the North Native Americans to the Australian Aborigines, from Druidry to Mongolian shamanism.

I wasn't one of those children who simply hated going to church or wanted to rebel against my Christian upbringing; on the contrary, I was very devout and believed wholeheartedly in the teachings of the Bible. But as I began to take an interest in history, story, and culture as well as science, I began to feel that the only real relevance the Bible held for me was the teachings of Christ himself, both in sermon and in action.

The stories had such a profound effect on me that I decided to look at why. The first story I remember having such an effect was of Jesus walking into a synagogue, seeing the gambling tables and the obvious hypocrisy in the building, flying into a rage, and dismantling the tables. The fact that Christ could feel anger and express it in such a way proved his humanity; it made him more real than simply the son of an ethereal being.

As I looked at the stories and practices of other cultures, I began to see correspondences between these and the stories of Christ, in particular the similarities between Christ's crucifixion and resurrection and that of the shamanic initiation experience. Also the fact that Jesus was born of a virgin echoed the births of other shamanic figures, gods, and demi-gods across the world, from Quetzalcoatl of the Inca, to Abai Geser of the Mongolians, and even to our own Myrddin (Merlin); all were born of virgins.

Let's examine the shamanic initiation experience. The first and most striking thing one notices when reading books on the subject of shamanism, such as *Shamanism: Archaic Techniques of Ecstasy* (Pantheon Books, 1964) by Mircea Eliade, is that the experience varies little across the globe, even among cultures who supposedly never had contact with each other.[123]

During the experience, the initiate ascends to the heavens usually by climbing a tree. There, he or she is dismembered, ripped apart, torn to pieces, and yet feels no fear or pain. It is said that the initiate then dies, though this death is metaphorical. During this "death," the initiate travels between the heavens and the underworld. The initiate learns all the skills he or she needs for journeying to the heavens or the underworld (the shamanic underworld is not a place of eternal torment; rather it is seen as the place to where all but the most remarkable of souls go). After this tuition ends, the initiate comes into a new life. He or she is said to be born as a shaman—someone who is able to remain in contact with the gods—to prophesy and to heal.

In the story of Christ's crucifixion he is placed upon a cross, violently nailed to it, stabbed in the side by a spear, and forced to wear a crown of thorns. On this cross, after three hours (an incredibly significant number in many religions and faiths across the world), he dies. He spends three days in hell before ultimately coming back to life and ascending into heaven. From heaven he is able to talk to his community, guide and protect them.

There are of course glaring differences. For instance, Christ did not willingly climb his tree, and he remains in the heavens. But the similarities cannot be overlooked.

An old practice of the Lakota still used today also mirrors this story: the practice of the sundance. In the sundance, the practitioners go through immense physical pain and distress, literally piercing their bodies with hooks, or cutting their chests, backs, or arms to tie thongs through them. They are then suspended from a tree in some situations, such as Sitting Bull's sundance before the battle of Little Bighorn in June 1876. The practitioner also cuts strips of his own flesh to offer to the Great Spirit (sometimes called *wakan tanka*, among many names). The object of the sundance varies; sometimes (as in the case of Sitting Bull) it is to ask the Great Spirit to bestow a great blessing, more than the average man could ask. Of course, Sitting Bull was praying that his people would not be slaughtered. In other cases, the sundance is used as a coming of age or initiatory rite. Once again we see the tree and the dismemberment.

Other practices, such as the Native American vision quest or the Australian Aborigine walkabout, echo Christ's time of isolation in the wilderness.

From his outburst in the synagogue to his time in solitude, his ability to heal and transmute water to wine, Christ shows both unusual mannerisms and extraordinary abilities. The same can be said for shamanic initiates, many of whom "suffer" from "mental disturbances" such as depression, rage, "schizophrenia," or epilepsy. In their youth, shamanic initiates show a preference for solitude, and are often marked for emotional outbursts.

I see Christ (as with Myrddin) as a great spirit guide, a shaman who has passed the greatest trial of all, surviving death in one way to achieve immortality. Through great wisdom, peace, and love, he teaches us how to be more compassionate and shows us through his stories how we too can enter a state of being intouch with the divine.

About the Author

James Carrington is an author, Druid, human rights activist, and active blogger. He gives workshops and talks on many areas of Shamanism and Druidry, and organises charity events and environmental action. He is the founder of the Grove of Yews, based in Buckinghamshire, and a member of both OBOD and the Loyal Arthurian Warband. His website can be found at www.thegroveofyews.blogspot.com

Sixteen

......

Encountering
the Galilean

by Stephen Critchley

In this short essay I am going to briefly consider aspects of historical "Pagan" views of Jesus and then conclude with a summary of some of my own views as a contemporary devotee of the Craft and initiate of the Western mystery tradition.

It is fairly well known that the term "pagan" is derived from the Latin *paganus,* which simply means rural, rustic, or "a country dweller." When Christianity began to be practiced as the state religion of the Roman Empire and Pagan temples were being closed and often plundered and vandalized by zealous Christian monks, it flourished first in the cities. The pagan (rural) areas were places that often lagged behind the cities when social changes occurred. The temples and shrines of the old gods in the countryside often survived a little longer than did their urban counterparts; hence the country-folk were generally devoted to the old gods for longer than the city-folk, though history has shown that the old ways survived in various forms, both in towns and in the countryside.

The shift towards the Christian faith (that was becoming statically systemized into a Catholic "*universal*" form rather than being an assortment of various cults or "Christianities") occurred during the reign of the Emperor Constantine I, who ruled from 306–337 CE. Constantine's nephew Julian, Roman Emperor from 360–363 CE, was raised and trained as a Christian but recanted that faith in favor of Hellenic Paganism and is thus often called Julian the Apostate. Julian was particularly devoted to the god Helios, "the Sovereign Sun"; to the solar divinity Mithras, as was common amongst the Roman military; and to the Mother of the Gods, known by many names. Eclecticism was as much a feature of ancient Paganism as it is of modern Paganism. One of the hallmarks of ancient "Pagan" society in the West, especially in late antiquity, was a tolerance of different ways of being devoted to spiritual experience and service. It is a noble tradition that individuals can serve and have special relationship with a deity or deities that they choose, or that choose them. Connection with the Divine through an aspect of it (a particular goddess, god, or some other symbol) is the basis of reflecting cosmic principles in personal contexts, which is a central aspect of priesthood as well as of initiation.

Julian was the last non-Christian ruler of the Roman Empire. He was politically tolerant of Christianity but opposed its supremacy as a state religion; he hated hypocrisy in Pagan as well as Christian contexts. He attempted, most often unsuccessfully, to re-establish the Pagan temples, shrines, oracles, and cults that had begun to wane. Many view it as one of his weaknesses that he was idealistic philosophically, in his personal views, and that he was interested in mystical philosophic-religious experiences. Julian was a dedicated student of Pagan philosophy, particularly Platonism, and was a practitioner of ritual theurgy in the style of Iamblichus. Julian worshipped the gods of his ancestors while also honoring the One and the Good—the ultimate God who was beyond all knowledge, description, gender attribution, or anthropomorphisation. Many "Pagans" throughout antiquity were much more than nature worshippers. They were pantheistic, and sometimes also animistic monotheists who understood that behind all goddesses was one Goddess, behind all the gods was one God, and beyond all was ultimately only One. Modern Hindus could in no way be called "Pagans," and their ultimate religious philosophy is very much what has just been described: the One is encountered at first through multiplicity in the phenomenal world. Many of the ancient "Pagans" would have seen worshipping a rock as just as much an act of superstitious idolatry as would a Hebraic monotheist—however, it would be accepted that one could worship the divine through the symbol of a rock.

In 361 CE Julian wrote a satire called *The Caesars*, in view of traditions surrounding the *Kronia* or *Saturnalia* festivities, when it was traditional to mock and invert all authority in jest and the gods permitted "man to make merry." In the satire several of Julian's forebears attend a banquet being hosted by Romulus in the netherworld to which several goddesses, gods, and heroes have also been invited. Part of the plot involves each of the assembled Roman Emperors choosing a guardian deity from amongst the gathering of divinities.

Julian depicts Jesus attending the gathering (as a deity) in the company of Pleasure and Incontinence, sported as minor deities. He writes of his uncle, who first began to entertain Christianity as a state religion, though he was not fully converted to that religion until the end of his life:

> *As for Constantine, he could not discover among the gods the model of his own career, but when he caught sight of Pleasure, who was not far off, he ran to her. She received him tenderly and embraced him, then after dressing him in raiment of many colors and otherwise making him beautiful, she led him away to Incontinence. There too he found Jesus, who had taken up his abode with her and cried aloud to all comers: "He that is a seducer, he that is a murderer, he that is sacrilegious and infamous, let him approach without fear! For with this water will I wash him and will straightway make him clean. And though he should be guilty of those same sins a second time, let him but smite his breast and beat his head and I will make him clean again." To him Constantine came gladly…*

> —(Julian, Caes. 336B, trans. Wright)

Here, Jesus—or at least the way in which Jesus was being used by the Church to proffer forgiveness to converts—is criticized. Julian's Pagan morality had a sense of honor at its heart in which people owned their sins and paid for them themselves. Admission of wrongs and attempted reformation of poor behavior was also held in high esteem amongst Pagans, especially those influenced by Stoicism, Platonism, and the codes of morality communicated in the Mystery cults. All human constructs are imperfect and open to abuse, including the Church. Julian was illustrating the sham of supposed forgiveness and salvation that even hypocrites seemed to be able to enjoy (or buy) through their patronage of the Church and receipt of baptism. Julian's *Against the Galileans* is an interesting short argument that encapsulates the anxiety of a Pagan who cared about Pagan heritage being obliterated by the political machinations and sophistry of early state-sponsored Christianity.

Early Christians sought to convert Pagan gentiles as well as Jews, and presented Christ in contexts that would appeal to their sensibilities and theological understandings. The Christ of the New Testament was constructed in narrative symbolic terms that Pagans as well as Jews could understand—this Christ was sometimes defined in Pagan terms and is a composite, in some respects, of other mythological figures. When the Apostle Paul preached in Athens—the only place where he preached and managed to attract only a few followers and failed to found a fledgling church—he appealed to the philosophically inclined Pagan audience to consider a statue to "an unknown god" amongst them. He also used some Pagan poetry, originally referring to Zeus, to introduce Christ to his hearers: "For in him we live and move and have our being. As some of your own poets have said, 'We are his offspring.'" (Acts 17:28) Also, when Paul wrote to the Corinthians, most probably referring to himself, that: "I know a man in Christ who fourteen years ago was caught up to the third heaven. Whether it was in the body or out of the body I do not know—God knows." (2 Cor: 12:2), he was appealing directly to his readers' interest in mystical experience—which they would have been familiar with through the initiatory teachings and rituals of the mystery cults and some of the temples.

The Gospel of John with its Gnostic overtones and explicit reference to Christ as the *logos* (John 1:1) meaning "word" (or as Erasmus translated it, "the conversation") was written to appeal directly to a Pagan audience that was already familiar with such mystical terminologies. There is a great amount of evidence that the Christ who is now so often enshrined in orthodoxy functions equally well in mystical, Pagan, and liberal contexts as a force for good.

A Pagan view of Jesus Christ must ultimately be an individual or personal opinion rather than an institutionally inspired or endorsed one. Contemporary Neopaganism is not a homogenized movement with a central core of creeds or doctrines, though there may be some similarities between individuals and groups that would be happy to term themselves as being "Pagan." Certainly not everyone in the Craft or amongst the various Druid orders (or in other groups that maintain, practice, and develop various revived mystical spiritualities and traditions) would identify themselves as Pagan. Some Craft folk and Druids happily practice forms of Christianity as well as more ancient mysteries or restored versions of them. Personal connection with the Divine through self-determination and the utilization of various mystical and sometimes arcane disciplines that contribute to individual and collective realizations of truth is of paramount importance in the Mysteries.

Jesus is often identified with other sacrificial (and sometimes solar) divinities, and is thus symbolically relevant and most welcome in some personal, and even communal, rites performed in grove, by stream, or where three ways meet beneath the moon—the White Lady of Dark Night. Equally, many of the Craft and those of other mystical persuasions can worship the Divine as easily in a church as they can outdoors in the temple of nature, a *temenos*, or an ancient shrine. It is the mindset that counts and the ability to use various sets of symbols as keys within the temple of the self wherever one is bodily present. Christ is a powerful symbol, as in accompanying biblical and ecclesiastical mythology, which was often borrowed from earlier "Pagan" mythologies.

The Christ can be used as a key and evoked powerfully in mystic rites that have roots far older than Christianity. The real essence of Christ is beyond orthodoxy or "systematic theologies," though it can be encountered within them. Many old churches and Christian works of art display symbols that pertain to the "old religion" and mystical paths of the past such as carvings, concealed artifacts, architectural designs and alignments, north doors that were bricked up for a reason, etc ... Many of the Craft could perform worship in their way beneath the noses of bishops and priests without causing any trouble and even being seen as devout—which they were in the context of their own inner illuminism. The Craft is often known as the way of the wise, true Crafters have never been fundamentalist zealots; rather, they are students of the alphabets of the mysteries which spell out the sacred ways in the symbol-structures of the words of many languages. The language of symbolism can lead to reunion with that which is beyond all representation, articulation, or description and this is the reason for the Craft's Arte; wisdom is the Craft's heritage.

ABOUT THE AUTHOR

Steve Critchley leads a Craft of the Wise group called *Folk i'the Wood* which is part of the Servants of the Light School of Occult Science. He is also an SOL supervisor. He was trained and initiated by Patricia C. Crowther in Gardnerian Wicca and led a coven in that tradition for several years before teaching and practicing his own synthesis of Wicca, Traditional English Craft, and folk magic within the SOL under the direction of Dolores Ashcroft-Nowicki. Steve writes and organizes public workshops as well as teaches privately from mouth to ear and free of charge, as is the traditional way. Visit his site at: www.folkithewood.co.uk.

Seventeen

······

The God from the
House of Bread

by John Michael Greer

I do not know much about gods," wrote T. S. Eliot in his poem "The
Dry Salvages," "but I think that the river is a strong brown god."[124] He
was a devout Anglican, but Eliot lived at a time when classical education
and a self-confidence long-since vanished from today's Christianity still
gave Christian thinkers and creative minds room to allow Pagan religious
metaphors free play in their work.

The same ease that allowed him and his Christian contemporaries
to move at will between Pagan and Christian religious visions was just
as common in the nascent Pagan scene of the time. Eliot's contemporary
Dion Fortune, whose writings played a central role in the birth of modern
Pagan spirituality, also wrote a work of Christian devotional literature—
Mystical Meditations on the Collects—without sensing, or being accused
of, the least inconsistency.[125] To Fortune, and in a different sense to Eliot
as well, Christianity and Paganism were simply different ways of talking

151

about spiritual realities and relationships that could not be reduced to a single symbolic formula.

Those times are unhappily long past. During the second half of the twentieth century, most Christian denominations in the Western world responded to the reemergence of Pagan religion by reviving centuries-old stereotypes of devil worship or, at best, restricting their efforts at interreligious dialogue to a narrow circle of "world religions" hedged in by definitions that exclude today's reborn Pagan faiths. Today it's almost impossible to imagine an Anglican poet anywhere this side of heresy wielding Pagan religious metaphors with Eliot's aplomb. The same narrowing of options can be found on the other side of the newly raised barrier, for that matter; Pagan writers nowadays are far more likely to pen extended diatribes about the misbehavior of Christian churches in the past than to explore, as Dion Fortune did, the interpenetration of Pagan and Christian religious experience.

It's anyone's guess when or whether this sorry state of affairs will end. Still, there are exceptions to the generalizations just made. Some Christians have made serious efforts to grasp the nature of Pagan religious consciousness, just as some Pagans have tried to understand Christianity as a valid religious expression that doesn't happen to be theirs. There are also those who feel called to a faith that blends Pagan and Christian traditions, and despite the hostility such ventures too often receive, their number is growing. From such initiatives, with luck and the blessing of the gods, a wider context of mutual tolerance and acceptance may someday arise.

My own background places me in a complex relationship to this hope. I am a Pagan even in the strictest Christian sense of the word; that is, I have not been baptized, nor have I ever belonged to a Christian church of any kind. I grew up in a comfortably secular milieu in one of the least religious parts of the United States; among the families on the block where I lived for much of my childhood, for example, only one went to church on Sundays.

When Christianity finally came to my attention, it was by way of the strident evangelical revival that swept over America in the late 1970s, and that movement's passion for dwelling on assorted motes in other people's eyes and ignoring the beams of intolerance, hypocrisy, and political op- portunism in its own did not exactly encourage me to take Christian- ity seriously as a spiritual option. Instead, like much of my generation, I explored other paths—atheism, Asian religions, a handful of the new religious movements—before finding my spiritual home; in my case this was on the far end of the religious spectrum, in that branch of the alterna- tive spiritual scene that embraces the name and draws on the inspiration of the ancient Druids.

The modern Druid movement has a complex and quirky history of its own, reaching back to the eighteenth century, when it evolved out of a collision between liberal Anglicanism, nature worship, and fragments of Celtic tradition.[126] It inherits from its origins a distrust of dogmatism that has made it a haven for eccentrics and a nightmare for would-be sys- tematizers. Even so simple a question as the number of deities Druids worship—one, two, many, none—finds nearly as many answers as there are Druids. At the core of most visions of the contemporary Druid way, though, lies a sense that living nature is the least murky expression of the divine accessible to human beings. We may not agree about much else, but the shorthand creed drafted by one Druid tradition wins almost universal assent: "nature is good."[127]

This apparent platitude has depths that may not appear to a casual glance. It's not a statement of fact, since nature routinely violates most conventional human ideas of goodness. Rather, it's the first postulate in a system of values. By taking living nature as our basic measure of the good, the qualities expressed by nature—wholeness, flow, spontaneity, elegance, and the like—become core values that can be expressed in the life of each Druid. Equally, the central role of nature in Druid thought makes symbols and imagery derived from nature equally central in contemporary Druid myth, ritual, and practice.

This may appear worlds apart from Christianity in its modern forms. In the hands of an almost forgotten tradition of nineteenth-century Pagan thought, however, it forms an unexpected bridge crossing the chasm that now separates the religious visions of Paganism and Christianity.

Very few of today's Pagans and even fewer contemporary Christians have ever heard of the redoubtable Welsh author and Druid Owen Morgan. In his day, though, Morgan—Archdruid Morien of Pontypridd, to use his religious title—was a prominent figure on the far end of British spirituality, with a substantial following in Britain and the United States.[128] Those who like to imagine the Victorian era as a glacial landscape of conformity and sexual repression should stay far away from Morgan's writings, especially his 1887 textbook of Druid philosophy and theology, *The Light in Britannia,* which argued that Christianity was a Pagan fertility cult.[129]

Morgan himself did not put the matter quite so baldly. He argued, rather, that the core of all true religion was the worship of the life force; that the most prominent emblems of the life force—in the macrocosm, sun, and earth; in the microcosm, the male and female genitals; in both, the activities that give rise to new life—were the foundation of all religious symbolism, in Pagan as well as Christian traditions; and that Christianity was simply a restatement of the old Pagan gnosis of fertility and new life. He considered himself a good Christian as well as a Druid, and saw nothing inappropriate in attending church regularly; for him, after all, the church was a stone representation of the vagina of the earth goddess, its portal facing east to welcome the virile and penetrating rays of the rising sun: the Bride of Christ, in another symbolism, eagerly awaiting her heavenly bridegroom.

Ideas such as these were far from unique to Morgan, or for that matter to the Druidry of his time. Behind his book lay more than a century of pioneering explorations of the origins of human religion, and the rise of two major schools of thought—one arguing for an astrological and seasonal origin to religion and myth, the other tracing all religion and myth back to what was primly called "the worship of the generative powers"—that many alternative thinkers of his time were trying to reconcile.[130] Some of these had already taken the final, daring step of including Christianity in their syntheses, though none ever quite managed to equal Morgan's flair or his genius for deadpan humor. Despite this, Morgan's own cultural impact has gone surprisingly unnoticed. You can read any number of histories of the rise of modern Neopaganism, for example, and never learn that *The Light of Britannia* was the first modern expression of a fertility religion that places a single god, a single goddess, and their sexual relationship at the center of its spiritual vision—a pattern that became popular after its publication, and eventually took definitive form with Gerald Gardner's invention of Wicca.

The broader tradition of seasonal and sexual religious interpretation has had a little more visibility in recent times, not least because it helped shape important works of scholarship such as James Frazer's *The Golden Bough* and iconic cultural works such as T. S. Eliot's *The Waste Land*. Still, such interpretations have been unfashionable in scholarly circles for some decades now. This is unfortunate, for however overblown some of the old analyses may have been—and Morgan's were among the most colorful, it must be admitted—they capture a crucial factor in ancient Pagan religions that is also amply present in the origins of Christianity.

The "strong brown god" in Eliot's "The Dry Salvages," mentioned at the beginning of this essay, offers a useful starting place. To any Pagan in ancient times, Eliot's recognition was so obvious that it scarcely required mentioning. Of course rivers were deities—gods to the ancient Greeks, for example, and goddesses to the ancient Celts. Other natural phenomena were equally full of divinity. An ancient Greek who wanted to comment on wet weather would as likely as not say "Zeus is raining."

Whatever else Zeus was in classical Greek religion, in other words— and Pagan gods and goddesses were richly complex beings, impossible to pin down with simple definitions—he was always, in part, the sky as a conscious and potent divine being. Poseidon was similarly the ocean, Demeter the fertile earth, Aphrodite sexuality in all its forms, Pan the raw unhuman presence of wilderness, and so on. Even through the elegant literary constructions of late classical myth, it's not difficult to see each god and goddess as a distinct force of nature with its own power to shape the weaving of the fabric of human life.[131]

The same principle applies in a different way to a class of beings the Greeks carefully distinguished from the gods—the heroes or demigods, who were born of loves between a god or goddess and a mortal. Each of these embodied one of the realms where the human and natural worlds fused into unity. The twelve labors of Heracles, for instance, echo precisely the seasonal movement of the sun through the signs of the Zodiac as reflected in the agricultural cycle—compare Heracles's labors to the tasks of the Greek farmer as outlined, say, in Hesiod's *Works and Days*, and it's not too hard to make sense of the myth. Heracles, half god and half human, is the divine spirit of farming as what we would now call an ecosystem, half natural and half human, contending with its seasonal opponents, bringing treasures from the underworld, and then dying in the flames of the burning stubble to be reborn. The Greeks called Heracles "son of god" and "savior," and since their daily bread depended on him, this was entirely appropriate.

Another god whose cult thrived in the late classical world had the same titles, of course, and the parallels linking the myth of Jesus with the seasonal cycle of agriculture are at least as precise as those that can be traced in the myth of Heracles. Just as Heracles had his twelve labors, for instance, Jesus had his twelve disciples, whose connection with the signs of the zodiac has been a commonplace of Christian symbolism for many centuries.

Yet the mythic narratives that surround Jesus have the greater richness one would expect from the classical Levant, where fertility deities who die and rise again had been a commonplace of Pagan religious thought for thousands of years before the rise of ancient Greece. It's for this reason that Jesus is paired throughout his myth with his alter ego John the Baptist. The two mirror each other seasonally; Jesus is born at the winter solstice and dies in the spring, the harvest time in the eastern Mediterranean, suspended above the earth like the ripe grain on the stalk; John is born at the summer solstice and dies in the autumn, the planting time, beheaded in a prison beneath the earth, like the seed that goes to its burial behind the plowshare's iron blade. "He must increase," John says of Jesus, "while I must decrease."[132]

Evidence for this interpretation of Christian myth is abundant in the Bible and other early Christian sources. Jesus's traditional birthplace is in Bethlehem, for example, a town whose name literally means "house of bread" in Hebrew, and the central act of traditional Christian ritual centers on eating the bread that is Jesus's body and drinking the wine that is his blood. (John has no similar ritual attributed to him, since one does not eat the seed corn or the rootstock of the grapevine.) "I have come that they might have life," Jesus says in the Bible, "and that they might have it more abundantly";[133] any other fertility deity could have said as much, and it's only the intellectual distance that separates us from the context of early Christianity that makes so many people nowadays think that the "life" Jesus spoke of is a spiritual abstraction.

Christianity, it must be remembered, had its birth in the bustling spiritual marketplace of the classical Mediterranean world, where religious metaphors of this sort were commonplaces of contemporary thought. The mystery religions, which offered salvation to those who sought union with a god or a goddess through rituals of initiation and communion, were among the most powerful religious forces of the time, and nearly all of them focused on exactly this kind of agricultural symbolism. Thus it's hardly a leap to suggest, as so many scholars of myth have, that the precise parallels between Christianity and the other mystery religions—and the rich agricultural symbolism of Christianity itself—show that the original Christian faith may well have been something not far from what Owen Morgan claimed it to be: a mystery cult venerating the life force in nature, expressed through a rich mythic symbolism that became associated through a complex historical process with the events of the life and death of an otherwise obscure Jewish religious reformer.

The relationship between the mythic role assigned to Jesus and the sparse historical traces left by his life is a challenging issue for many modern versions of Christianity. Some theologies refuse to draw any distinction between myth and history—if the Bible says that Jesus rose into heaven, according to these interpretations, then that's what happened—and if television reporters had been there, they could have filmed it for the eleven o'clock news. Others draw a distinction between the "Jesus of history" and the "Christ of faith," though data on the former is so sparse that it can be (and has been) redefined to fit any of a dizzying assortment of modern agendas. Still others have come to reject the idea that a historical Jesus existed in the first place.

If Christianity was originally a mystery cult focused on the life force, though, these confusions evaporate. Whatever historical reality might have formed the kernel around which the Jesus myth emerged—and in all probability no one will ever know what that reality was—the spiritual meaning of the myth is not dependent on that reality. In Morgan's sense, there is no question as to the factual nature of the resurrection of Jesus, since it takes place in every sunrise and in the sprouting of every seed. The historical figure around which the myth coalesced is simply not that important; there was doubtless some dimly remembered historical figure at the root of the myth of Heracles, too.

The claim that Christianity's dying and resurrected god was a historical person who lived in the very recent past rather than a wholly mythic figure played an important role historically in giving the newborn Christian church an edge over its competitors. When the fall of Rome dragged the classical world to ruin, however, the elegant mythic metaphors that had made Christianity the most successful of the Pagan mystery religions were reinterpreted in blindly literal terms. Later on in the Reformation and afterward, these metaphors lost the last of their original meaning and were transformed into bloodless ideologies completely detached from the seasonal and vegetative context that once gave them their power.

Nowadays, the obscure historical figure around whose life the original core of mythic narratives clustered lies in the distant past, and attempts to force a literal meaning out of those narratives have long since crossed over into absurdity. The widespread modern notion of the Rapture, in which believing Christians will soon be beamed up to heaven by some miraculous equivalent of *Star Trek*'s transporter beams, is a troubling case in point. It's a lightly disguised fantasy of mass suicide—when someone tells their children that Grandma has gone to heaven to be with Jesus, most people understand what that means—and its popularity suggests that the conflict between overly literal interpretations of Christianity's exuberant seasonal myths and the awkward solidity of a world that refuses to fit those interpretations may finally have become too great for many Christians to bear.

Efforts to reconnect Christianity with its origins as a mystery religion of life and fertility have been going on for more than two centuries now, and might have succeeded in revitalizing the old myths and rituals, except for one detail: nearly all these attempts aimed at discrediting Christianity as just another Pagan fertility cult, and therefore unworthy of respect.[134] It took a believer in a different Pagan fertility cult, Owen Morgan, to realize that the equation could be worked the other way. He saw, as a handful of visionaries since his time have seen, that the ancient worship of the life force is a potent and valid spiritual option in its own right, and that Christian ritual and symbols can readily carry this primal constellation of meanings.

It is only fair to say that many other interpretations of Christianity are possible; many people will find some other way of approach to the Christian faith more relevant to their own spiritual lives, and many others will find no need to approach the Christian faith at all. Central to old Paganism was the realization that different people are called to worship different deities, and the corresponding sense that each person has the right and the duty to pursue his or her own religious path within a context of respect and toleration for the deities of others. Still, for those who feel drawn to the rituals and symbolism of Christianity, the vision of Jesus as an image of the ever-returning life force, and of Christianity as a mystery cult that need not conflict with a wider reverence for the divine presence in the world, may offer unexpected possibilities.

ABOUT THE AUTHOR

John Michael Greer currently heads the Ancient Order of Druids in America (AODA), a contemporary order of Druid nature spirituality. A widely read author and popular speaker in the fields of occultism and alternative spirituality, he is also the author of the weekly blog The Archdruid Report, which explores the future of industrial society from a Druid standpoint. He lives in Cumberland, Maryland, an old mill town in the heart of the northern Appalachians, with his wife Sara.

Eighteen

......

Jesus, Horse of God

by Diana L. Paxson

In early Christian iconography, Jesus was called the Lamb of God. But an examination of his story from the perspective of Afro-Diasporic and other possessory traditions suggests comparison to something else entirely. When Maya Deren titled her book on Haitian Voudou *Divine Horsemen,* she was referring to the use of the term "mount" or "horse" for someone possessed by a loa. In those traditions it is also customary to refer to someone who has been initiated to a particular deity as the "child" of the loa. When I began to work with these traditions, it occurred to me that not only was Jesus the "son" of the Hebrew god in the sense that he was dedicated to him, but many of the incidents in his biography can be explained by the suggestion that he spent parts of his life and most of his ministry possessed by a particularly beneficent aspect of his god.

I should probably begin by explaining that by "possession," I mean an altered state of consciousness in which there is a dissociation of personality, the ordinary human persona being replaced to some degree by that of a spirit or god.

161

In an article titled "Cultural Variations in Multiple Personality Disor-der," Deborah Golub discusses the phenomenon of possessory experience within the context of personality dissociation in general.

> *The ability to dissociate appears to be a fundamental, ancient, and universal psychobiological capacity of human beings that is necessary for their healthy functioning, and multiplicity a normal condition present in all people (Beahrs 1982, Kripner 1987, Lampl-de Groot 1981, Ross 1991a). This ubiquitous "genetic endowment" (Good-man 1988) allows some members of all cultures to embody alterna-tive identities (Mulhern 1991); themes of fragmentation of self and transformation of identity can be traced throughout history*
>
> —(Golub, 285)

Possessory trance was certainly known in the ancient world. Most of the ancient oracles gave their prophecies as mouthpieces of Apollo. It is also possible that incidents such as the one in the *Odyssey* in which Athena takes the form of Mentor in order to advise Telemachus was actually a tem-porary possession, in which the presence of the deity was only recognized after she had gone.

The fourth-century Pagan mystic Iamblichus, analyzing the different varieties of religious inspiration in his book on the Mysteries, states that

> *There are, therefore, many species of divine possession, and divine inspiration is multifariously excited; thence, also, the signs of it are many and different. For either the gods are different, by whom we are inspired, and thus produce a different inspiration, or the mode of enthusiasms being various, produces a different afflatus. For ei-ther divinity possesses us or we give ourselves up wholly to divinity, or we have a common energy with him. And sometimes, indeed, we participate of the last power of divinity, sometimes of his middle, and sometimes of his first power. Sometimes, also, there is a partici-pation only, at other times, communion likewise, and sometimes a*

union of these divine inspirations. Again, either the soul alone enjoys
the inspiration, or the soul receives it in conjunction with the body,
or it is also participated by the common animal.

—(Iamblichus, iii:5, 123–24, iii:8, 128–29)

The typical African American ritual consists of a sequence of invocations in which a chant is sung to the drum beat associated with each deity. During this process, one or more of those present, especially those who have been dedicated to the divinity (orishas in Santeria, Umbanda, and the African traditions; loas in Voudou) are possessed by the deity. Once the possession is complete, he or she may be assisted to dress in the clothing and ornaments of the deity, who then moves around the room, spontaneously giving blessings, healing, or advice, sometimes interacting with other orishas, or answering questions. Although most possessions occur in the context of ceremonies, the folklore of Santeria and Umbanda includes many stories in which an orisha possesses his or her mount at other times, sometimes in order to discipline the mount or give a message to some other person. Those who work in these traditions report experiencing states ranging from a sense of shared consciousness in which the human personality is in control but is receiving information from the orisha, spirit, or god, to complete amnesic possession in which the spirit displaces the human entirely.

Given these definitions, how can we view the career of Jesus of Nazareth? Two points invite investigation. The first is the question of how Jesus defined his own identity, and the second is to look at the events of his life for clues regarding his state of consciousness.

Of the four Gospels, Matthew and Mark seem closest to the Jewish traditions. Luke includes more mythological elements, and John incorporates more mystical theology. It is in the first two Gospels, therefore, that we will find the most information about the historical Jesus. During the early years of Christianity, a great deal of time, energy, and sometimes blood was expended in attempting to define the exact relationship between Jesus and God. The confusion over his ancestry is apparent from the fact that Matthew and even Luke make a point of listing his ancestors in the paternal line back to King David and Abraham.

In the Gospels, he often calls himself the "Son of Man" or "Son of David," and refers to himself as a prophet. It is the spirits who are most likely to identify him as divine. The Gadarene swine call him "Son of God" (Matthew 8:29), and the unclean spirit, "the Holy One of God." (Mark 1:24) When the scribes accuse him of being able to cast out demons because he himself is possessed by Beelzebub, he points out that Satan cannot cast out Satan, but he does not deny being possessed by his god. (Mark 3:22–23) His ability to perform is affected by the belief of those around him—when his neighbors doubt him because they know his family, " … and he could do no mighty work there … " (Mark 6:5) As his ministry progresses, he begins to identify himself more often as the Messiah, a figure prophesied in Jewish scripture, although he very sensibly tries to keep that claim private until the very end.

To evaluate the description of Jesus as "Son of God" we also need to look at what was meant by "God," and the significance of calling oneself a god's child. The first thing we must understand is that the concept of a single All-Powerful, All-Beneficent Creator is a relatively recent one. The first Commandment does not state that there are no other gods, but only that the Hebrews must not follow them. The Christian insistence that the god whom Jesus proclaimed is the only one gives his claim to be the Son of God a weight that might not be justified in the context of the times.

At the beginning of the first millennium, the concept that an apparent human might actually be the child of a deity was a common way to explain heroic achievement. As the biography of Jesus became mythologized, it was natural to explain his miracles in that way as well. For the contemporary Pagan, the account of the birth of Jesus given by Luke would seem quite reasonable. In early Judaism, it was recognized that the god of the Hebrews had several aspects. El and Jah may have originally been separate deities, along with their consorts, within a Hebrew pantheon. For Jesus, his god is usually "the Father." Not only is Jesus himself the child of his god, but he promises in the Beatitudes and elsewhere that humans can become "sons of God," and consistently speaks of him as "your father in heaven." Jesus can therefore be viewed as the son of the Hebrew god in his fatherly aspect in the same sense as an initiate of Umbanda might be called the "child" of Xango or Yemaya.

What evidence can we find in the Gospels to support the hypothesis that Jesus was an extraordinarily gifted trance medium? Let us consider the following events.

1. The debate with the scholars in the Temple

   In Luke 2:46–49, we are told "After three days they found him in the temple, sitting among the teachers, listening to them and asking them questions; and all who heard him were amazed at his understanding and his answers. And when they saw him they were astonished; and his mother said to him, 'Son, why have you treated us so? Behold, your father and I have been looking for you anxiously.' And he said to them, 'How is it that you sought me? Did you not know that I must be in my Father's house?'"

   If Jesus had grown up with periods of feeling the influence of his god, entering the charged environment of the Temple might have been enough to shift his consciousness and give him access to the knowledge and verbal skills of the god. In the Gospel of John, we find a similar example when the scribes ask, "How is it that this man has learning, when he has never studied?" and Jesus replies, "My teaching is not mine, but his who sent me." (7:15–16) He claims a shared consciousness when he says, "It is not I alone that judge, but I and he who sent me." (8:16)and "…he who sent me is with me; he has not left me alone, for I always do what is pleasing to him." (8:29)

2. Initiation—

   the Baptism by John and the Forty Days in the Desert

   We know nothing about Jesus's life between the episode in the Temple and the day he shows up at the River Jordan, where John is baptizing those who wish purification from their sins.

One speculates, however, that by the time he reached the age of thirty, the tension between Jesus's attempt to live a normal life and his god-hunger had become unbearable. He went to John in order to make a formal commitment, and to undergo a ritual that would "open his head" and let the god fully in. Ritual cleansings are known in many traditions as a part of initiation, including Umbanda, where the head of the initiate is washed in a preparation of sacred herbs. In all the Gospels, the effect is described as being profound, and the response of the deity is perceived not only by Jesus himself but by John and many others who are present. "This is my beloved Son, in whom I am well pleased." (Matthew 3:17)

Having made his commitment, Jesus goes into the desert, as prophets and mystics have done before and since, for what is essentially an initiatory ordeal. It is reasonable to assume that extreme temperatures and lack of food push him past the boundaries of ordinary consciousness. He is tempted by demons and comforted by angels. When the forty days are done, he has succeeded in opening himself up to a point where he will be to some degree possessed by his god for the next three years.

3. The ministry

"And Jesus returned in the power of the Spirit into Galilee..." (Luke 4:14) After the ordeal in the desert, Jesus returns home to begin his ministry, teaching through parables and outright laying down the law. The thing that initially impresses people is the confidence with which he speaks. "...the crowds were astonished at his teaching, for he taught them as one who had authority." (Matthew 7:28–29). This is not the teaching of a scholar who cites sources and qualifies his conclusions, but the direct discourse that comes straight from the source. It is in fact the way that people speak when they are in trance for a god.

In John, he clearly states the source of this authority:

"He who has seen me has seen the Father; how can you say, 'Show us the Father'? Do you not believe that I am in the Father and the Father in me? The words that I say to you I do not speak on my own authority; but the Father who dwells in me does his works. Believe me that I am in the Father and the Father in me; or else believe me for the sake of the works themselves." (14:9–11)

Clearly, this indwelling is experienced as energy. "And Jesus, perceiving in himself that power had gone forth from him, immediately turned about in the crowd, and said, 'Who touched my garments?'" (Mark 5:30) He is clearly aware that not only he but others can become a channel for the god. In his prophecy of the coming disasters he refers to the "Spirit of your Father speaking through you" (Matthew 10:20), and quotes Isaiah, "I will put my Spirit upon him." (12:18)

After the death of John the Baptist his identification with his god seems to become more intense, and he has clearly had intimations of his fate. Jesus now speaks more violently, but with more authority. His miracles become more impressive. Walking on the waves of the Sea of Galilee, he is hailed by his disciples as Son of God (14:33). In Matthew 16:16 and Mark 8:29 he approves when Peter calls him "the Christ, the Son of the living God." He is not only claiming the status of a son of the Father, but the role of the Messiah, though the time has not yet come to claim that publicly.

4. The Transfiguration

In Matthew 17, Mark 9, and Luke 9, we find accounts of the Transfiguration. By this time, Jesus has been preaching for almost three years. His god has clearly shown him his fate, and he is preparing for it by opening himself ever more fully. On the mountaintop, "... he was transfigured before them, and his face shone like the sun, and his garments became white as light," and he walks with Moses and Elijah. "He was still speaking, when lo, a bright cloud overshadowed them, and a voice from the cloud said, 'This is my beloved Son, with whom I am well pleased; listen to him.'" (Matthew 17: 2, 5)

Such phenomena are known from the mystical literature of many lands. An excess of god-power is often perceived as light. It is interesting that in the vision, his disciples also see Moses and Elijah, two previous Hebrew prophets who channeled the words of their god. As at the baptism, proximity to this energy opens the disciples sufficiently so they hear the words of the god themselves.

5. The Crucifixion

During the third year of his ministry, Jesus includes a number of ominous prophecies in his preaching. Clearly, his god has been talking to him. This is not an unknown phenomenon. Most people who have active relationships with their patron deities have such conversations, which often include predictions and warnings. Those predictions that come true are offered as validation of the relationship. Those that do not are put down to misinterpretation or conveniently forgotten. Evaluating Divine Inspiration is difficult. The gods may have access to all knowledge, but trying to pour it into a human vessel requires a small funnel indeed, and the deity may be limited by what can be deduced from the database of the devotee and expressed by his or her vocabulary.

Admittedly, Jesus was able to receive more of his god's essence than most. However, while some of Jesus's predictions (such as his own fate and the destruction of Jerusalem) might have been foreseen by any acute observer of Palestinian politics, others (such as the Last Days) were eagerly awaited by the early Christian community but never arrived. It is my opinion that true prophecy is dependent on a fixed fate, and unless one believes in a deterministic universe, there is always the chance that things will change. Thus even the gods can only predict probabilities.

In any case, when Jesus goes up to Jerusalem for the last time, he is deliberately cooperating in a martyrdom that will immortalize his message. He sets the stage with the Last Supper and goes to the Garden of Gethsemane to wait for arrest. It is here that the constant support and companionship he is used to seems to falter.

"Then he said to them, 'My soul is very sorrowful, even unto death; remain here, and watch with me.' And going a little farther he fell on his face and prayed, 'My father, if it be possible, let this cup pass from me, nevertheless, not as I will, but as thou wilt.'" And then, "'My Father, if this cannot pass unless I drink it, thy will be done.'" (Matthew 26:38–39, 42). The deal has clearly been that he and his god will go through the sacrifice together, and suddenly he is alone. The spirit is willing, but without it, the flesh is weak indeed. Once more, he must consciously consent to become an instrument of his god's will.

From this point on, the strength of the connection varies. At his trial, Jesus affirms that he is the Christ. The energy carries him all the way to Golgotha, but the accounts of his time on the Cross suggest that it comes and goes. When he cries, "'My God, my God, why hast thou forsaken me," (Matthew 27:46) (Mark 15:34), the god who promised to bear the pain is clearly not with him. Luke, on the other hand, records the moments when the god returns, and Jesus is able to ask forgiveness for his enemies. Clearly, his performance is godly enough for the centurion to sense it and proclaim, "Truly this was a son of God!" (Matthew 27:54)

6. The Resurrection

Theories about the Resurrection are even more various than analyses of Jesus's ministry, ranging from the orthodox belief that Jesus reanimated his body after his spirit had left it and later discorporated to the idea that he (like those whom he "raised from the dead") were not clinically dead but only in a coma too deep to be identified by the means available at the time.

Most cultures have folklore about reanimated corpses, but there are also stories about divine manifestations that could explain what the disciples saw. Jesus, by completing his ministry, has effectively become a demi-god, like the "sons" of Greek deities who were welcomed to Olympus. Or in Voudoun terms, he has been assimilated to his head deity. Such figures can certainly communicate, either through a sense of presence, or possibly by speaking through someone else.

In several of the encounters, the disciples do not at first recognize Jesus, who reveals himself by his words and energy rather than his appearance. The post-crucifixion appearances are in format like those moments in Homer when Athena takes the form of someone else, and only later do those to whom she has spoken decide that this must have been a god.

Conclusions

Was Jesus the Christ? If by that we mean the Jewish Messiah, he did not end up fulfilling the role as it was envisioned at the time. But if the title means an aspect of the father-god he preached, the answer is most certainly yes. At least at times, Jesus was indeed God, or as much of that god as could manifest through a human vessel. In my opinion, the mechanisms through which he performed his miracles and taught divine wisdom are the same as those known in many cultures, past and present. How then do we account for his unique status today?

First, he was able to open himself more fully and consistently than almost any other religious figure of whom we know—the Buddha being perhaps the other example. Second, his story became easily mythologized to appeal to Pagan preconceptions. From that point on, the more people believed, the more vivid and easily-accessed his image became. As Dion Fortune points out,

> *To build up a group mind of any endurance some method of ensuring continuity of attention and feeling is essential. Whenever such continuity of attention and feeling has been brought about, a group mind, or group Elemental, is formed which with the passage of time develops an individuality of its own, and ceases to be dependent for its existence upon the attention and emotion of the crowd that gave it birth...*
>
> *When this process has been repeated regularly over considerable periods, the images that have been built up remain on the astral in exactly the same way that a habit-track is formed in the mind by the repeated performance of the same action. In this form the natural force remains permanently concentrated. Consequently subsequent worshippers need be at no great pains to formulate the simulacrum; they have only to think of the god and they feel his power.*
>
> —(Fortune, 19)

Thus, I have no difficulty in accepting that today, Jesus Christ is indeed divine. As a polytheist, however, I hold that although he is a god, both he and his father are only two among many who still speak to and through their worshipers today.[135]

ABOUT THE AUTHOR

Diana L. Paxson is the author of twenty-nine novels dealing with mythic and legendary themes, including the Avalon novels in the series begun by Marion Zimmer Bradley, and four nonfiction books addressing the runes, trance work, and Pagan religion. She is a consecrated priestess, a founder of the Fellowship of the Spiral Path, an Elder, and a former First Officer of the Covenant of the Goddess. Currently she is an Elder in the Troth, an international Asatru organization, coordinator of the Clergy Training

Program, and editor of the journal *Idunna*. She is also known as a pioneer in the reconstruction of the northern tradition of oracle work. Her book on the subject, *Seeing for the People,* will be published by Weiser Books next year. She lives in Berkeley, California.

Nineteen

......

I Have No Temple: A Consideration of Jesus as Pagan Teacher of Gnosis

by Marcus Katz

Introduction

As a pagan teacher and priest, I am interested in the way in which Christ taught his radical spirituality within the constraints of the orthodoxy of his time. I believe that as spiritual teachers ourselves within a minority and nascent religion we can learn much from Christ's teaching style. In order to illustrate this, I will present in this piece a singular example of Christ as a *Gnostic* teacher, one who perhaps taught spiritual knowledge both experientially and ecstatically.

I will use the lesser-known Gnostic text, *Hymn of Jesus,* a text translated by G. R. S. Mead and originally dated around the second century at the latest. Whilst we have no evidence that this is indeed a direct testament of the teachings of a real historical figure, and is possibly rather a mythic or allegorical account of a style of teaching practiced by his followers, we can use it here in either context. I will conclude by proposing a number of methods of teaching which can be utilized by Pagan teachers and priest/esses from the example of Christ within that hymn.

It is not intended to define Christianity, Wicca, Witchcraft, Esotericism, or Gnosis, which are subjects requiring detail far outside the scope and reach of this present piece. I use "priest/ess" as indicative of either gender in that role.

It is perhaps in the writings of the occultists that we find a more inclusive attempt to weave the Christian narrative into the tradition of Western Esotericism. Such occultists may be considered as influential on the Pagan movement, such as Dion Fortune (1890–1946), whose works in both fiction and non-fiction have shaped the imagination of many contemporary practitioners.[136] In one of her lesser-known works, *Mystical Meditations on the Collects,* she writes, "Christianity is very far from being a burnt-out cinder. Christianity must have a Gnosis as well as a creed … we need our Christian Mysteries—the deeper teaching that cannot be given save after dedication and purification."[137]

It is to this Gnostic conception of Christ that we will now turn to see a specific example of Christ as a radical and powerful teacher—one who teaches outdoors, using nature metaphors and physical methods in purely experiential teaching leading to profound personal mystical experience. It is proposed that through this ancient Gnostic perspective of Christ and his teachings, we can draw methodological similarities to contemporary Pagan practice.

The Dance and the Pipe

In the preamble to the 1907 *Hymn of Jesus,* translator G. R. S. Mead considers the text fragment as a "very remarkable tradition of the Gnostic side of the life of the Master; or, if it be preferred, of incidents in the 'occult' life of Jesus."[138] He goes on to assert that the theories of the Gnostics were based primarily on an actual experience of inner teaching, "made known to their consciousness in many marvellous ways"[139] after the physical death of the teacher. Indeed, in the Leucian teachings of John, it is stated:

I held firmly this one thing in myself, that the Lord contrived all things symbolically and by a dispensation towards men, for their conversion and salvation.[140]

This hymn is a short piece, which was later found in the practices of the Priscillianists in Spain, in the last third of the fourth century. This movement saw a primary importance in personal inspiration over doctrine and was one of many such movements later considered a heresy by the orthodoxy.

It begins with Jesus being in the centre of a circle, and the disciples holding hands to dance around him. They then answer the hymn at various points with Amens and other calls and responses.

As the Hymn commences, we see a teaching method of reconciled or reduced opposites:

I would be saved; and I would save
Amen!
I would be loosed; and I would loose.
Amen!
...
I have no place; and I have places.
Amen!
I have no temple; and I have temples.
Amen![141]

Compare this method of teaching with that employed by the Cad Goddeu, or "battle of the Trees" given in Graves:

I have been a word in a book,
I have been a book, originally.
I have been a light in a lantern...[142]

This teaching method seeks to reduce absolutism and generate a profound state of what the magician-artist Austin Osman Spare would call neither/neither consciousness.[143] As a mantra, it is peculiarly effective as it includes many nature-based references with which the practitioner identifies unconsciously as they chant. It can lift an entire group into the archetypal realm of what Henri Corbin would call the *mundus imaginalis.*[144]

The hymn also utilizes metaphor as a teaching method: "I am a mirror to thee who understandest Me."[145]

These simple metaphors can provide a deep contact with the Universe when delivered at the right point in a raising-of-consciousness exercise such as this dance. Note the *timing* of the delivery is of importance—a fact known by all good priest/esses and teachers. In either the drawing down of the moon or the raising of a cone of power, the art of priestcraft is in recognizing, incorporating, and utilizing the exact moment of potential where the ritual opens up consciousness into the divine realm.

The actual teaching content of the hymn is delivered in the middle of the text, particularly with regard to Jesus demonstrating the place of suffering—as being an exemplar for suffering as attachment:

Understand, by dancing, what I do;
For thine is the Passion of Man
That I am to suffer.
…

Know then how to suffer, and thou hast power not to suffer.
That which thou knowest not, I Myself will teach thee.[146]

That the dance and hymn are fully grounded in activity is a welcome remedy to the classical picture of the sterile teaching of Christianity through dry sermonizing. Mead clearly considers this hymn to make sense in the Gnostic worldview of hierarchical levels of the soul, but also points out the necessity to ground these experiences. That necessity is alluded to in the hymn by the symbol of the dance: "the manifestation in activity of real life and consciousness."[147]

The use of music and dance is particularly important in this prayer, which Mead suggests is a very early Christian mystery ritual, perhaps even the oldest Christian ritual of any kind.[148]

"I would pipe, dance ye all…who danceth not, knows not what is being done."[149]

This image and sentiment would not be out of place in Aleister Crowley's "Hymn to Pan."[150] There are other such poetic renderings of mystery teaching available to the Pagan teacher and Priest/ess, such as the ancient Egyptian ritual of the divine ass and the Greek hymns of Orpheus.[151]

In addition to the teaching through chanting and dance, the mystery processes of imitation, secrecy, and initiation are all alluded to as the hymn reaches its closure:

> *"Now answer to My dancing! See thyself in Me who speak; and seeing what I do, keep silence on My Mysteries."*[152]
>
> *"And having danced these things with us, Beloved, the Lord went forth. And we, as though besides ourselves, or wakened out of (deep) sleep, fled each our several ways."*[153]

This waking out of sleep should be considered as an initiatory statement. The allusion to a disassociated state ("besides ourselves") shows a powerful change has been experienced by the dancers of this hymn. In Christ's teaching of a Gnostic revelation through a method of dance, song, and piping, a state-change of consciousness is realized, held secret in experience, and then taken by the initiates to their "several ways." Here we see a fully experiential teaching, which is at home in Pagan circles as it is in many mystery schools.

Conclusion

The methods of teaching employed in this Gnostic conception of Christ, as in many other Hermetic teachers and teachings, is experiential and discursive.[154] It involves movement, engagement, challenge, and response to provoke a state-change in consciousness. It is a testament to the teaching methods of parable, metaphor, and ritual that the Christian philosophy took root and grew so dramatically. As contemporary Pagan teachers, we should embrace such methods in our own presentation of a Neopagan philosophy, rediscovering these and many other roots from which we have grown and continue to grow, and creating strong hybrids of spiritual experience. Christ could be considered as a radical teacher of his time in that he taught outdoors, used many nature-based metaphors, and in this Gnostic version, provided an experiential initiatory process through dance and chanting.

Through a Pagan's eyes, Christ appears here in this hymn as an initiator and an exemplar. He offers a model of a true teacher—one who is unafraid of his role, stoic in resolve, and concerned only for the lessons to be learnt. His suffering is only in the eyes of those who have yet to learn his lesson: we are all each both light and lamp, the book and the word, and even—in the initiation of all mysteries—both the circle and the cross.

ABOUT THE AUTHOR

Marcus Katz is the first student to successfully graduate with an M.A. in Western Esotericism through the University of Exeter. He is the author of *Tarosophy: Tarot to Engage Life, Not Escape It* and *After the Angel: An Account of the Abramelin Operation.* He is the co-director of Tarot Professionals, a global organization for Tarot readers, and co-founder of Tarot Town, a large social network for Tarot students. He has two innovative Tarot books forthcoming with Llewellyn, with co-author Tali Goodwin. He teaches Kabbalah, Tarot, Witchcraft, Thelema, and Spellcrafting through online and in-person courses at the Far Away Centre, based in the beautiful Lake District of England. He offers a unique online apprenticeship program in the Western Esoteric Initiatory Tradition, which is the subject of his next book through Salamander and Sons. www.farawaycentre.com

Twenty

......

The Fertile Christ
by Philip Carr-Gomm

The body, and it alone, is capable of making visible what is invisible: the spiritual and the divine. It was created to transfer into the visible reality of the world the mystery hidden since time immemorial in God.

—Pope John Paul II[155]

The image of Christ as a man being tortured to death is so unsettling and frightening that it has often been hard for me to sense the Christ who is associated not with death but with life and unbounded love, spoken of by mystics and even by those following Pagan and magical paths, such as Dion Fortune and my Druid teacher Ross Nichols. As a child, I remember being taken into cold and gloomy churches to sing the praises of a god who had allowed his son to be killed by crucifixion, and I found this sufficiently disturbing to make sure that my children never had to go through similar experiences.

When I was a teenager I went to Westminster School, which meant that every morning I had to sing in the abbey, whose magnificent stained glass windows and architecture inspired me. Despite my continued questioning of the central image of Christianity, I did have moments when I came to sense its mysterious power and even beauty. One morning, as I took the underground to school, I fell into a reverie and had a vision of entering a secret "hidden" church that stood in a side street near the abbey. As I entered it, there was Christ on the cross, but he was alive—and he was naked. Instead of looking tortured and as if he was dying, he somehow looked the opposite—as if he was becoming more alive. An image I had previously experienced as distressing and tragic had now appeared as one of great joy and giving to the world.

I didn't mention this experience to anyone for thirty years. Then, while being shown an exhibition of Dutch masters in the Hague, my guide turned to me as we gazed at a huge dark image of the crucifixion, and declared "Oh if only we could see Christ naked!" Her remark triggered my memory. I shared my vision with her, and we both talked about how we would like to experience Christ as someone who could bring us a sense of hope and renewal rather than pain and tragedy—someone who could allow us to experience the fullness of embodied experience—not denying the reality of suffering and death but expressing equally the joy of being fully alive in world as a being of flesh and blood, with the desire to love and even "make" love.

The Christ that I saw was dying, but at the same time he was fully alive and not dying at all, in a way depicted so well by Salvador Dalí's *Christ of Saint John of the Cross,* expressing directly the paradox of life-in-death and death-in-life that lies at the heart of Christianity. He was John Barleycorn, a harvest god being cut down but giving life as this happened.[156] Pared down to its basic symbolism, this seems straightforward and completely in line with Christian thinking.

The idea that depicting Christ naked is unthinkable can be dismissed by turning to history and theology: the three most significant events in

Christ's life—his baptism, crucifixion, and resurrection—occurred when he was naked.

In the time of Jesus and the Old Testament, the rite of baptism in Judaism required full immersion in the nude either into a river or a mikvah—a stone pool specially created for this purpose, and there is evidence that this had been the practice from as early as 1000 BC.[157] For this reason, when Jesus was baptized by John the Baptist in the river Jordan he would have been naked, and was portrayed as such in paintings and mosaics. In the Greek Orthodox church this moment is celebrated in a hymn which cries: "O compassionate Savior, putting on the nakedness of Adam as a garment of glory, Thou makest ready to stand naked in the flesh in the River Jordan. O marvellous wonder!"

When the Christian church created its own rite of baptism, it was based directly on the Jewish immersion rituals which required nakedness, and in c. 200 AD St. Hippolytus of Rome wrote of this, stating that total nudity was required and that women were also obliged to remove all jewellery.

In the final moments of Jesus's life, he was naked as he hung on the cross. The Gospel of St. John recounts: "The soldiers, therefore, when they did crucify Jesus, took his garments, and made four parts, to each soldier a part, also the coat, and the coat was seamless, from the top woven throughout, they said, therefore, to one another, 'We may not rend it, but cast a lot for it, whose it shall be;' that the Writing might be fulfilled, that is saying, 'They divided my garments to themselves, and upon my raiment they did cast a lot;' the soldiers, therefore, indeed, did these things."[158]

Crucifixion was designed to inflict humiliation as well as intense physical anguish, so stripping a victim of their clothes was simply one more way to make them suffer. Most crucifixes for obvious reasons depict Christ wearing a loincloth, but there are some notable exceptions, including the crucifix from the Convent of Santo Spirito in Florence, attributed to Michelangelo, and the work of another Renaissance artist, Benvenuto Cellini, who sculpted a naked Christ on the cross—this time in marble and life-size. It can be seen in the Escorial Monastery in Madrid, now draped with a loincloth and with a crown of thorns added to the head.

Spain is the location of another naked Christ that depicts him in his final, and arguably most significant role—as a resurrected savior. In 1598 El Greco carved a statue, clearly relying on the biblical account of the resurrection in which Joseph and Nicodemus were allowed by Pilate to take Jesus's body from the cross. They had wrapped it in linen, and placed it in a sepulcher which they then sealed with a "great stone." Later, four women including Mary Magdalene, on passing by the sepulchre saw that the stone had been rolled away and that there was no body in the tomb, simply the linen that had been used to wrap the body "as well as the burial cloth that had been around Jesus's head. The cloth was folded up by itself, separate from the linen."[159] In other words, Christ was resurrected without clothing. Michelangelo was also inspired by this account to sculpt a naked resurrected Christ for the Basilica of Santa Maria sopra Minerva in Rome, though now some linen has returned to cover his loins.

So much for religious art and history supporting the idea that Christ can, and perhaps should be, depicted naked. But what do theologians think? Michael Kowalewski in *Nudity and Christianity* writes: "Christ's nakedness is more than a historical fact; it is of theological significance. Christ's nakedness is sacramental. It visibly communicates the poverty of spirit and purity of heart required for picking up our cross and following Christ. A Father of the Church, St. Jerome, often said '*Nudus nudum Iesum Sequi*' (Naked, I follow the naked Jesus.)"[160] Pope John Paul II affirmed this sacramental view of the body when in his *Theology of the Body* he wrote: "The body, and it alone, is capable of making visible what is invisible: the spiritual and the divine. It was created to transfer into the visible reality of the world the mystery hidden since time immemorial in God."[161] Earlier, in his book *Love and Responsibility* he had written: "Nakedness itself is not immodest ... Immodesty is present only when nakedness plays a negative role with regard to the value of the person, when its aim is to arouse concupiscence, as a result of which the person is put in the position of an object for enjoyment."[162]

Theologians, historians, and artists—at least some of them—are comfortable with the idea of a skyclad Christ. But in addition to the image being historically and theologically valid, the image offers a specific, and I believe highly relevant, dimension to our appreciation of Christ. In seeing him naked, we can also see that he has the ability to be fertile—that he is truly a man. Viewing him in this way we can come to an appreciation of Christ that is radically different to the one that has dominated Church and world history for so many centuries.

The idea of a god who is sacrificed for his people is as old as the story of religion, and is rooted in an experience of the inner life as well as in the life of the natural world. In the Middle East this story of the sacred wounding and death of a god is depicted in a number of variations, including that of Ishtar and Tammuz, Venus and Adonis, and perhaps most notably in the story of Isis and Osiris. In all these variations on the same theme, the god represents the moment, the finite, while the goddess represents cyclicity and eternity. And in each of these stories the god is in relationship with the goddess, and passes on his seed for the cycle to continue and rebirth to occur. When the Christian version of the story appears, a significant detail is changed: the god is no longer fertile—he is born of a virgin and dies a virgin. In this way it can be argued that he is out of relationship with the embodied Feminine and with his own body, and because he does not pass on his seed, the re-flowering of the earth cannot occur. If you believe that the account of Christ's life is factually true, then the answer is simple: all the other stories were myths and legends, whereas this actually happened. But even those who believe the story is true hold to different versions, with some Mormons, for example, believing that Christ did not die a virgin but had children.[163] This idea lies at the heart of books such as *The Holy Blood and the Holy Grail* and *The Da Vinci Code,* and their success reveals how much the idea of a fertile (as opposed to virginal) Christ appeals to the contemporary world.[164]

Amongst the Bards of old it was apparently believed that you should never change the key details of an ancient story that was being handed down in the oral tradition. You could color it as much as you liked, changing minor details to suit the audience and the time at your disposal, but to change the basic structure of the story would be considered a fatal error that could have grave consequences. Could it be that by changing a key feature of an archetypal story, a chain of unfortunate consequences ensued through history? By depicting a god-figure out of relationship with the Divine Feminine and rendering him a virgin and hence effectively infertile, did the Church unwittingly initiate an era marked by a sterile and ferocious insensitivity to womankind, the Earth, and the sacred joys of embodiment? If the story of Jesus had been told as one of a man who died having passed on his seed, would events have turned out differently?

An old friend once told me that he was working on a book entitled *The World's Seven Greatest Failures.* It was going to start with a chapter on Jesus Christ. "Why was he one of the world's greatest failures?" I asked, but as I framed the question the answer came to me, and so I continued "Because he came to bring love to the world and instead so much suffering was perpetrated in his name?" My friend, a Christian, only nodded with a bitter smile.

What if we could change one detail and begin to repair the damage that has been done? The story of Christ currently requires two images: of his death and rebirth, but in practice it is the image of his crucifixion rather than his resurrection that is used as the central icon of the faith. As a result, however much Christianity wants to stress the 'Good News' of Christ's resurrection, it is his agonising death that occupies the centre-stage, and it is this focus on death that seems so unattractive to non-Christians and which may arguably have influenced the course of history in such negative ways.[165] What if Christ could instead be sensed as fully human: as a fertile being, as well as one who suffered, so that the message that suffering and joy are inextricably entwined in the experience of being human, of being embodied, could inform our experience of the Christian faith? This, I suspect, is a vision of Christ already embraced by many, including those Christo-Pagans who embrace a vision of life that sees sexuality as sacred, and honors the Goddess and the body as much as the God and the spirit.

About the Author

Philip Carr-Gomm helps to lead the Order of Bards, Ovates, and Druids and is the author of *A Brief History of Nakedness*, which explores the positive uses of nudity in religion, politics, and popular culture. Philip lives in Sussex, England, with his wife Stephanie and their children. From an early age, Philip studied with Ross Nichols, the founder of the Order of Bards, Ovates, and Druids. He has a degree in psychology from University College London, and trained in psychotherapy for adults at the Institute of Psychosynthesis, and in play therapy for children with Dr. Rachel Pinney. He also trained in Montessori education with the London Montessori Centre, and founded a Montessori school in Lewes. His other books include *Druid Mysteries, Sacred Places, The Book of English Magic* (with Richard Heygate), and *The DruidCraft Tarot* (with Stephanie Carr-Gomm).

Twenty-One

......

Jesus and the
"Devil's Picture Book"

by Sarah Kral

He [the Fool] is a prince of the other world on his travels through
this one-all amidst the morning glory…

—A. E. Waite[166]

Throughout the centuries people's perspectives on Jesus have changed dramatically. The stories have come into contact with science and reason, the demands of a modern technological age and vastly different cultures and emerging ideologies. The stories are two thousand years old, yet they still speak to the hearts and souls of people of all ages, creeds, and cultures. They are being read and re-examined in new ways, and this is also very true of the tarot. Like Jesus, the origins of the tarot are shrouded in mystery and myth; no hard facts and no real knowing exists of "why" people connect with seventy-eight pictures. Some stories mention ancient Egyptians, others the travelling gypsies across Europe. Other tales mention magical orders and occult traditions keeping the seventy-eight cards secret and hidden from view until the initiate is ready to safely dive deeply into the mysteries. The bubble-bursting reality is that Jesus was just a bloke who got on his soap-box a bit, and the tarot was a parlor game of playing cards for fun and gambling in courtly Europe. Why do these two myths speak so strongly to people, and more interestingly, why should Jesus and the tarot be linked together?

There are many ideas about who Jesus was. Was he a wise man, prophet, fictional character, mythical figure, or the human embodiment of God? The stories in the New Testament and in the recently discovered Gnostic Gospels speak of a Jesus who was a mortal being. Like you or me, he was a human being, plodding through the ups and downs of life, trying to make sense of all the chaos we feel and perceive, yet trying to connect to it all on a deeper spiritual level. The essences of these stories are truly no different to our own personal struggles through life. The biographies in these gospels are no different to the holy book of the tarot, which can offer guidance, insight, and comfort as we ponder life's great questions or seek inspiration at times of great joy, confusion, and sadness. The only difference is that the tarot is written in symbols rather than words; it speaks to our intuitive and subconscious minds first, rather than words on a page that have to pass through the defenses of our over-critical and analytical "thinking" minds. Many magical orders, practices, and occult figures have highlighted the importance of using the tarot as a way of connecting to our higher selves, or our own holy guardian angel. The tarot can be a way of linking and developing a relationship with our own inner Jesus—the questing soul. Rather than an unreal figure in a book, the tarot can offer us a way of connecting to the man who, like us, faced the great questions of life, and felt the joy of family and the bitterness of betrayal. Recent concepts of a Jesus who was trying to manage a love life as well as a spiritually fulfilling life illustrate the balance of being a teacher and a guide, walking his own path and learning from his own mistakes.

The tarot reflects these same fundamental experiences and archetypes of human experience, especially the major arcana. These are twenty-two cards starting with the Fool and ending at the World. They are not linear stages of experience, but cyclical and pertinent; similar to how we can honor and mark the birth, growth, death, and rebirth of Jesus every twelve months. It is not a huge leap to link the life experiences of Jesus to the common human experiences of the tarot. The following ideas on some of the major arcana cards are ones I have developed through my own under-standing and relationship with life, the symbols of the tarot, as well as who Jesus was and what he means to me. These are not definitive ideas, and I welcome other people to expand and develop their own ideas compar-ing Jesus and the tarot! The tarot is a very deep symbolic language that is being reinterpreted and revitalized constantly with every new deck on the market, yet its wisdom is ageless and profound to our spiritual journeys. The symbols may speak to you differently than they do to me, just like the stories of Jesus speak to us differently individually or develop new mean-ings at different times in our lives. What I am offering here are some seed thoughts that may deepen your understanding of Jesus, tarot or both, for both of them help us understand and navigate our way through life. Let me show you some of my own thoughts comparing Jesus and what has sometimes been wrongly portrayed as "the Devil's Picture Book."

Fool

Jesus the man was born as innocent as all babies are. There was no divine revelation; he didn't come out of the womb spouting the word of God from his manger. His soul was like all souls who live in a place of unknow-ing bliss, unaware of all the joys of the universe, until that soul is put into a body to experience life. The fall of the Fool, the impending edge of the cliff in most decks, is like Jesus coming into the world.

The Fool also reflects the awe and wonder that Jesus brought by his "innocent" thoughts, questions, and point of view. As Jesus grew up, he would ask the same questions and the same direct observations of a child—not clouded in judgment or "what should be." Sometimes on our paths of self-discovery we need to retain that wide-eyed joy of the Child Within that lets us fall in love after failed relationships, take that leap of faith in a project, or discover Divinity.

Magician

Jesus is the Magician in so many ways—the conjurer, the alchemist, the healer, the showman, the public speaker. He is the conjuror that creates wonder, performing miracles or tricks like turning water into wine. To do things such as turn water into wine, heal the sick, or cure the blind, he would have to believe in himself and his own ability to do it, as well as possess a strong belief in the connection between him and Divinity. The Magician card shows how we too can connect to our own power, believe in it, and believe in the source of that power or Divinity. Jesus demonstrates that when we channel our focus—the will of our being and our soul's journey—magic happens.

The Magician card empowers us to realize that we are just like Jesus, a humble mortal being. We can perform such miracles too. The power of prayer, which science today is starting to accept, has the ability to heal the sick and change the lives of many. The connection of intention and Divinity, be it through prayer, ritual, spellwork, and/or magic, is simply the ability to recognize the divine within us (the soul, the divine spark, the holy guardian angel, and in all its other guises) and to connect and speak to it for energy to flow without worry, thought, or judgment. So we might not be able to turn tap water to wine, but the metaphor points to the truly amazing possibility that, through intention and will, we can perform such alchemy on our own souls, transforming our own dross into gold.

High Priestess

The obvious connection is to that of Mary, the virgin queen of heaven— and mother of God. Mary appears in the stories to be a very intuitive figure. Her mindset and spirit is open in that she is receptive to the words of the angels and the intention of God without question, reason, and science affecting her intuitive abilities. Humanity was still cynical, always seeking to understand the universe through observational and measurable science, yet the Bible is littered with stories of prophetic dreams and of how God spoke people through their intuition, offering guidance and help. Mary, the High Priestess, reflects the truth that if we are not prepared to listen or open our minds to the possibilities around us or the wisdom of our dreams and gut instincts, we are unable to have a conversation with Divinity. If we close ourselves off from the impossible, the unexpected, the unseen, and unreal, we are depriving ourselves of the vast potential of the universe—the wisdom veiled behind the High Priestess's curtain.

Empress

Again, the natural thought here to is think of Mary the mother; however, Jesus was the Empress in a lot of ways. He often spoke in a way that makes him the nurturer of love, life, and the potential around us. If we only think of Jesus as being a man who is unable to demonstrate motherly characteristics, then we are confining his symbolism and message by our own stereotypes and cultural standards. Like a single father who must be both mother and father to a child, so Jesus is within the stories. People often connect to Deity when they need love, support, and encouragement to bring projects into fruition such as writing a book, understanding parenthood or relationship issues, or needing confidence or reassurance in life—the gifts of the Mother. The unconditional love that Jesus spoke of, and shared with his followers and those that have been touched by the stories, is the gift of the Empress—nonjudgmental, always giving, always revitalizing.

Emperor

Much of modern Paganism may associate Jesus (or rather the religion inspired by him) with the negative qualities of the Emperor—control, authority, power, dominion. Using any faith as a form of social control has been a longtime method the ruling elite have employed, none more famously than Constantine selecting the gospels for the bible that created his ideal ethos for society, an ethos that could be unquestionable such as the Emperor being chosen by God to rule and dictate over us all.

The lessons of the Emperor, of the fatherly part of Jesus are far removed from that, however. The fatherly qualities of Jesus are seen throughout the stories—of the provider, the protector, as well as being father-like to the children he met and to the followers he gathered. There are many instances of Jesus being like a shepherd, who keeps an eye on his flock with diligence and compassion, and searching for the lost sheep. The role of the Father of unconditional love and never giving up on his children, no matter how lost or prodigal, is a powerful archetype that the Emperor reflects of custodian and protector.

Hierophant

The Hierophant is a card of tradition, which for Jesus was the Jewish tradition. I often wonder what Jesus would think of the Christianity that was born in his name—and if he only saw himself as being a small addition to the Jewish prophets and teachers. The Hierophant is the Teacher archetype, the Guide, and even the storyteller whose stories offer us insight into life's complexities. The books are filled with examples of Jesus speaking, instructing, and guiding people, especially through the medium of stories or parables, much like the Celtic Bards keeping the history and lore of the land alive through poetry, story, and song.

Of course, the simplicity of Jesus the Teacher can get very lost when today we see the Hierophant as the Pope or representing the Church as an organization with a sordid past and unlearnt mistakes. It can be difficult to separate Jesus the Teacher from those who seem to manipulate those teachings for their own desires and power. However, Jesus the Teacher would remind us that no matter our degree or priestly rank, we are still learning and need support to make sense of our mistakes and find truth. This is easier said than done, as is the way of any spiritual guidance dealing with the darkness of the soul.

Lovers

The newly discovered Gnostic Gospels offer us a new way of looking at Jesus which should have always been blindingly obvious: the Lovers with Mary Magdalene. The possibility of Jesus loving her more than the other disciples, of kissing her on the mouth, or even having a child with her, has caused a great deal of interest and intrigue in religious communities over the years. Within the Pagan community we can see how Mary the Virgin can be paired with Mary the Lover, a female counterpart or consort to Jesus, the meeting of God and Goddess. Here we can recognize the power and interplay between Male and Female within the Jesus mystery that causes friction and ignites passion to bring forth life. Between Mary and Jesus there is balance to power and a sexual chemistry that can only be sacred and blessed.

There is another way of viewing the Lovers, as in the traditional meanings of the tarot. Do we go with our spiritual purpose, our life's journey, and the direction of Will, or, do we go with our emotions or ideal of what will make us happy? The Lovers is a card of hard choices between two paths that seem equally rewarding and tempting—in traditional decks, the female figure is trying to decide between the Angel or the man, seeking divine guidance about whether being with that particular man is really the right choice for her. If we apply it to Jesus, is it not easy to see how he would wrestle internally with being dedicated to his role of as Teacher and a prophet or the ability to be loved by a woman like Mary so completely without causing competition or stirring jealously amongst his followers. Aren't these the worries and concerns of us in the modern age of loving—someone who distracts us from our soul's journey or who overtly tries to stop us from doing so out of jealousy or fear? From even these few cards we can clearly see a correlation between the cards and the stories that are moving and poignantly modern.

Chariot

The symbolism of the Chariot card, the rider being led away from the confines of previous institutions or thought, is often portrayed in tarot decks as being all about the rider or the vehicle itself. However, it is the road, the path of life itself that offers us experiences and insight into human nature and spirituality. This can be seen very literally in the stories of the Bible. The stories of the Good Samaritan or the appearance of the blinding light on the road to Damascus reflect how when we are travelling on our spiritual journey, even in the most mundane parts of life, we have to keep our desires, principles, and ethics close at hand. These are the things that we carry as we travel through life. They bring us wisdom as we apply our principles of loving thy neighbor, equality, etc., in a very hectic and insecure world. The Chariot card reminds us that we need to always be "aware" on our journey through life. Spirituality and belief do not stop at the temple door; we don't stop being spiritual beings when we go to work or buy our groceries—our beliefs, ethics, and philosophies are carried wherever we go.

Strength

Would you say that Jesus was a strong man? I see Jesus as being a character of great personal strength—strength of will and of soul purpose. The stories offer us insight into how Jesus was a man of great personal strength who had great compassion and understanding of people without either dictating to them or demeaning them. Strength is a card of putting aside our own difficulties so we can help others; this can be through use of being very direct by intervening in an obvious way, or gently with patience and compassion. Jesus often displayed this characteristic as the man who would dine with tax collectors, who would talk to the sick, and treat the thieves, robbers and prostitutes with respect and dignity, without a goal, without wanting to "convert" them. This gentle approach to an ideological revolution inspired so many as he treated the "piranhas" as a precious part of Spirit and worthy of love, respect, and dignity. How often can we honestly say that we do that in our modern lives, where fear and "privacy" keeps us from speaking to our neighbours, or our judgment prevents us from talking to young people or those who have been convicted of a crime? Do we too have that compassion to be able to talk to, help, and treat those people like everyone else?

Hermit

Even Jesus had moments of when he needed to be alone, to listen to the darkness of his soul. Either by escaping into the wilderness for forty days and forty nights or at the Garden of Gethsemane, where he needed to be alone to listen to the voice within.

We all have times when we need to retreat, take a break from the world, isolate ourselves from stresses and strains. As spiritual beings, we need to take time to reflect, assimilate, listen to the dark thoughts as well as the good ones to process and integrate them. In our modern lives, this tends to happen when we are forced to do so, by taking days off work and being ill with a cold or flu virus. These are brief moments of retreat, yet vital to our beings and to our soul's journey. Like us, Jesus would have moments of doubt, of questioning life and the will of the Divine in the ups and downs of life, and we need time alone to do that. Otherwise the Universe will enforce that time on us by way of something like the common cold, connecting us to what is important and reminding us of the Great Work and our soul's evolution.

Wheel of Fortune

The Wheel of Fortune is sometimes referred to as the Hand of God because it reflects the unpredictable way that life tends to happen. But it is not the events themselves that define us, but how we deal with the lot that we have been given. Are we gracious winners, humble and demure? Or are we sore losers who let such negativity bite at our very souls, making us bitter and hurtful toward those around us? Or do we seek to try and improve on what we have been given? Are you empowered to create change in our world through prayer or magick?

Jesus had no choices in life with regard to social status. He was born into the country, the "class" and tradition of fate. He experienced things in life that were the decision of fate, and he even died by the decision of fate—as destiny had marked him to be the Dying God on the crucifix. It was how Jesus dealt with it, as a human with upset and suffering, yet with great strength, compassion, and humility that makes the stories of the stations of the cross, or the moments leading up to his death, the most profound and illuminating stories of Jesus (in my opinion). They demonstrate that it is not the role of fate you must fear, but the way in which you deal with it that is important.

As a Pagan, I like to see the Wheel of Fortune reflecting the turning of the Wheel of the Year from sabbat to sabbat, festival to festival. These moments in time give us the ability to review and reflect every six to eight weeks on how our lives are developing, where we want them to go, and how we can deal with changes. We can also ask the spirits of the time of year to help us process or even change the events that are happening in our lives. Watching the Wheel of the Year reminds me of the ever-changing nature of the Universe. Nothing is left to stagnate unless we resist the powerful transformations that are around us—and I think Jesus the man would probably agree.

Justice

The concept of justice in the Bible is one that people turn to when they feel angry, hurt, or violated by someone or something. The quotation of "an eye for an eye" often is seen as the best form of justice. Alternatively, justice is seen as something decided upon death, whether you go to Heaven or Hell. These are harsh absolutes that are very difficult to process in theory, let alone in everyday practice, for how can you cut the hand off the thief who stole bread to feed his family, or worse, condemn his soul to eternal torture just for trying to provide for his children?

Jesus spoke about forgiveness, acceptance, and learning from our mistakes, which is difficult if you are full of negative emotions such as betrayal, anger, and the desire for retribution. The card of Justice reflects the concept's complexity, of how every action has a consequence, and at the same time, a lesson and an opportunity to learn and grow. Although forgiveness is incredibly difficult, the anger and hurt is not beneficial for the betrayed *or* the betrayer. In holding on to hate or a sense of retribution, we damage ourselves by locking out our hearts from the gift of love. The act of forgiveness can therefore be healing for all involved. If every action has a reaction, would you rather your action produced positive consequences or negatives ones?

Hanged Man

The most well-known image in the "Devil's picture book" of Jesus is that of the Hanged Man. Some decks actually depict some sort of crucifixion whilst others only show a figure suspended from a tree. The card can be one of suffering, being restricted, helpless, and hopeless to your fate. However, it can also be a card of deep inspiration, or how in stillness we can find great clarity and peace. When we "suspend" our belief in science and the way things "should" be, we get a greater understanding that can be incredibly illuminating.

The Hanged Man is a card of sacrifice, for Jesus was a sacrifice to his beliefs and teachings. He could also be seen as a sacrifice to make sure that sacrifices will never need to be made again. The Dying God is the symbol of how even Divinity has to give up that which is most precious in order that enlightenment and wisdom come forth.

We may think that sacrifice is always the big thing—sacrificing a family life for a good career, or sacrificing love for the freedom to be who we are. Sacrifice seems too big, too much, or never enough when we think of sacrifice within a spiritual context. When time is a valuable commodity as it is in our modern world, the sacrifice of twenty minutes each day to pray, meditate, contemplate, and connect with Divinity can seem too difficult. Television tries to entice us to watch all the programmes on its schedule, and society says we should be going to the gym or finding a partner in a club that seems more like cattle-market. We have to work longer hours to get a better career, so the offering of twenty minutes to our spirituality becomes the most difficult task. However the great sacrifice it may seem to be, it can offer the most deep and profound wisdom and clarity, be they in our relationship to Divinity or our priorities in life. In the stories, Jesus offers the tool that gives other perspectives, posing pertinent questions that cut to the core. It is here within sacrifice that we can be aware of it.

Death

The Death card is among the most feared and least understood tarot card to the masses, for we all fear the concept the physical death. All that is born must die, and Jesus was no exception. Was he afraid of dying? Of course he was! As he walked in the Garden of Gethsemane he felt conflicted, as though he was betraying his faith by his fear of the dying process and what lay beyond. The possibility of having to let go is difficult, especially letting go of a life that has friends and loved ones and that offers us such happiness and joy. But it is a lesson we all go through, a natural transition that Pagans honor with the festival of Samhain—the death of nature as winter rules and those precious to us who have died.

Death needs to occur, for it is through death that we can be reborn. In various initiation rituals, a person experiences "death" of his or her old life in order to be reborn into a new life, phase, role, awareness, or mindset. It is through the symbolic death of Jesus that we are given the gift of rebirth at Easter and the hope that carries us through the most grief-stricken times. We will have joy and happiness once again.

Temperance

The essence of the Temperance card is the way I tend to view religion/spirituality in any context. The depiction of the angel of temperance in most decks highlights the ability of balance, moderation, and finding a connection to all the aspects of life and putting that into a complete whole. You cannot truly separate Jesus the man from Jesus the teacher, or Jesus the magician, or Jesus the Dying God, as these are all part of who he is and what he was in the stories. To do so would be to divide and diminish his essence—just as it would be to separate our roles of brother/sister, mother/father, profession/spiritual belief. We may want to carve out the bits about

Jesus we don't want to see, but in its totality there is such wisdom and learning that gives us so much, if we are open to experience it.

Devil

Naturally, the stories of the Bible depict a creature called the Devil. Some Pagan authors have tried to suggest that the image of the Devil was a political move by the Church to vilify the Horned God of ancient Pagan religions in an attempt to increase conversions to the Christian Church. However, most Christians even now will admit they do not believe in a "devil," but more that the figure is an archetype or representation of humanity's darker aspects—lust, power, greed, and dominion.

The binds of materialism and temptation have long been lessons for humankind. The story of Jesus destroying the tables and stalls of wealth and commerce in the temple is enough to remind us of how we can so easily become distracted by materialism and greed. Not even modern Pagans are free from the powers of the Devil card, being tempted to spend hundreds on (for example) an athame or wand that will be the envy of all, rather than finding or making a tool that is best suited to them.

Here we can be reminded that it isn't how much we spend, owning the latest technology, or binding the right "sort" of partner to you in marriage that is important. They are but distractions, pursuits to fill the empty void or ones that seem less difficult than the journey of self-awareness and spirituality. The pursuit of money, power, or sex for its own sake is a superficial quest that prevents us from learning the deeper lessons in life. Such freedom can happen when we take off those chains.

Tower

The Tower card reflects those moments when our faith is questioned and when the things we hold dear are shaken or pulled from under our feet. It must be similar to how the disciples must have felt when their teacher and guide—their rock—was no longer with them. In grief and loss, their confidence, faith, and what they had built their lives around was left in rubble. A "Tower moment" can be an action, word, or thought-form that pierces through your defenses and hits the very core of your being, shaking the foundations of who you are and what you value in life. How could you not be as shaken, upset, and confused as the disciple Thomas who doubted that Jesus had been reborn?

In modern life you may experience this feeling as being made redundant, when a partner of thirty years leaves you, or if you have a crisis of faith in yourself, your ability, or even your spiritual philosophy. However, it can be a positive experience, for it is the moment that cuts out the unnecessary and the distractions, so all we are left with are the core truths of our lives, the core friends who love and help us when life turns difficult, or the belief that keeps us strong.

Star

The Star is a card of renewal and new hope, as the essence of the old is taken and from it a new way is begun. This can be seen in so many ways, such as when Gardner took the essence of ancient Pagan religions and the essence of magical practice to form a new tradition called Wicca. Within the context of Jesus, books such as this one show how the essence of Jesus's story has been taken in the hearts and minds of so many; such truth has been found within the stories in a new way. Even this addition to the book opens a new insight into the man via the tarot's symbolism. Throughout the ages, the teachings Jesus has shared with us have been carried and reinterpreted, which make the essence and truth of the stories transcend time itself. Is the essence of the teaching "love thy neighbor" really so different to the essence of Crowley's belief that "every man and woman is a star" or that "Love is the Law, Love under Will"? We are all part of Divinity and worthy of love, and by following our divine inspiration we are working for our own development and the betterment of everyone else.

The beauty of time is that the stories' essence can mature, the waters of the Star can cleanse away the dirt and leave us with shining truth, transcending the politics and religious lines of old. The acts done in the name of Jesus can no longer tarnish the truth within the pages and between the lines and so we can accept the essence of who Jesus was and what he had to share with us all.

Moon

The Moon card reflects a world of dream and illusion, the shadows that play and torment you, and the wolves that howl, and whose light hides behind a cloud when you least want it to. The realm of Shadow, our fears and anxieties, is one that we fight against, and yet at the same time we are tantalized by it—hence the gothic horrors of vampires, ghosts, ghouls, and werewolves. Within the Jesus stories, we see Jesus facing his own inner demons and anxieties at Gethsemane; he wanted his disciples to sit and hold a vigil for him, to be guiding his light and soul through the darkness. However it is only you who can navigate your way by understanding it, listening to it, and knowing what to react to (versus what is only your mind tormenting you).

The Moon is also a card of great mystery, signifying ancient people who wondered why the moon waxed and waned, how it affected the coming and going of the tide, and how it influenced plant growth. Sometimes we spend so much time asking why, when really it is the mystery of that power that is more important. For myself and my connection to the Jesus myth, I often ask myself why I feel a connection when I follow a Pagan path; I am Druid and a Witch, but it is the essence of that mystery and the energy and inspiration I get from it that is the most wonderful gift, and one I am not too keen on rationalizing with psychology.

Sun

Although not a part of the Jesus story itself (despite the many attributions you can make between the Sun card and Jesus in his role as the light of the world), I feel here we have a connection between ourselves and the Jesus figure. The Sun card is of radiating light, positivity, and potential, just like the disciples felt when they received the blessing of the Holy Spirit. They were filled with love and joy, and felt ready to be teachers to others in life. When we think of the stories, ourselves, the man, and how we are all very similar, there is a huge rush of joy and exuberance. And there is nothing wrong with feeling the love of Divinity and simply letting that energy radiate through your entire being. Be it through a teacher like Jesus or another spiritual figure, seeing that connection can only be a joyous experience that vitalizes the soul. There is a moment where we don't see Divinity as being the only light of the world, but our own souls are too—we are Jesus, God, and Goddess, all found within shining brightly when we recognize it.

Judgement

In most decks is the Judgement card. Although in modern Pagan decks it has been renamed, such as Rebirth or Karma, the essence of the card is Judgment, the Last Day, when the dead receive their promise of eternal life. However, the card's deeper meaning is being beyond judgment, beyond the confines of "the Matrix." Here is the essence of rebirth, the transformation that happens when we realize we are powerful beings and can be extraordinary. Here we can rise to any challenge from the lessons and learning of the previous twenty cards. This was the nature of Jesus's "rising from the dead" and his spirit and legacy speaking to us rather than quoting every word or action he did.

Through Christ's rebirth we have the possibility of recreating and redefining ourselves. New projects and new horizons expand like never before. Jesus was asked to rise to the challenge, and he did. Like in the Lovers card where there were choices and indecision, the Judgement card is that moment you realize it was not the path that you chose which was important, but the way you conducted yourself along that path, what you learnt, and what you have shared and will share again. We don't all have to be like Jesus, the disciples, Christians, or even of any faith to find worth and truth in the Jesus stories, for truth will always come forth.

World

In some decks, the World card is renamed the Universe. This is the precious transcending moment of honoring the union of the Jesus within us and the Jesus in the story. The spirit within us and the Divinity without are both the same thing. This feeling is beyond words—it is awe and wonder, perhaps lasting for a fleeting moment before it ebbs away. As the World is the last of the major cards, it marks the end of our journey connecting the life and stories of a man with the major arcana. Hopefully you're now filled with a moment of insight, clarity, and perhaps the urge to step on the path again.

The spiral of creation continues, the journey is never ending. Although I have written some ideas, thoughts, and insights about the cards, there are perhaps many more you could think of and perhaps more for the elemental Ace cards, the rest of the numbered minor arcana, and even the court cards as facets of Jesus or figures within the stories. So much can be related and woven together because there is so much truth. The symbolism of the stories of the Dying God are throughout cultures throughout time. The tarot's symbolism works effortlessly between us and our spiritual selves. There is much left to explore, such as Jesus and the Kabbalah or astrologically through signs and planets, but I hope you have picked up enough "tools" on the way. You can now be like the Fool—leap into your own journey of Jesus and "the Devil's Picture Book"!

ABOUT THE AUTHOR

Sarah Kral lives on the Welsh borderlands. Her Catholic background prompted her search for spirituality. From listening to the hills, seeing the magic of trees, and studying the tarot she came to her Pagan path in her early teens. In 2004 she joined the Order of Bards, Ovates, and Druids and is currently befriending her Darkness in the Ovate grade. (Mark's note: She doesn't like me saying this [for she's far too humble] but I call her a "Tarot Reader Extraordinaire.")

Twenty-Two

······

Soul Friends: A Wiccan/Jesus-based Spirituality

By Erin Dragonsong

Perhaps it seems paradoxical that many Witches may honour or even venerate Jesus. But it's not so far-fetched. Wicca spirituality actually has much in common with the teachings of Jesus.

Jesus the Nazarene was one of the world's great spiritual leaders. He exposed as fraudulent the established religion's hypocrisy and ignorance. He daringly broke the stranglehold of orthodoxy and advocated the individual's search for reunion with the Divine. He exemplified this search with his own life and shared the path with those who chose to follow.

The profound value of his teachings are timeless—as relevant and revolutionary now as they were two thousand years ago.

In this piece, we will look at Jesus's core teachings and how Wicca fulfills them.

Before we can look at the similarities between Wicca and Jesus's teachings, however, we must define our parameters: what sources are we drawing upon?

You will not find much Wiccan philosophy in sacred texts. Wicca is not a dogmatic religion and has no designated "gospels." It is an experiential spirituality, a way of living—just as Jesus lived and *demonstrated* his truth, rather than writing treatises on the matter. So here we will be looking at what is commonly taught and practiced in Wicca.

Also, we will examine the spiritual essence of Wicca—that which transcends the superficial variations in practices—rather than any particular Wiccan sects or rites.

Similarly, we will bypass the popularized revisions of Jesus's teachings and go to what Christian scholars have identified as most likely to have actually been said by Jesus. These are based primarily on *The Jesus Sayings: The Quest for His Authentic Message,* which quotes the most noted authorities on Jesus's original teachings.[167] (The footnotes identify the biblical sources of these teachings. Please note that biblical references in footnotes may not be comprehensive.)

The Written Teachings

There are two bodies of teaching Jesus left us. One is written by his followers, presumably spoken by him. The other is demonstrated through his actions, though not put into writing (or if it was, it did not survive later editing).

This first section refers to the written works passed on by Jesus's followers in the church-sanctioned version of the Bible as well as the Gnostic Gospels.[168]

In the headlines below, I've paraphrased the teachings in modern English. The footnotes will lead you to the actual quotations.

The kingdom of Heaven is right here, right now,[169] *but it is subtle and most people don't notice it.*[170]

Heaven is not a place. Heaven is a quality.

Jesus likened it to the nourishing grain that falls unheeded from a crack in a jar or leaven spread throughout masses of flour.[171] It is a subtle thing that goes unnoticed as we hurry from task to task. But it's right here, all around us, sustaining and nourishing the world.

One of the primary characteristics of Wicca is that it celebrates the Earth and all material existence as "Heaven"... that is, beautiful, balanced, loving, sacred—the body of the Divine.

That means the Divine is all around us. Not waiting somewhere far away in space and time, but here within us and within everything and everyone else—right here, right now.

It is our practical experience in Wicca that the magickal, spiritual realm coexists with the mundane realm... in fact, it underlies the everyday world we know. With a shift in awareness we can enter this realm at any time. We need only choose it and practice it to live in the kingdom of Heaven every day we're on Earth.

That is what we do with every ritual, every magick act, every prayer, and every moment of awareness.

Seek the Divine,[172] and you will find it where it has always been: within you.[173]

Another fundamental of Wicca is that we humans embody the Goddess and the God. The Divine lives within each of us; it is our duty to seek that, and incarnate the Divine in the world through our actions.

The Charge of the Star Goddess[174]—one of Wicca's few "gospels"— states it explicitly: "I call upon your soul to arise and come unto Me... And if you find Me not within you, you will never find Me without. For behold, I have been with you from the beginning..."

Commit fully, now, to the Divine.[175]

Traditional initiations are optional in Wicca spirituality, but there is still the tradition of a year and a day's study and practice before one is ready to take one's place as a Wiccan. This ensures that we are committed to spiritual development, through all phases of the Moon and seasons of the Sun.

Commitment to the spiritual life is vital. Otherwise we are merely practicing dogma—the letter that killeth. And Wicca is not a dogmatic religion: it is real, experiential, and personal.

Wicca spirituality teaches that the spiritual life must be lived in every moment... not just during religious celebrations or when in need. Commitment to the Divine permeates every aspect of a Wiccan's life.

Share what you know about the Divine and how to find it. Speak out; show others. [176]

I have never met a Wiccan who wasn't happy to share information, ideas, and tips on how to be more successful in the practice of the Craft. In this tradition, we often learn from each other more than from a few designated authorities.

I think it's true of any spiritual path that once we've experienced the joy of connecting with the Divine, it multiplies the joy when we share it with others.

Moreover, we know that since we are all united in one energy system, until we are all free none of us are free. [177] We do what we can, to help others along spiritually. In what is the essence of this rule, we let our actions and way of life shine as an example of living in connection with the Divine.

Act on your knowledge. Your actions, not your words or rituals or even your beliefs, show you for what you are and what you've committed to: the Divine or Error. [178]

Although Wicca spirituality and Witchcraft are not entirely the same, Wicca is a Craft. It is not sufficient to simply think and talk about it. It must be *practiced and experienced.* And the necessary skills must be developed.

Action is one of the four Powers of the Witch. Belief is necessary, but not sufficient in itself.

Whatever we act on is what we really believe.
And how we act becomes what is true.

Action arises from power, and generates empowerment in turn. Wicca spirituality teaches that action is what counts … and that action includes our thoughts, emotions, and speech.

The only test for whether a religion is true and good is how close it takes us to the Divine. Even two thousand years ago people knew that talk is cheap. It is our actions that prove our beliefs. In Biblical terms, we are known by our fruit.[179]

All these miracles that Jesus does, you can do … and more![180]

In Jesus's time, miracle workers were not so rare. There were many spiritual seekers who did miraculous deeds which we today would call magick. Working miracles—or magick—is an integral part of Wicca, though not every Wiccan casts spells.[181] Through making magick, we come to perceive a deeper level of reality and understand who we really are—a core purpose of Jesus's and every enlightened teacher's message.[182]

All Jesus's disciples were expected to work miracles, especially in healing the sick. The early church itself practiced magick—practices only thinly disguised as today's orthodox rites and rituals.[183] It was only later that the Christian orthodoxy, determined to keep control of the religion, began judging what was an approved miracle; whatever they didn't approve was labeled "demonic" and "Witchcraft." The distinction lay in whether the miracle served the religious hierarchy or challenged it.

It's important to realise that the language itself has altered much through the centuries, as the perception of miracles changed. Words that originally were free of stigma became used to suggest evil. For instance, an archaic word for magick is *gramarye*[184]—the same root word that gives us "grammar," "glamour" (as in enchantment), and the Witch's "grimoire."[185] Writing itself was considered an act of magick.

So too the word *daemon (demon)* meant a god, goddess, divine power, genius, or guardian spirit, rather than an evil creature.[186]

In other words, although public perception of magick and miracles has changed, there is nothing inherently evil about them. And as Jesus taught, magick can and should be used to help people.

Be merciful. Take care of people. If someone is sick, offer what healing you can.[187]

I have yet to be at a ritual where healing wasn't offered, either to the Earth and the soul of humanity, or to someone who is in need. I have never met a Wiccan who didn't routinely offer spells and prayers for the well-being and healing of others, and offer herbs, hands, and ideas to those who were ill.

Wiccan philosophy states that we are all children of the Divine, and even moreso that we are all *part* of the Divine, inseparable. So of course we should care for each other. But there is more to it.

When we can feel another's pain as if it were our own, and when we know that we are not really separate at all, it follows logically that we will do whatever we can to alleviate another's suffering. The sensitivity one develops in spiritual practice (or the natural sensitivity that leads people to Wicca) automatically creates this desire to care for others.

Love everybody, not just family and friends, whom it is easy to love. Love your enemies too.[188]

The Charge of the Star Goddess states what I consider to be the only Wiccan Law: "For My law is love unto all beings. By naught but love may [the Divine] be known."

In the Wiccan point of view, all people—indeed, all beings, animate and inanimate—are children of the Goddess and God. We are all equal in

Their eyes. Therefore everyone is our sibling, deserving of our love, loyalty, and protection.

And more than this: We are each a literal Temple of the Divine.

If this is so, how can we think of anyone as an enemy? We'd be rejecting an aspect of the Divine. Therefore we must find a way to honour the Divine even in the form of those who seem on the surface to be antagonists.

Wiccans believe, as Jesus did, in a Divine Force as the creator of the universe, and that this force is not merely loving, but is Love.

In Wicca spirituality, we know that hate is going the wrong direction.[189] The way to the Divine is through love. The Three-Fold Law and the Wiccan Rede both make that clear.[190]

As Wiccans have always declared, we come to the Divine through Perfect Love and Perfect Trust.

Forgive those who harm you.[191]

The Three-Fold Law states that whatever we give out returns to us. If we judge and resent others, we will incur judgement and resentment. Same with anger, blame, hatred … forgiveness, compassion, love, etc. Thus it is necessary to rise above harmful emotions and practice compassion and forgiveness.

Of course, that's a simplistic version. Seldom is the return so obvious. Even so, there is truth in this, because when we feel anger and hatred we are the first to suffer from feeling it.

And if our "enemy" is in truth the Divine in another role, it suggests that even the hard things in life are meant to be gifts. Our enemies are those who give us the gifts we least want to receive. These are, however, the gifts that hold the most power. Wiccans know the power of energy and that emotion is energy. There's a Wiccan saying: Where there's fear, there's power. That is true of every strong emotion.

Any strong emotion binds us to the object of that emotion. When we send energy to another in this way, we bind them even closer to us. Doing so leaves us two choices: hold our enemies near and in our minds, continually enduring their presence, or forgive them and let them go. Aside from "earning" forgiveness by being forgiving, Wiccans recognise that forgiveness is the only way to be free of the harm done to us... to avoid continuing to perpetrate harm upon ourselves.

Deal with your own shortcomings rather than worrying about other people's flaws.[192]

Because Wicca isn't a religion of rules but of personal spiritual experience, there is very little room to judge others. Everyone's experience of life and spirituality is absolutely unique. So how can we compare and find fault? Without rules, one can't point fingers at rule-breakers. The only thing we can really concern ourselves with is our own experience and how well we live up to our own values, and how well we love and serve as the Divine asks us. It is necessary in Witchcraft to know ourselves and to polish our rough edges... to hone ourselves to be a clearer vessel for the Divine. It is this practice that makes Wiccan ritual and magick powerful.

Remain humble.[193]

Humility is a natural consequence of Wicca. When we honour all of nature and every being—animate and inanimate—as our sibling, teacher, and the Divine, we don't foster superiority complexes. When we dismiss judgement and self-righteousness—when we love even our enemies—there is no room for arrogance. When we love ourselves as a Temple and Aspect of the Divine, the pure self-esteem we generate does not require anyone else's inferiority. I believe this is what Jesus meant when he admonished his followers to be like little children.[194] Children epitomize humility. This humility gives them three characteristics that are vital to spiritual pursuit:

1. They accept the limitations of their knowledge and are thus highly receptive.

2. They look on the world as the magical, wondrous, Divine place it is.

3. They have an innate belief in the Universe as a loving, supportive deity.

Wiccans, as mystics, share these childlike traits. We cultivate awe in the wonder of life, death, and rebirth. We believe in—and experience—the loving care of the Goddess and God. And we know that what we know is only a tiny fragment of the whole Truth. We are always open and receptive to new wisdom.

Don't worry about your comfort, your clothes, or what you have to eat.[195] *Be generous; give what you have to everyone who asks.*[196] *The Divine provides for your needs.*[197]

There is a generosity of spirit that comes from Wicca, especially among those who practice magick and manifestation. The Divine does provide in abundance, as we become more adept at asking for what we really want and allowing ourselves to receive. As we learn to trust this abundance, sharing occurs naturally. When we have plenty, it increases our joy to share it with others. Even when we have little, sharing increases the abundance of the whole community.

The Feasting that Wiccans do at the end of every ritual is in token of this abundance and generosity. Taking care of each other is a way to express our thanks to the Divine for all our blessings.

Which, as the Three-Fold Law tells us, increases our own blessings![198] There is physical as well as intellectual humility, and this is what Jesus preached when he reminded us to give away what we have. Don't pay attention to the trappings of the world; focus on your inner journey.

The truly radical part of this message is that Jesus was speaking to the poor, not the wealthy. He was saying that it doesn't matter that you have little, but that you share what you have, and trust the Divine to take care of you. The Wiccan Three-Fold Law and now-popular Law of Attraction agree:

*Put aside dogma and rules of conduct. Don't make rules for other
people and beware those who seek to force their rules on you.*[199]

Personal authority is the essence of Wicca. It is so crucial, it is one
half of the only "law" in Wicca: "Do as ye will." The Way to the Divine
is through our devotion to our deepest truth, rather than established rites
and doctrines. In other words, it's not about *acting* as if you're pious, but
about *being* pure in your heart.

Wiccans perceive that the Divine lives in each person's heart. So only
your heart can guide you along the path right for you. The same is true for
everyone else. Therefore everyone's path is unique, and equally valid. No
one else can say what's right for us, just as we can't say what's right for anyone else. In Wicca, it goes against our fundamental principles even to try.

*Beware religious authorities who take the keys to the spirit but don't
enter and won't let you enter.*[200]

Binding others with rules is especially destructive in matters of spirituality. By definition, religious authority usurps an individual's divinity. It
claims that an ordinary human can't know the will of God. But if that is
so, who can? Who among us is not human? Who among us isn't ordinary
and extraordinary at the same time?

Religious authority claims that only certain superior people have the
franchise on speaking for God and determining good and evil, and thus
can insist on obedience to their rules. This separates the rest of us from the
Divine, as if Divine will wasn't our own heart's deepest desire. Thus it is
inevitable that religious authority "takes away the key" to personal experience of the Divine, substituting rules and rituals in its place. In their desire
to keep hold of the key, they become easily diverted from spirit themselves.
Many religious leaders so fondly hoard the key to Heaven and in doing so,
mistake it for the door! This is what Jesus was warning us about.

But rules are not what liberates us.

According to Wicca, Jesus, and other great spiritual traditions, it is our
responsibility to attain to the Divine personally.[201] In Wicca everyone is

her or his own priestess and priest. We are each our own spiritual authority. That means that every human being has the keys to the state of Heaven Consciousness, and the responsibility to enter. Let those who have eyes see, and those who have ears hear.[202] We all have the ability to perceive truth and discern wisdom, and are born with minds capable of understanding the world around us. Wicca insists that we use them. We can't take other people's word as gospel; we must find the truth for ourselves.[203] Others can only speak *their* truth. If we don't find it ourselves, it will never be our truth, merely a belief we hold. This concept is fundamental to Wicca and all Mystery religions, as the original Christianity was.

Wake up. Pay attention. Notice what is around you and discern what is real. Get out of your preconceived notions and beliefs, and perceive what is *really* being shown to you. Jesus repeatedly urged this. Wicca also insists on it.

Be wise as the serpent and gentle as the dove.[204]

This is one of Jesus's most intriguing and provocative teachings, deliberately overturning millennia of religious bigotry. Along the way, it has served to align him with Pagans all over the world. Even in his own time, the dove was an ancient symbol of peace. Being as gentle as the dove means to not hurt anyone or anything, including ourselves. The Wiccan Rede, primary and only "commandment" of Wicca, agrees: Harm none.

The dove was a common symbol in Judaism. It could be expected that Jesus would use it. But the serpent was maligned and condemned most vehemently by Yahweh, according to Biblical stories. Why would Jesus overturn that doctrine? What was he telling his followers?

The serpent is an ancient symbol of wisdom. It is the wisest of all creatures. It knows the mysteries that the Gods themselves know: having eaten of the Tree of Knowledge *and* the Tree of Life, the serpent owns the ninefold wisdom. It knows *right* and *wrong*, and the *truth behind* this duality. It knows the secrets of *life, death*, and *rebirth:* the ever-evolving transformation of soul. It knows all the worlds, travelling into the *underworld,* across the *Earth,* and up into the branches of the World Tree in the *heavens.*

In other words, the serpent knows the truth of its Self, which is the truth of the Divine and all the universe. Accordingly, the serpent follows the path of its own wisdom and will not be deceived by any other's beliefs, choices, or demands. It is no wonder the serpent is reviled by the dictator-God Yahweh.[205]

According to Pagels in *The Gnostic Gospels,* Jesus and early Christians recognised knowledge and self-knowledge as the key to returning to the Divine.[206] Wicca also values self-knowledge and knowledge of all worlds. The Charge of the Star Goddess likewise encourages us to recognise the Source of life and Its existence within each of us. Only within ourselves can we find the Divine for which we yearn.

Wicca advocates the wisdom of the serpent. It requires knowledge of the manifold worlds and the ability to enter each with ease, as the serpent does. It requires eating the fruit of Knowledge for ourselves to make informed free choice and take responsibility for our actions. It requires an understanding of deeper reality, the Wheel of life—a fundamental philosophy of Wiccan religion.

Christ in Action

The following principles were not recorded in Jesus's words, per se. It could be that he spoke of them and no one wrote it down, or it was excised at a later date. Nevertheless, these teachings are what he showed by example and demanded of his disciples. I am indebted to Pagels's *The Gnostic Gospels* for these teachings.[207]

Men and Women are Equals in the Pursuit of God.[208]

In Wicca, women hold positions of leadership. In Wiccan Circles, priestesses are honoured as conduits for the Goddess—the feminine aspect of Divinity.[209]

Women are revered in Wicca—as in ancient religions—as representatives of the awe-inspiring Creative Power of the Goddess. The menstrual cycle shows women's innate connection to the cycles of life and the Powers of Creation. Childbirth and lactation, for all that we take them for granted as commonplace, are profound mysteries that science has not yet begun to comprehend. Women are by nature open to the subtle realms and deep wisdom (not that all women cultivate or even notice this gift).

It is through women that humanity begins to access divinity: as creator, as nurturance, as compassion and loving kindness, as Mystery, as sexual transcendence. The early Christians, following Jesus, also honoured women as spiritual disciples and leaders. In fact, it was common for early Christians to follow the teachings of Jesus's female disciples, including Mary Magdalene, and for women to act as priests and even bishops.[210]

As all beings are aspects of the Divine, it is ludicrous to imagine that one half of humanity is incapable or undeserving of spiritual evolution, let alone leadership, as patriarchal religions insist.

Jesus made clear his position when he taught in Bethany, for instance. Mary (most likely Mary Magdalene) sat attentive at his feet among his disciples. Her sister, Martha, asked if she shouldn't help care for the guests, and Jesus replied that Mary has chosen the one important thing—spiritual devotion.[211] Thus he put aside for all time, one would hope, patriarchy's convenient belief that only man can aspire to God, while woman exists merely to assist him.

Death is meaningless, when you transcend separation from the divine.[212]

For Wiccans, death isn't the big drama it is for many people. We know that death is just a doorway we pass through many times, in both directions. The door is not solid, more like a veil than a wall; there is actually much communication that flows back and forth between the two realms. It is only when we think of ourselves as solidly in the ego and body that we fear death, clinging to this life.

Wiccans travel between the worlds frequently, and thus experience personally that we are not the body nor the mind we think of as ours. We experience transformation with every ritual.

Death loses its power over us. We know it is not the end; it is not even a complete severing from this world. It is not actually death at all, but a rebirth to a more natural and wonderful state of existence than we have here on this tumultuous, limited, yet thrilling plane. When we are aligned with the truth of the Wheel of life, death can actually be a graceful and beautiful transformation.

Personal experience of the Divine is the goal. Don't worship; BE the Divine.[213]

The crucial thing to realise about Jesus is that he never advocated being a Christian nor following dogma; quite the opposite. Jesus insisted that his followers *be as he was,* rather than worship him as an idol.[214]

Wicca likewise requires more than a statement of belief; it requires living in accordance with fundamental spiritual truths…in essence, following in Christ's own footsteps.

Like early Christianity, Wicca is a mystery religion of personal enlightenment. In such a religion, it's our evolving *experience* of God that matters. We don't show devotion through obedience to religious authority or worshipping a deity as far beyond us. We don't prove our faith or love of God through merely "believing" in things. The original apostles received secret teachings from Jesus, initiating them into higher levels of understanding and God-realisation—teachings they could not share with those who were not ready for them.[215]

Belief is another word whose meaning has changed dramatically; originally it referred to much more than clinging to a pre-chosen mindset. It meant being committed to something you dearly cherish. When told to *believe* in Jesus, it meant to cherish him and commit to being as he was…in other words, to experience Christ Consciousness, i.e., Divinity, personally.

The practice of Wicca *is* a personal experience of the Divine. Every Wiccan ritual is designed to facilitate this direct communion. We invoke within ourselves aspects of the All: gods and goddesses; qualities and energies. We intentionally submerge the ego-identity that stands between Self and Divinity, and merge for a time with our Source. We become channels through which the Divine enters the world.

A Difference of Semantics

Reading between the lines in Jesus's teachings and Wiccan philosophy, the underlying framework of both becomes clear:

We are all One, and that One is the Divine.
Our purpose is to remember, experience, and embody this truth.

I believe the major differences between Jesus's teachings and those of Wicca are merely semantic. The limitations of verbal language, translation, and cultural perspective make it seem as though Jesus's teachings and the Wiccan path are worlds apart.

Going beyond those limitations, however, the teachings show their unity. Though the methods may be somewhat different, the goals and the purpose are something Wiccans share with Jesus and his original apostles. Why is this so? We might say it's because modern Wicca arises out of a Christian context and has adopted its best values. Or we might say, as *The Pagan Christ* documents most convincingly, that it's because Jesus's teachings arise out of Pagan traditions.[216]

I believe the truth lies deeper than either of those theories. As individual as human cultures and religions are, there is only one Source, understood as divine. And regardless of the way we interpret the Divine, there exist certain core qualities which every sincere spiritual seeker discovers, no matter in what religion they are trained.

When we embody these qualities to the best of our abilities, we find the Divine hidden behind all the rules and dogma. We are worshipping the Divine in the footsteps of all the greatest spiritual teachers, including Jesus.

This is all they ask us to do, and is exactly what Wicca spirituality excels at.

ABOUT THE AUTHOR

Erin Dragonsong is a modern mystic and a leader in the field of evolutionary spirituality. Her award-winning website, www.Wicca-Spirituality.com, serves over half a million visitors a year from more than 140 countries. Her writings and workshops highlight the connection between our individual experiences and the planetary transformation now underway. Erin inspires people to awaken to the beauty and power of the Divine within ourselves and the Earth. Her publications include the Personal Mandala Starter Kit, the Spiritual Mandala Templates Kit, online 'zine *The Silver Chalice,* and two previous magazines, **Sparks* and *Navel Gazing: Bellydance Spirituality.* She is currently finishing her latest books: *The Natural Connection: Discover Your Animal Spirit Guides and How They Can Help You* and *Energy-Field Survival Guide For Highly Sensitive People,* among other works-in-progress. Her online spirituality school launched in late 2011. You can find her on Facebook (WiccaSpirituality) and Twitter (WiccaSpirit).

Part Three
Thirteen Interviews with Respected Pagan Elders

☸ † ⏚ ∝ ⊗ ✳ ⚥ ☥ ✝

Christians can learn from Paganism that there is no one religion for all people; that love is the most important thing of all; that all things are living and have spirit; and to remember the Golden Rule at all times.

—Raymond Buckland,
The Father of American Wicca[217]

Pagans can learn from Jesus that to follow a spiritual path and the promptings of one's heart and conscience is perilous.

—Vivianne Crowley,
University lecturer, psychologist,
and teacher of Wicca[218]

Introduction

......

What follows is an astonishing collection of conversations with prominent clergy and teachers from the worldwide Neopagan movement. Not all of them agree, but the purpose of this section was not to portray the Pagan world as harmonious in its attitude to Jesus. Indeed, if this were thirteen conversations with Christians of different denominations, I doubt there would be much more harmony. What the following pages demonstrate is that there are a whole host of ways that various Pagan men and women can view Jesus and Christ. I have to say that, while I do not subscribe to everything said here, I learned an incredible amount from these discussions. I hope that you do too.

Twenty-Three

......

Maxine Sanders

The very first of the thirteen respected elders I had the privilege of interviewing was Maxine Sanders, who describes her spiritual tradition in terms of being a "Witch and Priestess of the Goddess." I can't begin to express how excited and honoured I felt when Maxine agreed to this, for she is without doubt one of the world's most well-known and well-respected witches. Her late husband Alex was the founder of one of the two largest Wiccan traditions, known as Alexandrian Witchcraft. Maxine's latest autobiography, *Firechild,* is a truly fascinating adventure for the reader, as she lifts the curtains in a world rarely glimpsed by the uninitiated. As with all the other sections, at the end of each interview is a brief biography.

MT: Maxine, first of all I must thank you for taking the time to speak with me. I do appreciate it.

MS: You're very welcome, Mark.

MT: Perhaps I might begin by talking a little about your incredible autobiography, *Firechild ,* and some of the amazing experiences you describe in relation to Christianity and certain "followers of Jesus." For example, you experienced both extreme fear, even hatred from some Christians, and yet also kindness, acceptance, and affection from others.

MS: Indeed, an example of the former would be an occasion when I came home to my mother's house and was met by the local Catholic priest and two of his large and very adult altar "boys," who proceeded to attempt an aggressive exorcism of sorts, deafening me with prayers, drenching me in holy water, and forcing me to the ground.

MT: My gosh! As a teenage young woman, that must have been terrifying. And yet there are other stories of a much more accepting relationship between you, Alex, and the Catholic Church. For example, is it right to say that at one point in time, the robes for your coven were made by the nuns of a local convent in return for Alex's mediumship skills and the séances he'd perform for them?

MS: Yes, that's true.

MT: Amazing. Anyway, we must get onto the main subject of this book, which is not so much the Church or Christianity but Jesus himself, who of course was not a Christian but a Jew. So let me ask you, was the figure of Jesus, to a lesser or greater degree, part of your upbringing as a child?

MS: Christianity was the religion of my childhood; Church of England until the age of seven, when my mother converted to Roman Catholicism. I was devout in my faith and loved the ceremonies, particularly Benediction.

MT: But did he [Jesus] feel important to you at all?

MS: No, not really, and especially not now. I have found an enjoyable sense of peace based in the realms of nature and the seasonal rituals of Witchcraft.

MT: If you were to imagine Jesus, how is or isn't his spirit reflected in the modern-day Church? Do any Pagan traditions or concepts reflect the spirit of Jesus better?

MS: Christianity is obviously still a religion that gives a sense of belonging and peace to many. The spirit of Jesus is needed and, whilst that need is met by Christianity, it clearly has worth. Paganism is not fulfilling for everyone.

MT: What feelings or thoughts does the Christmas story conjure up in you?

MS: Memories of Christmas Eve midnight mass, drunks reeling up the aisle, incense, mince pies, sherry, and feelings of joy that the Christ brought light into the world.

MT: And Easter?

MS: Sensations of hunger brought about through the fasting until after 3 p.m. on Good Friday and thoughts of the crucified Christ reeking of emotional blackmail to be good.

MT: If you have one, what is your favourite story, parable, teaching, or symbol of Jesus?

MS: Stone throwing comes to mind; I think it was one of the best and least listened to.

MT: Who do you think Jesus was? For example [was he] a simple Jewish teacher, a divine prophet, a valid deity of the Christian pantheon, a miracle worker, a magician, etc.?

MS: I see him as a teacher, prophet, miracle worker, and valid deity of the Christian pantheon. Who am I to deny the Christ's validity? Although, having known many magicians, Jesus strikes me as far more secure in his being than those magicians.

MT: Wonderful. And what lesson do you feel the modern-day church needs to hear from the person/teaching of Jesus?

MS: Having suffered the stone throwing and deafness, the church's hypocrisy is loud. They are experts at teaching/pontificating, sadly lacking in priestly listening.

MT: This is a controversial question, not only for Christians but also within the Pagan world. Do you consider it possible to be both Christian and Pagan?

MS: As a practising witch I found no conflict when for a while, ritual within the circle of Witchcraft was my religious practise on most days of the week. On Sunday morning, the mass in the Liberal Catholic Church was most enjoyable and uplifting.

MT: So what, if anything, can modern-day Pagans learn from the message/person of Jesus?

MS: Modern-day Pagans could learn a tremendous amount from the message of Jesus, although rather less from the interpretation of modern-day Christian clergy.

MT: And what, if anything, can Christians learn from modern-day Paganism?

MS: Unless they want to, nothing.

MT: Maxine, it's been a real pleasure to speak to you about these things. Once again, I do thank for your time.

MS: You're welcome, Mark.

ABOUT THE AUTHOR

Maxine Sanders was initiated into Wicca in 1964. The High Priest was Alex Sanders, known throughout the world as the "King of the Witches." He and Maxine were Handfasted in 1965 and married in 1968. They became household names during the sixties and seventies, bringing modern Witchcraft into global consciousness. Today Maxine is a highly respected

Priestess of the Sacred Mysteries and has encouraged, enabled, and inspired many students and Initiates. Several of Maxine's pupils have become accomplished teachers of esoteric knowledge and work internationally. Maxine's vocation as a priestess includes talking to audiences who wish to listen and counseling those who are in need of kindness, truth, and hope.

Twenty-Four

......

Selena Fox

MT: Selena, I can't tell you how delighted and excited I am to be interviewing you for this book. Your work has influenced people of not only the various Pagan paths but also right across the faith spectrum, and I know that you hold a very broad spiritual vision and see interfaith bridge building as of extreme importance. Thank you so much for allowing me this little glimpse into your personal thoughts about Jesus.

SF: You're very welcome, Mark.

MT: Perhaps I ought to begin with something about your own spiritual tradition. Selena, you founded the Circle Craft path of Paganism. For the benefit of those who do not know, can you explain a little about it?

SF: The Circle Craft tradition began taking form in 1971, with its primary influences being ancient Greek and Roman Pagan religions; American adaptations of European folkways imported from Scotland, Germany, and Latvia; and American folk magic practices from the Appalachian and Ozark mountain regions.

Central to the Circle Craft tradition is communion with the Divine through attunement to Nature. Also essential is developing and sustaining of spiritual relationships with the Divine as Unity and Multiplicity—both as a great interconnecting Spirit, and with multiple sacred forms, including Deities, Ancestors, Elementals, and Nature Spirits. Deities honored include both Goddess and God forms and forms that transcend gender.

The Circle Craft path is animistic and shamanistic. Practitioners develop sacred alignments with the Spirits of particular plants, creatures, and places. The Circle Craft worldview is panentheistic, recognizing the sacred both as immanent, or indwelling, as well as transcendent.

Whenever possible, Circle Craft rituals are held outside in a Circle, representing community and unity, in natural settings. Seven sacred forces, realms, and directions are invoked and honored in rituals: Earth in North, the physical realm; Air in East, the mental realm; Fire in South, the behavioral realm; Water in West, the emotional realm; Cosmos for Above, the universe; Planet for Below, the biosphere; Spirit in the Center, the all-encompassing spiritual realm and the interconnecting center that is Divine Unity.

Initiation by a teacher or group is not required in order to be a Circle Craft practitioner, but this is an option for those who complete a course of study and meet other requirements, including a preparatory outdoor vigil in a natural setting. An important part of personal and group spiritual work is healing and wellness for others, self, and planet. Work with dreams, meditation, and intuition are also important to Circle Craft study and practice. Circle Craft principles include: Harm None, Be of Service, and Live in Balance.

MT: So to my passion and subject of this book. Was the figure of Jesus part of your upbringing as a child?

SF: Yes, Jesus was an important part of my upbringing. I was raised Protestant Christian and was a member of a fundamentalist Southern Baptist congregation in the Washington, DC, area for the first seventeen years of my life. My family has been and continues to be devoutly Christian. As I grew up, I regularly attended Sunday services and other church activities with my family, read and studied the Bible, memorized Bible passages, sang in church choirs, was part of Sunday School and Training Union youth groups, prayed several times daily, and endeavored to follow Jesus's teachings in daily life. I had a series of mystical experiences involving Jesus, including when I was nine years old, when I "went forward," became a member of the congregation, and was baptized in the full body immersion rite of Southern Baptists.

MT: Most Pagans I've spoken to with that kind of a Christian background ended up rejecting it completely and Jesus along with it. So is Jesus still important to you at all?

SF: Yes, Jesus, along with his embodiment and teachings of Divine Love, continues to be important to me. He is important because of his loving essence and wise teachings. He also is important to me as well as to many others because his spirit, lore, and symbology have been a way to perpetuate and transmit sacred knowledge and wisdom from a variety of ancient cultures and religions. In addition, he is important because of the effect, positive and negative, those who call themselves Christian have had and continue to have on the world.

MT: Do you think of Jesus as a historical person?

SF: Yes, I think that Jesus was a historical person. And, as Jesus Christ, he was and is a sacred iconic figure with mythic and mystical dimensions.

MT: So do you see any difference between the terms "Jesus" and "Christ"? Many progressive Christians and Pagans see Jesus as a fully human being and Christ as a more cosmic "spark of deity" within all things. Do you have any thoughts on this?

SF: Yes, I make a distinction between Jesus and Christ. Jesus is the name of the incarnated human being. Christ is the name of the Divine love and wisdom that manifested and expressed itself through Jesus during his birth, life, death, resurrection, and eternal presence.

MT: And are his [the historical Jesus's] teachings reflected in the modern-day Church?

SF: The loving spirit of Jesus is part of many Christian practitioners and is reflected in some Christian groups, communities, denominations, and institutions, but not all. The ones that most embody the spirit of Jesus are those that exude his radiant spiritual essence and lovingly help others. This unconditional loving service is shared with others regardless of their spiritual orientation and without requiring recipients to listen to Christian preaching and/or convert to Christianity. I have encountered many such Christians through my interfaith work locally and globally. I am appreciative of these manifestations of Jesus Christ.

However, there have been and continue to be some who call themselves Christian and Jesus-followers who engage in behaviours that are contrary to the divine loving, caring essence that was his spirit and central to his teachings. These "Christian" individuals and institutions spread hate and discord rather than love. They have harmed and continue to harm and battle Pagans and those of other faiths with their chauvinistic, arrogant ego-driven attitudes, words, and actions. Instead of being loving, humble, caring servants of Christ, they are hateful, egotistical, oppressive, self-righteous, dogmatic, bigoted, and mean-spirited.

MT: Do any Pagan traditions or concepts reflect the spirit of Jesus better than the Church?

SF: The spiritual practices of communing with the Divine in natural settings, and of unconditional positive regard for others regardless of their religious/spiritual/philosophical orientation—which are central to the spiritual practice of Paganism, Witchcraft, and Nature religion that I and many other Pagans practice—these better embody the loving kindness and mystical wisdom that is the spirit of Jesus than problematic, mean-spirited forms of "Christianity."

MT: What feelings or thoughts does the Christmas story conjure up in you?

SF: I enjoy the beauty, magic, and mystery of the Christmas nativity story, and understand and respect how it is an important spiritual foundation for many Christians today. However, the nativity story for me also embodies ancient sacred motifs from Pagan religions, cultures, and peoples that pre-date Jesus's birth. When I see a nativity scene, I also view it as the archetypal dynamic of the Great Mother with Divine Child. I see the Divine Child of Light not only taking the form of Jesus and Jesus Christ, but as Pagan deities such as Horus of Egypt, Mithras of Persia, and Sol Invictus of Rome.

MT: And the same for Easter?

SF: Reflecting on the Easter story of the crucifixion and resurrection brings forth a mixture of perspectives and feelings for me. As with the nativity story, I respect and understand it as an important foundational story for Christianity, but I also view it in an archetypal way as a sacred motif often reflected in Pagan teachings and traditions. It calls to mind the cycle of life, death, and rebirth that is central to most Pagan paths. And it calls to mind the sacred stories of the resurrection/return to life of Kore/Persephone, Attis, Osiris, Dionysus, and other deity forms.

From a historical perspective, the story of the crucifixion is a sad reminder of the cruel behaviours that some humans and human societies have engaged in across cultures and through the ages. It also is a powerful example of the problems that can arise when church and state are one instead of separate among a people. From a psychological and mythic viewpoint, however, the story of the resurrection can be one of hope. From an environmental perspective, it is a reminder and metaphor of the renewal of life.

MT: Do you have a favourite story, parable, or teaching of Jesus?

SF: One of my favourite parables of Jesus is that of the Good Samaritan. Although Jews and Samaritans often were at odds in that time, in this parable, a Samaritan aided a Jew who had been mugged by robbers and left for dead. Two others, both Jewish, had passed him by. I like this story because it not only teaches the importance of helping others, but it encourages helping others regardless of their culture, religion, race, nationality, and other differences.

MT: Who do you suppose Jesus was? For example, was he a Jewish teacher, a divine prophet, a miracle worker, or what?

SF: Jesus was—and is—a spiritual teacher, a Nature mystic, a healer, a Jewish social change activist, a visionary, and a sacred way-shower. And as Jesus Christ, Jesus was and is a manifestation and incarnation of Divine Love.

MT: That's very beautifully put. What lesson do you feel the modern-day Church needs to hear from Jesus the person?

SF: Focus on resonating with and expressing the loving consciousness that was and is the spirit of Jesus. Release from the distorting and counterproductive confines of dogma. Come to understand that when Jesus said he was the way, the truth, and the light, he was referring to Love, not some imperialistic edict to proclaim and enforce Christianity as the only religiously, morally, and politically correct way to be.

MT: Is it possible to be both Christian and Pagan? Why?

SF: Yes, it is possible to be both Christian and Pagan in personal spiritual practice. It also is possible to be both in some spiritual communities. Paganism and Christianity have many shared spiritual values and virtues, such as love, liberty, service, charity, hope, courage, honesty, humility, perseverance, and compassion.

Within our Circle Sanctuary community, in addition to Wiccans, Druids, Heathens, Pantheists, and other Pagans, we have Christian-Pagans and Pagan-Christians, including those who are Roman Catholic nuns and Protestant Christian teachers and musicians.

As for myself, although I am primarily identified as Pagan at this stage of my life's journey and ministry, there continue to be Christian dimensions to my spiritual practices well as Pagan ones. In addition to being senior minister of Circle Sanctuary, from time to time, I am a guest minister in various Christian and Unitarian Universalist churches. At the core of my soul is Nature mysticism, which transcends the boundaries of religion. My ministry includes spiritual service to Pagans of many paths, but also to those of other religions and those with no religion at all—and to the greater Circle of Nature of which we are all part, not only here on planet Earth, but also the larger cosmos and universe.

MT: What, if anything, can modern-day Pagans learn from the message of Jesus?

SF: Contemporary Pagans can learn from Jesus and his teachings the importance of humility, forgiveness, kindness, inner peace, selfless service, courage, and Divine Love.

MT: And vice versa, can Christians learn from modern-day Pagans?

SF: Yes. First of all, it is important for Christians to recognize and respect the contributions that Christianity has received from various forms of Paganism—symbols (such as the equal-armed cross and the five-pointed star), sacred stories, ceremonial tools, holiday customs and lore (Christmas from Winter Solstice, Easter getting its name from Ostara, St. John's from Summer Solstice, etc.), and sacred forms (some of the Saints actually embody Pagan deities' forms such as St. Brigit from Bride/Brighid, Santa Lucia from Lucina, St. Mary from Isis/Auset).

In addition, Christians can learn and have been learning from Pagans and Paganism: (1) the importance of living in harmony not only with other humans, but the larger community of life on Earth and in the Universe; (2) communing with Nature as a spiritual practice; (3) attuning to natural rhythms by celebrating the cycles of the sun, the seasons, and the cycles of the moon; and (4) celebrating life passages, including honouring the passages into senior adulthood with croning and saging rites.

The concept of living a good and virtuous life is an important part of Paganism today as well as in the past. A quote from the Pagan Roman philosopher, writer and emperor Marcus Aurelius (121–180 CE) is an example:

> *Live a good life. If there are gods and they are just, they will not care how devout you have been, but will welcome you based on the virtues you have lived by. If there are gods, but unjust, then you should not want to worship them. If there are no gods, then you will be gone, but will have lived a noble life that will live on in the memories of your loved ones.*

MT: Selena I can't thank you enough. You've been a real delight and have given me much to think about.

SF: Thank you. You're very welcome, Mark.

ABOUT THE AUTHOR

Selena Fox is a Pagan priestess, teacher, environmentalist, counselor, and psychotherapist. Rev. Fox is senior minister of Circle Sanctuary, a legally established Shamanic Wiccan church that has been serving Pagans worldwide since 1974 through publishing, networking, festivals, and other endeavors. Selena is one of America's best-known Pagan rights activists and is Executive Director of the Lady Liberty League. She is active in regional and global interfaith endeavors, and is a guest minister at Unitarian Universalist fellowships, Christian churches, and other religious centers. For many years, Selena has served as a cultural and religious diversity trainer and consultant to a variety of institutions, including hospitals, military installations, campuses, correctional facilities, and state and federal government agencies. Selena's writings, rituals, meditations, chants, and photographs have been published in a variety of sources, and she travels widely presenting workshops and facilitating ceremonies. She is founder of Circle

Sanctuary Nature Preserve, located in southwestern Wisconsin, USA. She also is director of Circle Cemetery, a national Pagan cemetery and one of the first Green cemeteries to be established in the United States. More information about Selena and her work: www.selenafox.com; www.circle-sanctuary.org.

Twenty-Five

......

Raven Digitalis

MT: I must begin by thanking you for the experience of interviewing you for my book, and also for the wonderful exchanges and sharing of ideas we've had over the few months I've known you as a "Facebook friend." For the sake of the readers I must point out that we often refer to each other as "my brother priest," and that though we come from vastly different traditions of priesthood, there is a deep level of mutual appreciation and respect between us. Perhaps it would be good to begin with a brief explanation of the particular Pagan path to which you belong and serve as a Priest?

RD: Yes, you are certainly my brother and fellow Clergy member, and someone I am happy to count as a friend! As for me, the spiritual group I work with and co-run is rather eclectic, so I'm technically an eclectic Neopagan Priest (specifically, Eastern Hellenistic Neopaganism, within the spiritual training group Opus Aima Obscuræ in Missoula, Montana, USA).

MT: Can you briefly say anything more about that group?

RD: Sure. We integrate teachings from numerous spiritual paths by drawing on the ideologies of Alexander III the Great. I mean this in the sense that King Alexander intricately understood the interconnection of the religions in the various areas he "conquered," which reached as far as India. We expand this idea to include other mystical Eastern paths in our practices including Taoism and Buddhism; we regard all religions and progressive spiritual paths as sacred and valid. As a ritual group, we observe the cycles of the moon and the sun, with monthly ceremonies for each, alongside the traditional Wiccan and European Pagan holidays (from which Catholicism and Christianity align many of their holidays) and regularly perform Cottage Craft or Hedge Craft events that work on honing old world skills.

MT: So to the theme of my book, was the person of Jesus part of your upbringing as a child?

RD: Not at all. My immediate family is non-religious, though I wouldn't say that they are non-spiritual. Jesus was never emphasized in my life as anything more or less than a historical figure recognized by many religious groups in the world. The same would have been said for the Buddha, Mohammed, and so on.

MT: Even so, does Jesus hold any important to you now?

RD: Absolutely! Jesus Christ is an incredibly powerful force. The energy of this deity—and indeed he is a deity—has had an incredible influence on humankind. One should keep in mind that as with all deities, their interaction with humankind depends on one's interpretation. Gods, spirits, deities: entirely interpretive. I occasionally call upon the Christ in my own Pagan rituals, depending on their intention. For example, because the Christ is a solar deity, I feel comfortable calling his presence alongside that of Ra, Horus, Mithras, Helios, and so on. Archetypes transcend time and culture.

MT: That's all very cosmic and mythic. In your opinion, was Jesus a historical person?

RD: I tend to take the Buddhist view of the Buddha in terms of my view of both Siddhartha and Jesus, which is that we simply do not know whether or not they were actual, physical people, or if they were "regular" people whom heavy mythology was structured around (this was common in ancient Egypt and innumerable other ancient cultures), or whether he is simply a mythical figure. I am also subsequently of the belief that it simply doesn't matter either way! These forces exist in the present regardless of their history, and the Now is the most supreme moment of all time.

I do believe that many churches lovingly and accurately attune themselves to the compassionate energy of the Christ. At the same time, so many do not, which is especially obvious in America. Christ is love, healing, and wisdom; politics are (quite frequently) built around fear, greed, and discrimination; sometimes the two spheres become confused—this is the danger zone.

MT: What feelings or thoughts does the Christmas story conjure up in you?

RD: The linguistic origins of the words "Santa" and "Satan" are rooted in the same Latin roots, and the red suit of Santa Claus is based on the red blood of Christ. Nah, not really. However, Santa's clothing and mythical history is interesting history in itself!

Christ is another mythical example of the Holy Child; a child seen across cultures and throughout time in different forms. Christmas is the retelling of a mythology that is as old as humankind itself.

MT: This is one of the things I especially enjoy about you, Raven, your zany humor. In that light, what about Easter?

RD: Why, Cadbury Christ, of course! He laid the chocolate eggs at the foot of the cross, which in turn created the mythology of Jesus's mystical hare-shapeshifting qualities. As a matter of fact, we find the origin of the word "rabbi" and "rabbit" being of the same linguistic foundation. Joking again. I tend to get goofy when I'm sleep-deprived. Which, come to think of it, is actually most of the time.

The mythology of the murdered-and-resurrected god is seen in numerous pre-Christian cultures, and is indeed the foundation of the Easter mythology. The mythology of the Sun has always been as such: He is born (or, rather, reborn) as the Holy Crowned and Conquering Child, gathers strength, and is then killed and enters the Underworld, which is where we get the cold and dark part of the year. This mythology is as ancient as humankind, and the Christian reinterpretation is no different nor any more or less sacred!

MT: Fabulous. Now, if you have one, what is your favourite story, parable, teaching, or symbol of Jesus?

RD: I resonate with Christ's Discourse on Judgmentalism as given in the Sermon on the Mount. If only more followers would listen to their alleged prophet! Sadly, it seems that many self-proclaimed Christians, wallowing in their fear and hatred, are the ones furthest from the light of God.

MT: In your opinion, who was Jesus in terms of being a teacher, a prophet, a deity, or a magician?

RD: I think Jesus was a teacher of the Mysteries of Life; he was a man. Mohammed and the Buddha said that they themselves were only men, and spoke against people idolizing them. To this day, human depictions of Mohammed are forbidden in Islam because of the belief that one will tend to focus on the messenger rather than the message. In very early Buddhism, soon after the delivering of the Dharma (or Dhamma: life teachings of the Buddha) and Siddhartha's Paranirvana (death or transcendence), you will find that the only artistic depictions of the Buddha himself were, for example, a simple footprint or a spiral rather than a human image of a guy meditating.

MT: What lesson of Jesus stands out to you as something of which the church needs to take note?

RD: Modernize! Adapt! Cultural appropriation! The world has changed and scriptural politics must also flow with change, which is the nature of existence. People need to separate the wheat (the teachings of the Christ) from the chaff (the politics). (Or separate the wheat from the chavs, depending on location.)

MT: Is it possible to be both Christian and Pagan?

RD: I think the purest form of Pagan Christianity, or ChristoPaganism, is actually Gnosticism. This early form of Christianity was very much Pagan or mystical, though a bit nihilistic for my personal tastes. Early Coptic Christianity and the Hellenistic Greco-Roman-Egyptian-Christian fusion paths are also worth a historical mention. I think a person can balance Christianity with Wicca and other forms of Paganism if—and this is a big if—he or she is able to recognize Christianity as a mythological system that is very similar to other religions and mystical systems the world over. Of course, doing so requires the person to throw away the politics and pseudepigraphic rubbish: i.e., dogma and hatred!

MT: What, if anything, can modern-day Pagans learn from the message of Jesus?

RD: Plain and simple: Love is the Law.

MT: Nicely put! What, if anything, can Christians learn from modern-day Paganism?

RD: They could learn to understand the similarities that exist between positive spiritual paths (such as views of the Divine, community service, humanitarianism, magick, and prayer). As well as, ideally, a bit of their own history. The majority of modern Christians seem to gravely lack an understanding of Christian history: I see this as extremely dangerous and spiritually incomplete. The path to God is many.

MT: Well, this has been a wonderful discussion, Raven. Thank you again. I'm very grateful indeed to you for sharing so much of your time, wisdom, and humor.

RD: You're welcome, my brother!

ABOUT THE AUTHOR

Raven Digitalis (Missoula, MT) is the author of *Planetary Spells & Rituals, Shadow Magick Compendium,* and *Goth Craft,* all published by Llewellyn. He is a Neopagan Priest and cofounder of the "Eastern Hellenistic" magickal system and training coven Opus Aima Obscuræ, and is a radio and club DJ of gothic and industrial music. Also trained in Georgian Witchcraft and Buddhist philosophy, Raven has been a Witch since 1999, a priest since 2003, and an empath all his life. Raven holds a degree in anthropology from the University of Montana and is also an animal rights activist, black-and-white photographic artist, tarot reader, and the co-owner of Twigs & Brews Herbs, specializing in bath salts, herbal blends, essential oils, soaps, candles, and incenses. He has appeared on the cover of *New Witch* magazine, is a regular contributor to *Dragon's Blood* and *The Ninth Gate* magazines, and has been featured on MTV News and CBS *PsychicRadio.* He can be found at www.ravendigitalis.com.

Twenty-Six

......

Sorita D'Este

MT: Sorita, first of all thank you so much for your hospitality and for allowing me to interview you. Perhaps it would be a good idea for you explain the terms "Gnostic Theurgist."

SD: Thank you, Mark. Over the years I have found religious and spiritual "labels" to be more of a hindrance than a help. So I decided to try to find a term which describe my own personal beliefs and practices in a way which is unlikely to change as I grow in knowledge and experience of myself and therefore would not restrain me. The term "Gnostic" comes from the Greek meaning "knowledge" and "theurgist" being one who practices theurgy, which also comes from the Greek, referring to the practice of rituals performed with the aim of achieving henosis with the Divine. Therefore a literal meaning might be "a practitioner of rituals with the aim of achieving union with the Divine and a seeker of divine knowledge." The knowledge in this context being a type of mystical or divine revelation, achieved through experience of the Divine.

MT: Fascinating. You also use the term "Devotee of the Seven Wandering Stars."

SD: When I refer to myself as a Devotee of the Seven Wandering Stars it's a reference to the Mysteries—the Seven Wandering Stars, or the "Deathless Gods" (Classical planets—i.e., Sun, Moon, Mercury, Venus, Mars, Saturn, and Jupiter) have been around since the beginning of time and play an important role in most of the religious traditions of the West, as well as elsewhere in the world. The Mysteries here, being not just the Mystery Traditions of the ancient world, but also those "truths" which are universal to all spiritual traditions, for me keeping a focus on that allows me to see past the boundaries of the traditions in which they are respectively worshiped or evoked as Gods or Spirits, under many different names, but instead see what there is to learn and gain from the knowledge they have to teach us. Alternatively, I could also just be called an "old-fashioned, stubborn wild woman"; people usually remember that better.

MT: Last time I was here, I also met David Rankine, a well-respected authority and author on (among other things) the Qabalah. I remember the three of us getting into a fascinating discussion on the Qabalah and the significance of Jesus's death on the cross (which I shall to come back to in a later question). First, however, can you tell me whether the figure of Jesus was to a lesser or greater degree, part of your upbringing as a child?

SD: Jesus was an absolutely intricate part of my childhood. I was raised in the Dutch Reformed Church (Nederlands Gereformeerde Kerk), whilst also having parallel Roman Catholic influences on my views and beliefs along the way from a young age. As a child I had what I now realize to be a series of profoundly spiritual experiences that led me to study the only religion I was familiar with at the time, Christianity (I was raised in Cape Town, South Africa, during the apartheid years). I prayed to Jesus at least as much as I did, instinctively, to the moon, sun, stars, and winds; but it was the moon, sun, stars, and winds who answered my prayers more often and stole my heart.

MT: So does Jesus still feel important to you?

SD: From a personal spiritual perspective, not at all. From a historical and cultural perspective, I consider Jesus to be an important symbol which has been understood, misunderstood, interpreted, misinterpreted, reworked, and reinvented by each successive generation. Jesus is a phenomenal power of both good and evil for those who believe in him for their salvation, and for those who encounter those who follow his traditions. From a magical perspective, Jesus is important as an example of the perfected self, who has unified all of their being. In Qabalistic terms, this is expressed through the union of the three parts of the soul, the Nephesh (animal soul), Ruach (breath), and Neshamah (higher soul). This unification was described in the major thirteenth-century Qabalistic book, the Zohar, which declared "Man is a threefold product of life (Nephesh), spirit (Ruach), and soul (Neshamah), by the blending and union of which he became a living spirit, a manifestation of the Divine." Jesus represents that manifestation of the Divine achieved through this union.

MT: Amazing. I think people will be absolutely fascinated by what you've just said. So, you do see Jesus as a historical person then?

SD: I believe absolutely that there was a historical person at the centre of the Jesus-myth. His message was clearly one of acceptance and love, and of change—whilst at the same time reflecting a strong sense of humble respect. I am not really qualified to speak on behalf of the different Christian churches today; their beliefs and practices are something I am only marginally familiar with.

MT: Who was Jesus the historical man? For example, was he a simple Jewish teacher, a divine prophet, a miracle worker, a magician, or even a literal Incarnation of God?

SD: I perceive Jesus as a man who reached a state of enlightenment and then sought to share the vision of perfection he had experienced. This is born out repeatedly through his teachings, if we interpret the kingdom of heaven as perfection, and appreciate that Jesus always encouraged people to manifest that kingdom on earth through their thoughts and deeds. Jesus also emphasised that he did not come to change the existing laws, but to change the perspectives of people. In this he can be considered a teacher, but certainly not a revolutionary, and the frequency with which Jesus quoted Scripture and used it to make a point demonstrates the strength of his heritage and his foundations in it. I feel that in his death, Jesus achieved an apotheosis, something demonstrated by the Qabalistic symbolism of the crucifixion. Jesus was crucified between two thieves, so he represents the balance and harmony of the Middle Pillar of the Qabalistic Tree of Life, with the two thieves representing the outer Black and White pillars. However the location of Golgotha ("place of the skull") was also key, as it was the place where Adam was said to have been buried. When the blood of Jesus dripped to the ground and permeated it, he redeemed the original sin of Adam by willingly giving of his life and showed that perfection on earth was possible.

MT: Sorita, during the research for this book I've become more and more aware of a difference between the two terms "Jesus" and "Christ." Many progressive Christians and Pagans see Jesus as a fully human being and Christ as a more cosmic "spark of deity" within all things. Do you have any thoughts on this?

SD: To me there is a very clear difference between Jesus and Christ. In fact, I would go so far as to separate them into three distinct terms—Jesus, Christ, and Jesus Christ. I see Jesus as the historical figure, the man who was a Rabbi and teacher, who gained enlightenment and sought to bring his vision of heaven on earth into manifestation in the physical world around him. Christ, or maybe more accurately the Christ Force, is the power that has been strengthened and empowered by centuries of prayer and devotion from millions of Christians—in magical terms, it is an egregore, an astral form which has become manifest as a storehouse for the energy directed at it over the centuries—whether by simple peasants, church bishops, saints, or sinners—their combined hope for salvation and a better future has brought this force into life, shaping it through the centuries. It's a reservoir of energy, which allows for communion between all those who are able to access it through prayer and the pure force of their faith. Then finally, Jesus Christ to me is the figure who has been shaped by the Church to present their view of what he represents. As such Jesus Christ is a gateway image to access the Christ (or Christ Force), which reminds me of the line from the Gospel of John (14:6), "I am the way, and the truth, and the life. No one comes to the Father except through me." In this regard one can also see Jesus the historical figure recorded in the gospels as being a gateway image to the Christ Force too, but with the difference that it is a simpler, humbler gateway. Speaking from a magical perspective, I believe this gateway to be an easier and more direct door to the Christ Force, as it can be accessed based on an individual's personal understanding and interpretation of Jesus's life, rather than an enforced (and often political) point of view which might be enforced by a particular Church tradition. Through the examples he set in his life, Jesus presents us with a pathway to God, a pathway which is incredibly simplistic and much in keeping with the teachings of many of the other spiritual traditions of its time, as well as those who went before. In order to perceive that pathway, however, we have to put prejudice aside and look at what is before us. A force which cannot be owned by any institution or any individual, but rather which can only be accessed by those who have overcome their own fears and who are able to achieve their own personal union with God through their faith.

MT: Do you think Pagan traditions or concepts sometimes reflect the spirit of Jesus better than Christian ones?

SD: I do think that individuals of all religious and spiritual traditions are able to reflect his core message and philosophies and carry his proverbial light into the future. I think individuals have the innate ability to serve one another and share in spiritual awakening, and it is my opinion that individuals are able to achieve this through belief and through absolute spiritual conviction. I don't think that the particular religious tradition an individual finds themselves to be joined to, whether through birth, life's journey, or choice, is really that relevant. Spiritual conviction, faith, and belief manifest themselves regardless and sometimes even in spite of these traditions. All you need are strength of will, desire for knowledge, courage to dare, and the ability to appreciate silence within and without. The Demiurge does not belong to a religious tradition; it is universal.

One of the most significant recorded and surviving oracles given by the goddess Hekate was recorded by Porphyry, and commented on Jesus and Christianity. Porphyry, a Neo-Platonic philosopher of the third century CE who followed the works of Plotinus, also studied Jewish scriptures and attended lectures by the Christian theologian Origen. The oracle from Hekate was probably in response to his own questions, for he was the author of the most significant intellectual anti-Christian writings of his age, *Against the Christians* and *Prophecy from Oracles*. In some ways, the words of this oracle also reflect some of my own views on Jesus:

> *And to those who ask why he [Jesus] was condemned to die, the oracle of the goddess [Hekate] replied, 'The body, indeed, is always exposed to torments, but the souls of the pious abide in heaven. And the soul you inquire about has been the fatal cause of error to other souls which were not fated to receive the gifts of the gods, and to have the knowledge of immortal Jove. Such souls are therefore hated by the gods; for they who were fated not to receive the gifts of the gods, and not to know God, were fated to be involved in error by means of him you speak of. He himself, however, was good, and heaven has been opened to him as to other good men. You are not, then, to speak evil of him, but to pity the folly of men: and through him men's danger is imminent.*
>
> —(*Prophecy from Oracles*, Porphyry,
> c. 3 CE, trans. J. R. King)[219]

MT: We've just seen another Christmas come and go. What feelings or thoughts does the Christmas story conjure up in you?

SD: For me it's always been a nice story, but with an avid interest in mythology since childhood it didn't take me long to find out that the story itself is not unique to Christianity. The solar God Mithras, for example, born from the virgin Goddess Anahita, predates the Christian myth by quite some time and has some remarkable similarities. For me the most interesting part of the story is the manifestation of the archangel Gabriel and the three Magi. I love incense and ascribe that to a fascination with frankincense and myrrh inspired by this myth.

MT: And the same for Easter?

SD: Easter for me is about light and new life; it's springtime here in the Northern Hemisphere, after all. The symbol of the sacrificed and resurrected God is one which is often associated with this time of the year, so again it is no surprise to find such a myth in Christianity. It is the time that seeds buried in the ground magically comes to life, bursting through from the darkness into the light—awakening new hope, as life is literally "resurrected."

MT: What about the actual stories Jesus told. Do you have a favourite story, parable, teaching, or symbol of Jesus?

SD: My favourite of Jesus's teachings is probably the "first remove the log from your own eye before you remove the speck from your neighbour's." It is such a simple phrase and yet so eternally relevant, offering a simple path of behaviour. The phrase reminds us that it is all too easy to fall into criticism of others, and that we all have failings. If we address our own weaknesses and turn them into strengths, then we may find that the quality that irritated us in another person was really irritating us in ourselves, and the person was a mirror that showed us. It also implies that if you do have a criticism to make of another person, it can be done in a positive and constructive way, which improves that person's perspective (removes the speck).

MT: Wonderful. So what lessons do you feel the modern-day church needs to hear from the person or teachings of Jesus?

SD: I think that modern followers of Christ, in addition to Christians who express their faith through a church, should go back to basics. There are so many misunderstandings and so much hearsay passed down as fact that I think more than often, people are blind to that which is obvious and staring them in the face. This is true for Christians as much as it is for followers of many other religious traditions around the world, so it might be as much a human condition rather than one specifically inherent in the church.

MT: In your opinion do you think it's possible to be both Christian and Pagan?

SD: This is a big question in a short sentence. Personally, as an outsider to both religious traditions with experience and insights into both, I would say that it depends on your definition of "Christian" and your definition of "Pagan," which as anyone who has ever studied religion will know is not as straightforward as it might seem. There are so many different strands of Christianity today that it might more rightfully—as some scholars have suggested—be referred to as "Christianities" and thus become an umbrella term for all the various strands, some of which are a lot more accepting and progressive in thinking than others. "Pagan" is a much-disputed term, today often taken by adherents of the modern forms of it to be a Nature-based spiritual path, but which of course historically has been used more often than not to mean someone who is specifically non-Christian. So there is a dilemma with terminology. However, if you mean "Pagan" to mean someone who has a respect for and sees divinity as being inherent or expressed through nature, and "Christian" a follower of Christ in the same way as the early disciples, learning from his words, and studying his teachings rather than that of a particular institutionalised form of Church Christianity, then I would say there is nothing stopping someone from being a follower of Christ with a strong affinity for the divine expressed through nature. In fact, if you look at iconography and if you read the texts of the Bible it is clear that a strong respect for nature, and an affinity with the natural world as an expression of the Divine has always been an inherently essential part of the teachings presented therein. This is in keeping with other spiritual, religious, and philosophical teachings of the time which were contemporary with those of the books now included in the Bible (New Testament).

MT: Are there any lessons that modern-day Pagans can learn from the message or person of Jesus?

SD: Modern Pagans can learn a great deal from Jesus the person. The most obvious lesson from his actions is knowing when to act and when to do nothing. Jesus always encouraged people to act based on their faith rather than simply spoon-feeding them. This is particularly emphasised when he pointed out he had not come to help the virtuous or righteous, but those who needed help. Jesus showed that a light provides illumination, but it is still up to the individual to walk their path and ultimately provide their own light. The ability to not apportion blame and to accept people's failings, i.e., selfless compassion, is perhaps the most important lesson Jesus can teach modern Pagans.

MT: And can Christians learn from modern-day Paganism?

SD: I think that institutionalized Church Christians would benefit from taking on a more holistic view of the world, being more open to the beliefs of others and knowing that by learning about the beliefs and religious practices of others you can strengthen your own. They could also benefit from the idea that studying the roots of your beliefs can enrich your understanding of those beliefs.

MT: Well, this has been an amazing discussion and huge learning experience for me. Thank you again, Sorita, for your wisdom, hospitality, and ... cakes!

SD: You're very welcome Mark.

ABOUT THE AUTHOR

Sorita D'Este is an esoteric researcher, author, and Priestess who manifests her knowledge of the wisdom of the ancient world into the modern age through her work. Her areas of expertise include the Western Esoteric Traditions, European Mythology, British Folklore and the Grimoire Tradition; with particular passion for the magic and mystery of the Seven Wandering Stars, Graeco-Egyptian Magic, and the goddess Hekate. She is probably best put in a box with the label "Mystical Enchantress, Priestess, Author, and Esoteric Researcher." She is a prolific writer and passionate researcher who has authored/co-authored fifteen books on magic, mythology, and mysticism to date. These include *Hekate Liminal Rites, Practical Planetary Magick, Practical Elemental Magick,* and *Visions of the Cailleach.*

Twenty-Seven

......

Caitlín Matthews

MT: Well first of all, Caitlín, it is such a pleasure to meet you. I was so delighted when you agreed to this interview. Having been aware of your amazing work for many years, I can't wait to hear your thoughts, opinions, and wisdom on the subject we are about to discuss.

CM: You're very welcome, Mark.

MT: But before we do get onto the theme of Jesus, perhaps I might just ask you a question with regard to your spiritual tradition. You refer to yourself as an animist, but also a "shamanic servant of all traditions when necessary." Can you say any more about that now, or should we make a note to come back to it later on?

CM: Let's see if it comes up naturally.

MT: OK, that's fine. So, was Jesus part of your upbringing as a child?

CM: Jesus was not taught, depicted, nor portrayed with any vigour, though he did seem to have the biggest club or gang which it was obviously shameful not to be part of, or so it seemed when I was growing up in the fifties.

From a nominally Anglican family, I discovered that the divine primarily showed itself to me through feminine forms since I was a child. Religious Education lessons presented a picture of the divine that was largely masculine. So I just kept quiet about what I understood and perceived until I was of an age to leave school and home and seek others of my ilk.

The stained glass and plaster Jesus of Brownie church parades—virtually the only time I was ever in a church as child—did not appeal to me, being designed along the "gentle Jesus, meek and mild" line. Divinity for me was rather more raw and passionate than these depictions, and the occasional Lady Chapel didn't inspire me either. Neither of these images resonated in any way.

Our RE teachers in the fifties generally taught from the New Testament once we were past eight years old, and the teachers made poor work of it. I yearned after the delights of Babylon and Sumeria, which were both historically described and most attractively depicted in our Old Testament workbooks. The testy divinity of the Israelites didn't appeal to me anything like as much as those inveighed against by the prophet Jeremiah. Still, you can't have everything!

MT: And does the figure of Jesus hold any significance to you today?

CM: So much of our ancestral traditions, culture, and civilization are shaped by Christianity, it has been essential for me to understand Jesus's teachings intelligently from both within and outside of the context of the church that formed around him.

Every spirituality has at its heart a figure in whom love is manifest. If we walk through the world with this knowledge in our souls, then we can be welcome everywhere we go. The priests, priestesses, and congregants of any spirituality are, to my mind, most faithful to the Beloved (whoever he, she, or it may be for them) when they give the Beloved's unconditional welcome to visitors. How often have we found this lacking? How many circles, meditation groups, churches, or congregations have you visited where you felt immediately not only unwelcome but perhaps a little less shiny, prayerful, or spiritual than anyone else already ensconced? Spiritual hospitality is the queen of virtues.

When someone comes to my shamanic practice for healing, I try to discover where love is already seated in their lives—this might be in their fervent religious belief, a vague but hopeful adherence to some spirituality, a love of nature, or whatever. I cannot work without the spirit of that love: that is what will dispense the healing they seek, not me, be it ancestral or divine in nature. I work completely across all traditions and so I must have proper access to spiritual sources of love in order to be of service.

MT: Ah, so going back to my first question, this is precisely what you mean by a "shamanic servant of all traditions when necessary"?

CM: Exactly. Shamanism and ancestral understanding of the earth is the undercarpeting of nearly all religious traditions. It remains the bedrock upon which all traditions or lack of them can be understood and accepted because we all derive from our ancestors and they from theirs, back on down.

When people come for shamanic help, I try to discover what has set the wheel of their life turning, rather than trying to fit my own wheel to their cart or to invent a new one. If someone is enthusiastically Jewish, we have Jewish prayers before I work; if someone is Catholic, we might pray the rosary and put some holy water about. Hell, if someone is turned on to the love that lights their life through Elvis, I would sing an Elvis number for them when I pray for help and healing, if it would help! Some people don't have a faith, though, and my work is primarily with them, which is when I have to return to that shamanic bedrock for inspiration.

I was taught a fine lesson about this many years ago when I went to Cornwall to bring a ritual of reconsecration to some women who had been raped or abused. I turned up with my nice ritual and explained that it needed some spiritual leverage for me to customize it for them: what was important for them? One by one, the women began to tell me that they didn't have beliefs at all, absolutely none. I probed deeper: when they were in deep trouble, what then did they turn to for support and consolation? Each of them spoke of some place in the land that gave them strength.

Accordingly, I spoke prayers and words of consolation in the name of a cliff-walk one woman took, or in the name of an oak tree that offered wisdom to another, and invoked the spirit of Barbara Hepworth's sculpture garden in St. Ives for another woman. The power of that ritual remains forever with me. When everything else fails, it is love that matters. What brings us consolation, support, and blessing is what we love: it also loves us. That is the basis for all spiritual relationships.

MT: Beautiful. So Jesus was a historical person for you?

CM: Jesus lives in time as well as eternity, being—as I understand it—an embodiment of divine wisdom. Since the church is supposed to be the body of Christ, his followers are (or should be) his mediators, because that was the spirit in which he taught. It's a lovely, ancestral-style kinship, but, like many families, it has its own hidden loyalties and exclusions. I've found Jesus's same wisdom and respect for others in animist and ancestral traditions, but then I would respond to it wherever it showed itself, in whatever place, having long been accused of "spiritual promiscuity."

MT: What feelings or thoughts does the Christmas story conjure up in you?

CM: Stories of hope must always be told at Midwinter, and this is one that reminds us, as the Neo-Platonist Macrobius's *Dream of Scipio* tells us, that this is the proper midwinter gateway through which incarnating saviours always show up: Mithras, Dionysus, etc. The ancient Welsh converts to Christianity saw Jesus as "the Maiden's Mabon"—a concept that the Anglo-Welsh poet David Jones explored in his long poem *Anathemata*.

The welcoming of the Child of Light is so easy for people everywhere because it is infused with ancestral as well as more recent midwinter rituals for welcoming the returning light.

MT: And same with Easter?

CM: The Easter Triduum of Holy Week packs all the punch of an ancient mystery religion. Anyone who wants to know about what these were like and what the word *anamnesis* really means should attend. The death on the cross, the harrowing of hell, and the resurrection are three mighty things. The dying and rising gods of the Mysteries—Dionysus, Tammuz, Adonis, and Osiris—received similar rites at the same time of year. The hermetic tradition of Isis looking for the lost parts of Osiris is but a mystery story of how things fall apart and are gathered back together again. This mystery is enacted again at Easter: "they have taken away my Lord and I know not where they have laid him" still echoes down the centuries, whether you think of Isis or Mary Magdalene.

MT: If you have one, what is your favourite story, parable, teaching, or symbol of Jesus?

CM: The new commandment of "Love one another" is pretty impressive and hard to live up to still. The Beatitudes speak to the soul in all its conditions. Those who keep the keys of the kingdom should indeed go in more often and allow others to do so, as commanded. I love the everyday metaphors and parables that help make the understanding of esoteric and spiritual mysteries that much easier—I use this way of speaking myself. His parable of the yeast in bread is a great Sophianic emblem for the spirit working invisibly within us. I love the way Jesus goes apart to pray—I couldn't live without this regular communion with silence either.

MT: So was Jesus a simple Jewish teacher, a divine prophet, a valid deity of the Christian pantheon, a miracle worker, a magician, or what?

CM: He was all of those, as well as Gnostic Saviour, King of the Mysteries, Jewish prophet, fulfiller of prophecy, healer of *harmatian* fractures. Harmatian or "missing the mark" is more descriptively accurate than "sin." I've never been a fan of St. Augustine and original sin, and wrote my retelling of Genesis, *The Blessing Seed,* against it to back up our wonderful native heretic, Pelagius, and to promote a more Sophianic view of the Fall, as a myth in which the stealing of wisdom is the result of a foreseen human curiosity.

MT: What lesson do you feel the modern-day church needs to hear from the person or teaching of Jesus?

CM: Jesus welcomed everyone unconditionally. He also spoke clearly about what his disciples were to do if they themselves were not welcomed when they went through villages healing: "Shake the dust from the soles of your feet." Tribal-style Christianity often wishes to inflict itself on the world whether we want it or not. Proselytizing evangelism is, for me, on the level of an advert that demands that we eat a product whether we have a taste for it or not. Jesus's remarks on salt come to mind: "Ye are the salt of the earth: but if the salt have lost its savour, wherewith shall it be salted? It is thenceforth good for nothing, but to be cast out and trodden under foot of men." (Matthew 5:13 English Revised Version) If the message doesn't have any savour, we can't hear it!

Mature or gnostic (with a small *g*) Christian wisdom, on the other hand, is available to anyone who is receptive and who finds welcome in Jesus's company. Accepting people for what they are in their souls, as opposed to categorizing or judging them for their appearance, rank, occupation, or gender, seems to me to be the only way to go. The Church could try respecting the spirit of Jesus's wisdom, not just the letter.

MT: This is a controversial question, even among Pagans, but is it possible to be both Christian and Pagan?

CM: Yes. The Russians have a lovely, untranslatable word, *dvoverie* or "double-belonging," for those who espouse both. Most people I know (including Christians) travel under that sign, for ancestral traditions are always part of us and grow through the revealed traditions we accept later in life. So it is quite possible to be a church warden and a morris dancer, for example, or a priestess of the sacred earth and a communicant. "Love is not love that alters when it alteration finds—it is an ever fixéd-mark," to quote one of my favourite dramatists. Christianity rather set the tone for this kind of thing in its earlier centuries by borrowing Pagan sacred sites and taking over Pagan festivals and divinities—what were we not supposed to like? As part of our ancestral tradition, Christianity has grown up through the deeper soil of Paganism—we can't really pick and choose our ancestry, can we? It's always part of us.

MT: What, if anything, can modern-day Pagans learn from the message or person of Jesus?

CM: Service, unconditionality, care of others not of our tribe, nonviolence, non-competitiveness, and generous sharing might be some areas for improvement, as could a lot more self-clarification. Much of what we regard as Paganism today was actually preserved within the church, and Pagans could well learn a little about that, such as beating the bounds rituals, for example, and the physicality of spiritual practices like fasting, prayer, and vigil—all of which were used in ancient times but which most Pagan people think was exclusively Christian, for some unfathomable reason.

MT: And what, if anything, can Christians learn from modern-day Paganism?

CM: Respect for all species of life, not just humans; acceptance and equal respect for the spiritual viability of other faiths; and the living priesthood of all human beings. More flexibility in the rituals offered, especially as modern life develops into some areas not previously covered by existent services. Less transcendence and more embodiment would be ideal, though I would hate to see a further impoverishment of the mystery—the vernacular and chummy vicar sets a jarring tone, when what is needed is beauty, dignity, and the spiritual hospitality of welcome.

MT: Well this has been an amazing discussion. You've brought up so many ideas and possibilities for further study that it's going to be difficult to keep me out of the library. Caitlín I can't thank you enough for your willingness, wisdom, and hospitality.

CM: Mark, you're very welcome.

ABOUT THE AUTHOR

Caitlín Matthews is the author of over sixty books including *Singing the Soul Back Home, King Arthur's Raid on the Underworld,* and *Sophia, Goddess of Wisdom.* She teaches shamanism, spirituality, and ancestral traditions spanning many faiths, both Christian and Pagan, across the world, and has a shamanic practice in Oxford. She is co-founder of FíOS, the Foundation for Inspirational and Oracular Studies, which promotes the restoration of the sacred arts. www.hallowquest.org.uk

Twenty-Eight

......

Janet Farrar

Janet Farrar and her husband Gavin Bone are two of the most well-known Wiccan teachers and authors today, travelling far and wide with their progressive tradition of modern Witchcraft. I interviewed them both separately and I can't begin to express how delighted I was that they agreed to this. On top of being teachers, Janet and her first husband Stewart gave the Wiccan world some of the most sought-after books on the Craft.

MT: Janet I'm so grateful to you and Gavin for allowing me to speak with you both. I've seen so many clips of you on various television documentaries that I feel like I know you. May I begin by asking you about your own journey into Wicca, for I believe you were quite a strong-minded Christian before that?

JF: Well, Mark, let me explain. Back in the late 1960s I started working in the music industry and was surrounded by some very brilliant people, and of course they were interested in things like tarot cards, ouija boards, and everything the hippy generation was into! So that influenced me as well, but the important moment came after a dream I had one night. At the time I was a good Christian, a Sunday school teacher. I dreamt that

Jesus came knocking on my front door and he was having a street party, so I went out and joined everyone, and he said, "Hey, you've got to come and meet my mum!" He led me down to where the local baker's shop was, which was also the post office. Outside was one of the old red London post boxes and sitting on the box was the Virgin Mary. Instead of having the bleeding heart image you would usually associate with her, she opened up her robe and over her heart was five-pointed star inside a circle—the pentacle. At the time it made no sense to me, as I had never seen that symbol and had no idea what it meant. Jesus said to me, "You'll understand what it means later, as it's going to play an important part in your life!"

MT: That's amazing, so in a real sense Mary and Jesus led you to Wicca? How astonishing. So let me ask you, was the figure of Jesus, to a lesser or greater degree, part of your upbringing as a child?

JF: Jesus was very much part of my upbringing as a child, as I was raised by my father, grandfather, and maiden aunt after my mother died when I was five years old. My grandfather was a very strict Christian. He never qualified as a theologian but he studied theology, and he was also the church warden for Emmanuel Protestant Church in Leyton, East London. When I was growing up, he was a great influence on my life, and he allowed me to look at his library. He never once dictated to me how I should react to some of the books that I came across, so I was studying the Gnostic Gospels from an early age. He had the Gospel of Thomas there, as well as the rest of the books from the Apocrypha, the books removed from the Bible. He also had some of the great Church theology books. Although much of this knowledge was way beyond my ability to understand at that age, they did influence me in the way I saw Jesus. So I very much saw him as a protector of children and as a very nice, gentle person.

MT: And does Jesus still feel important to you?

JF: I prefer to use the name "Christ" rather than "Jesus." I see two aspects: the historical figure of Jesus and what some refer to as the "Cosmic

Christ." The Cosmic Christ I believe to be the true concept behind Christianity; an all-embracing Christian figure who is a divinity in its own right. Yes, that part of it is important to me, but not so much the historical figure of Jesus. I view him purely as a figure of academic interest.

MT: Wonderful. Yes I share your opinion there. In fact, I've written about precisely that distinction in the first section of this book. Back to Jesus the historical person: what about him as a person? What do you think he was like?

JF: Are you asking me how would I imagine him?

MT: Yes.

JF: Well, I don't really see his spirit reflected in the modern-day Church. What has happened over the generations is the Jesus I knew as a child and the Jesus people talk about in the Church today are two very different characters. I do not see the spirit of the human Jesus reflected very much in a lot of Christianity, with certain exceptions, one of these being the Quakers. With the Quaker families I have known personally, I have found them to be very sincere Christians.

MT: Would it be fair to say that Pagan traditions reflect the spirit of Jesus better?

JF: I think Pagan traditions on the whole—and I am not talking about every individual Pagan—do tend to reflect more the legendary and historical Jesus teachings, especially when it comes to caring for your fellow man. Certainly in my tradition and my covens, part of the work we do is service to the community, and that includes being there to minister as a priestess or priest for not just other Pagans, but also for the ordinary man or woman in the street, regardless of religious background. This certainly isn't in conflict with the teachings of Jesus.

We see the divine as a many-faceted window, rather like a rose window in a church; Christianity is just one of the aspects of that window. A Pagan sees him- or herself in that window viewing all the other world religions, giving them a chance to express themselves and not judging them, and I think this is the problem. Too many people judge other world religions against their own. You see this constantly in modern-day Christianity, which I think is a great tragedy. I think the historical Jesus would be very disappointed about what has grown up around him. I certainly don't think he would approve of the wealth of the Church or some of the attitudes it shows. Certainly, some of the aspects of Christianity that have come to light are not very pleasant at all, especially in their dealings with the impoverished and the innocents of this world, the little children. The quote from Jesus "Suffer the little children to come unto me and forbid them not" I think a lot of people have forgotten in the Church, and I am not talking about the ordinary worshipper, but the some of the priests and ministers, and the terrible things which have come to light over the years.

MT: What feelings or thoughts does the Christmas story conjure up in you?

JF: I think very much in terms of the Winter Solstice. It is the time when Mother Earth is about to give birth to new life, and I think the Christmas story for little children is absolutely charming. I think it gives them a focus at the Winter Solstice, which if properly observed is a time of family communion. So, in a Christian sense, take all the glitz out of the shops and take away all the garbage that has been attached to Christmas and you end up with what it is really about. That is, a time of family feasting, family joy, and a family united. As Pagans, we certainly use that time of the year, the Winter Solstice, for exactly that in our religious rites and home lives. The Christmas story for me still plays a part of that. I mean, we still put a candle in our windows even though we're not Christians, just in the case the Holy family wanders by and needs somewhere to stay. This is a very Pagan custom. It's the night of the Mother, Modranacht, and should be for be for mothers all over the world as well as Mary, the Christian mother. It is midwinter, when you welcome strangers to the fire, feed them, and give them somewhere to rest their head, protected from the bitter winter cold. This is a traditional Pagan custom.

MT: And the same for Easter?

JF: Easter to me is not so important. My deceased husband, Stewart, used to say that it is a much better for a child entering a church to understand Christianity through the baby in its mother's arms and the loving father looking after them, than to see the terrible image of a crucified man on a cross. I do not believe Jesus came to save our souls, but for us as Pagans, it is again a time of renewed life with parallels in the Christian concept of the resurrection. For me, though, this is symbolised best by a chick emerging from an egg. A concept, by the way, Christianity took from Paganism.

We view Easter as a Christian Festival; it is their festival, and Ostara; the Spring Equinox which of course Christianity took the term "Easter" from, is ours.

MT: If there's one favourite story, parable, teaching, or symbol of Jesus for you, what is it?

JF: I think my favourite stories comes from what I read about Jesus as a child. When I was a teenager I was a hippy, as well as a Sunday school teacher. My favourite parables at the time were about Jesus's attitude towards the creatures of the Earth, the flowers of the field, etc., and to the children. It's this statement from him again: "Suffer the little children to come unto me and forbid them not for such is the kingdom of heaven." I think it's a way of trying to make people understand that religion is something which should not be rammed down a child's throat. A child should be able to embrace divinity and consider it as a "friend," not a social obligation. I've always visualized Jesus in that story as having children climbing all over him and playing ball with him, and (being the son of a carpenter) carving toys for them. He was somebody who had a love of life, and love of the innocence of children. Because of this, I think even he realized that one day they would have to grow up and face the harsh realities of the world, but in the meantime, in childhood, he believed that they should keep their innocence. His other statement, which I love and have often quoted, best sums this up: "To enter the Kingdom of heaven, ye must be as children."

MT: Was Jesus the man a simple Jewish teacher, a divine prophet, a valid deity of the Christian pantheon, or something more akin to a magician?

JF: Well, I don't believe he was a simple Jewish teacher. I wouldn't call him a divine prophet, but I do believe he was a prophet. He is a valid "deity of the Christian pantheon" because from a Pagan viewpoint, if he wasn't, Christianity wouldn't exist! Was he a miracle worker, possibly? Certainly from the perspective of his time. Like his cousin John the Baptist, I believe he was an Essene, and had learnt much from the teachings within that tradition. He was performing a form of medicine, which to the average man in the street would have seemed to be a miracle. So, I wouldn't call him a magician, but for his period he was considered a miracle worker. I do think that he had glimpses of the divine, which is why he tried to point out that the "Kingdom of God is within you"; it's not out there, it's not in the clouds, not unreachable, but reachable within ourselves. I think this is what he was trying to explain, making him a prophet for his time, as any of us have the potential to be "prophets for our time." He was trying to make us all understand that we, like him, are *all* sons and daughters of God, and it is inside of ourselves we find our answer to the mysteries of divinity and how to link with the divine. I always call it divine DNA; I believe the ultimate is totally unknowable, just as in the Jewish tradition. But we can see it reflected through teachers like Jesus, Buddha, and Muhammad. You realize that although you cannot understand the ultimate, you can become close to it in your life through their teachings.

MT: What lesson do you feel the modern-day church needs to hear from the person of Jesus?

JF: I think the first thing they need to learn is a little more humility, and that the hoarding of worldly possessions is not the important thing. Throw away your gold, open up the windows of your churches and temples, and feed the world! Open up your arms and realize that every man, woman, and child living on this world is divine, and when they are starving, war-torn, and when young boys and girls are forced to hold guns and kill, converting them is not what the world needs! At these times the Church needs to feed and educate them, and turn this world into a better place. I think that is what Jesus was trying to say. Sadly the church has lost it's understanding of this. One of the saddest sights I ever saw in my life was in the cathedral in Toledo, Spain. There is a beautiful statue of the Madonna, the mother of Jesus. Amongst the ritual regalia she wears is a beautiful emerald. That emerald was stolen by conquistadors from a child, who when he refused to give it to them, was killed. They took that emerald to Spain and placed it in the crown of the Madonna. When you look into the face of that statue, she is one of the saddest ladies I have seen, as she wears the blood of a child on her brow. To me that is a travesty of everything that Jesus tried to teach. If the Christian story was true, and if Mary was a virgin and Jesus was the divine son of God, can you imagine how that lady would feel, to wear the blood of a child in the crown that is suppose to be the Queen of Heaven's? It's appalling!

MT: Do you feel it's possible to be both Christian and Pagan?

JF: Some Witches would say no. I, on the other hand, would say yes! I know people in the Craft who are both Christian and Pagan, and what they have found is that Paganism has given them a greater understanding of Christianity. So, they have looked to the Cosmic Christ rather than the historic Jesus, and made him their god figure. Why not? In the United States there are Pagans who call themselves "Jew-witches"! They are from a Jewish background and have learned to combine their cultural background with that of Paganism. I see no reason at all why a Christian and Pagan cannot exist in the same person.

Although I am a witch, I believe I am "multi-religious." Witchcraft is my religion, but if I was to go into a mosque I would veil my head; and if I was to go into a synagogue I would wear a hat or scarf. If I was to go into a Catholic church, I would make sure my arms are covered, and if I was entering a Hindu temple I would first give the appropriate offerings to Ganesha before going to worship any of the other gods. To me, the whole world—both inside the religious buildings and outside—is a temple to the divine, and so we should respect each other's religions when we go into their places of worship. There is no reason why a Pagan should not offer up a prayer to the Christian Madonna; she is, after all, no different from our own Queen of Heaven, the Goddess. Historically, they are exactly the same Lady. If I were to go into a synagogue, I would respect the Jewish teachings and go along with the doctrines laid down by the Rabbi, and sit with the women. I don't find that offensive or any different to being a Pagan. All true religious faiths are welcome in my temple, and I hope I am welcome in their temples as well.

MT: What, if anything, can modern-day Pagans learn from the message of Jesus?

JF: I think I probably, to a certain extent, have already answered that. What we can learn is an understanding of a different faith. Jesus wasn't always a "sweetness and light" character; after all, he did cast out the moneychangers from the temple. I think his example can teach us to stand by our principles. I have only once found myself in a situation in a foreign country where I suddenly realized that I would be willing to die from my beliefs, to die for my beliefs. I think that this is something Pagans can learn from Christianity, that level of sacrifice for your principles and beliefs.

MT: And what, if anything, can Christians learn from modern-day Paganism?

JF: I think I've also answered that. They could learn tolerance. Generally, Paganism is a very tolerant religion, although even we lapse sometimes. But I'm not just talking just about tolerance for the practises and beliefs of our fellow man, but for the Earth itself. Some Christians have changed their attitude, but still some believe that animals have no souls and that the Earth is a consumable resource given to us by God to do with as we will. Oh, how wrong they are! I think Christianity and other world religions could learn that we live on a beautiful planet the divine has given us to nurture and care for. We need to treat every living creature on it with respect, because God/Goddess is in everything: from the leaf on the tree, to the worm that lives under the stone, and even the slugs that destroy your lettuces! Christianity needs to learn to live in harmony with nature, realising that we are not separate from it but all part of it in "God's master plan"; that we need to give back to it if we are to live in balance with it. Connection with divinity doesn't start when you go to church on Sunday evening and end after services; it needs to be part of our lives every day. We need to leave for our children a good and wholesome world for them to live in. Part of this is caring and respecting this planet, and this is vitally important; now more than ever!

MT: Janet, it's been an absolute delight to hear you explain your thoughts with such clarity and wisdom. I am so very grateful.

JF: It's been my pleasure, Mark.

ABOUT THE AUTHOR

Janet Farrar was initiated by Alex and Maxine Sanders in 1970. She first became involved in the Craft after a friend started regularly visiting the Sanderses. Janet, being from a Christian background, went along to dissuade her friend from becoming involved, but was impressed by the moral structure Wicca had and joined the Sanderses' coven.

Stewart Farrar and Janet first met when Stewart was asked to script and narrate *A Witch Is Born*. After receiving their Third Degrees from the Sanderses, they left Alex and Maxine's coven to form their own. They married in 1972 and moved to the Republic of Ireland in 1976. Stewart passed away in February 2000 following a series of illnesses, but Janet has continued her work as a priestess and author.

With her late husband she has written over a dozen books on the Craft to date. Titles include *Eight Sabbats For Witches, The Witches' Way* (one of the first books to suggest the Southern Hemisphere turn of festivals in

Australia), *The Witches' Goddess, The Witches God,* and *Spells and How They Work.* Janet has also had one book published jointly with Virginia Russel, *The Magical History of the Horse,* and with her current partner Gavin Bone, several books: *The Pagan Path, The Healing Craft, The Dictionary of European Gods and Goddesses,* and their latest work, *Progressive Witchcraft.*

Twenty-Nine

......

Gavin Bone

MT: Gavin, thank you and Janet for agreeing to talk to me. I mentioned at the beginning of Janet's interview that you teach a progressive form of Wicca. Before we move on to the interview itself, are you first able to briefly give an example of what that means?

GB: Sure, Mark, and thank you for inviting us to be part of such an interesting project.

With regard to our work, I'm not sure all Pagans think the way we do. We're not what you would call "Orthodox Wiccan." We've worked with a host of different religions over the years. My favorite story comes from the US. A lone witch was looking for a coven or group in Sacramento back in the early '80s but couldn't find one. In desperation, he started going to the local Hindu temple, a new temple which had just been built—the Indian community is well rewarded for their hard work in the U. S., and are well respected for it. Well, he was noticeably this small impoverished white face, who would turn up in his battered car for every paja, while everyone else was either an Indian businessman or a member of the businessman's family. After several weeks, the priest finally approached him and asked if he was Hindu. Our friend replied, saying, "No, I'm Wiccan," and started to explain what that meant to him—the conception of deity, the system of festivals, etc. The Indian priest listened intently, nodding his head the way Indians do. Then when our friend finished, there was brief silence as the priest thought about what he had said. Then, looking at our friend intently, he said, "Ahhh... you're a Hindu!" He now works permanently in the temple by the way, as the priest's assistant.

MT: Oh, that's wonderful.

GB: By the way, Mark, we read some of your other books, and Janet really loved the "spare a talent for an ex-leper" story, as did I! Well, I can say that we have a sense of humor. Old saying: "Take what you do seriously, but not yourself." This is our mantra. Unfortunately, some Wiccans tend to be a bit serious and lack humor. Our view is that divinity must have a sense humor; look at the duck-billed platypus!

MT: Fabulous! So let me now talk to you about this strange and entrancing man we know as Jesus. Was he part of your upbringing as a child?

GB: Yes, he was part of my upbringing. I was brought up in a normal, regular C of E [Church of England] family. We weren't strict Christians. I think I only really attended church a couple of times with my grandmother. Of course, there were the compulsory school events at Christmas and Easter, etc. I wouldn't say he was ever an important figure in my life, and my religious life at this time revolved around the events which were of a social rather than religious importance.

MT: And does he feel important to you today, even if you don't know why? Is he of interest?

GB: Is he of interest to me? Yes. Does he feel important? I have to say no. I did briefly start going to church in my late teens, where he did begin to figure importantly, but I became very dissatisfied with the teachings the church purported to be his. I should point out that at the same time, I was also examining other religions such as Hinduism and Buddhism. I came to the conclusion that Krishna and Christ were, from a spiritual viewpoint, pretty much the same figure.

MT: So, in your understanding, was Jesus a historical person?

GB: Yes, I do believe there was a historical Jesus, but I don't believe that he is the person they really talk about in the Bible. I believe there are three Jesuses: the historical Jesus, the Jesus of the Christian Church and the Bible, and the "Cosmic /Astral" Jesus—the real "Christ." From what I have researched and read, I believe that the historical Jesus was more than likely to have been a "rebel" Essene priest, with many of his teachings originating from the Egyptian tradition. Many people seem to forget that Palestine and Canaan were originally part of the Egyptian empire before they were Roman. He became a focus for all sorts of already-existing myths, and the Church even managed to merge some of the teachings of other figures with him such as Apollonius of Tyana.

I believe that all three figures are very different. The "Cosmic/Astral" Jesus has more in common with such figures as the Norse Baldur, the Welsh Mabon, and the previously mentioned Hindu Krishna than he does with the Jesus of the Bible. I think most Pagans find it easier to connect with someone who is "part of their land" than a figure who came from several hundred miles away. This is because it allows them to connect with both the spirituality of the figure and their connection with the Earth itself.

MT: Yes, as I said to Janet, I do go along with the view that Jesus and Christ are two very different personas, sometimes bridged together in one literal yet mythic story. For example, the Christmas story: What feelings or thoughts does that conjure up in you?

GB: I see it as an analogy for the return of the Sun; after all that's why the Church set the Christmas story on the Winter Solstice. They managed to merge it with the already-existing Norse Modranacht (Night of the Mother) on December 24, Saturnalia, and the birthday of Mithras. You have to hand it the early Church fathers, they were very clever! For me, it is still a message of hope, regardless of what tradition it is from. It just depends on how you want to interpret that message.

MT: And the same for Easter?

GB: Sorry, I'm a Monty Python fan! Easter will always be tainted by *The Life of Brian* for me! I just wish some Christians had really understood what [the movie] was saying, as it wasn't really about Christ. It was about how they had misused his teachings. Perhaps that's why it got banned in some places, while the hideously violent and anti-Semitic *Passion of the Christ* wasn't. Again, for me, Easter/Ostara is about the solar cycle, in this case the Spring Equinox.

MT: If there's one favourite story, parable, teaching, or symbol of Jesus that stands out for you, what is it?

GB: The parable of the Good Samaritan, but not for the reasons most would think! The Church has so distorted the true meaning. They say "it's about being good to your neighbour," but they don't point out the impact this story would have had on a Hebrew at the time. It would be like the Samaritan being a radical Muslim cleric who had found a Jewish Zionist lying in a ditch and had not only given him first aid but then taken him back to his house and given him food and water. It was saying that there is good in all people and in all religious persuasions.

From what I see, this is the problem with many of the stories in the Bible. They are not taken in context of the time they were written. A good example is "turn the other cheek." It's not saying that you should passively accept whatever is dished out to you; quite the reverse. To "turn the other cheek," to face an aggressor was in original Hebraic tradition an act of defiance. Basically it was saying "you get the first hit free, now try that again!"

MT: Gavin, who do you think the historical Jesus was? For example, might he have been a divine prophet, a miracle worker, a magician, perhaps?

GB: I believe him to have been one of many supposed messianic figures who was roaming the Holy Land at the time. Sorry, we get back to that *Life of Brian* image of the square with all the prophets in it! People forget that Terry Jones, the writer, was an academic Oxbridge historian. Jesus was most definitely an Essene priest, as I mentioned earlier, just as John the Baptist was. This is where the act of Baptism came from. Was he a healer? Most definitely. He knew all the secret healing techniques of the Essenes which had been absorbed from the Egyptian traditions. These would have appeared "miraculous."

Was he a divine prophet, a miracle worker, or a magician? I think he was as much one of these as Gandhi was. To use the Hindu term, I believe he was an avatar. He was a genuine spiritual person who had merged with the true spirit of his divinity. I think we are all capable of this, and this is what he was trying to teach us.

MT: What lesson do you feel the modern-day Church needs to hear from Jesus?

GB: TOLERANCE! I don't really need to say any more than that. All his teachings point to this, but for some reason they seem to dwell on the Old Testament teachings rather than his. Sorry, can't find anything in the New Testament saying Witches should be condemned or there can't be gay marriages.

MT: Is it possible to be both Christian and Pagan?

GB: If you mean Christian by following the REAL teachings of Christ, then I think most good Pagans are good Christians by default. But, if you mean following the Jesus of the Bible and the Church, then no. If a Pagan can work with Krishna, Baldur, or the Mabon, then why not Jesus the Cosmic Christ?

MT: What can modern-day Pagans learn from Jesus?

GB: A lot of Pagans immediately dismiss him as a figure, which is a shame. The first thing they can learn is that you do need connection to personal deity. That is what is meant when he says: "I am the way, the truth, and the Light." That doesn't just mean through him, but through any of the major deity figures. When he says "I," take it not to mean Jesus's own ego, but of the divine he is channelling when he says it. Likewise, I think Pagans can all learn to connect directly to divinity in this way. Jesus wasn't saying to follow his teachings, but to follow him, follow what was happening to him. We all have the potential in us to be "Christ"; to be able to bring divinity into us and bring healing to people and the Earth.

Pagans might wonder why I am talking like this. This is because I went through my own "born again" experience with the divinity I work with—my real initiation, as I call it. After that, I understood what Christ was talking about and what born-again Christians experience. The major difference between them and myself was through my magical training; I understood what was happening to me. I think this is something that both Pagans and many Christians can learn from.

MT: And what can Christians learn from modern-day Paganism?

GB: Well, they can learn how to do ritual properly, for a start! Christianity is already learning from Paganism, through the back door, from figures like Matthew Fox, who was responsible for introducing the doctrine of "Creationalist Spirituality" into the Episcopalian/Church of England.

There is of course, that word "tolerance" again! They need to learn that the other spiritual paths to God—or Goddess—are just as valid.

MT: Gavin, thank you so much for taking the time and being such a delight to talk to.

GB: You're very welcome, and Mark, we're honored to be part of your project.

About the Author

Born in Portsmouth, *Gavin Bone* was originally initiated into Seax-Wicca in 1986. He trained as a registered nurse, is a practising spiritual (naturally empathic) healer, and a trained reflexologist. He developed a fascination with the theory that Wicca's roots are in tribal shamanistic healing traditions rather than medieval ritual magic and their related secret societies. He has studied shamanism in a Northern European context, with particular focus on the runes.

He met Janet and Stewart Farrar in 1989 at the Pagan Link conference in Leicester and moved to Ireland in 1992 after accompanying them on a tour of the United States. He co-authored *The Pagan Path, The Healing Craft,* and *The Complete Dictionary of European Gods and Goddesses* with Janet and Stewart.

In the UK, he was both a Pagan Link and Pagan Federation contact in early '90s, and this led him after his move to Ireland to set up the Pagan Information Network, a contact network for Pagans in the Republic and the North of Ireland.

Like Janet, he is an honourary member of the Strega tradition, and ordained third-level Clergy with the Aquarian Tabernacle Church.

Thirty

......

Oberon Zell-Ravenheart

MT: Oberon, it's truly marvelous to be able to talk with you about this strange, first-century wandering prophet, healer—or was he a magician?—called Jesus. Thank you so much for giving me some of your precious time. Let's begin with a question that I feel is very appropriate to direct at you. As a Wizard—in fact, as the head master of a real-life Wizard School—what fascinates you most about Jesus the miracle worker?

OZ: His congruence with other famous Wizards—especially those of his own time, such as Simon Magus (fl. 20–50 CE), Apollonius of Tyana (c. 30–96 CE), Cailitín (first century CE), Elymas the Sorcerer (first century CE), Jean (first century CE), and Veleda (first century CE). I find it fascinating to compare and contrast all of these "miracle workers"!

MT: I wish we had the time to explore all those congruences now, but alas, we don't. Perhaps that's a future book for you or me?

OZ: Yes, maybe!

MT: So was the figure of Jesus, to a lesser or greater degree, part of your upbringing as a child?

OZ: Yes. But then, so were all the figures of Greek mythology as told in Ovid's *Metamorphosis*—a significant and influential book in my childhood. I've always been fascinated with all myths and legends, and I explored those of the Bible as deeply as those of the Greeks, Egyptians, Celts, Norse, Hindu, etc. I had a perfect attendance record at Sunday school until I left home to go away to a college prep school for my senior year.

MT: Yes, I can totally relate to that. For me my earliest memories of the power of mythic epics were the Greek and Roman masterpieces. I was turned on to such literature years before I'd ever noticed the Bible's stories. But can I ask, does the figure of Jesus feel important to you now, in any way at all?

OZ: Not particularly. I mean, I'm a Pagan, not a Christian. I think the figure of Merlin has always felt more important to me than that of Jesus.

MT: Do you consider Jesus to have been a historical person?

OZ: Yes, I think Jesus really lived.

MT: So when you imagine the historical Jesus, is his spirit reflected in the modern-day Church?

OZ: I don't think his spirit is reflected at all in most modern-day Christian churches (with a few exceptions—perhaps the Quakers, Seventh-Day Adventists, Unitarians, Congregationalists, Unity, etc., might come closer...). As a teenager, I took confirmation classes in my family's church (Congregational), where the most important thing I learned was that "Christian" means "Christ-like." So I always evaluate Christians by that criterion of comparison: "What was Christ actually *like,* and how closely does this person match?" Oddly, I find that most Pagans seem to be more "Christ-like" than most Christians! For the first three hundred years, it seems the early "Christian" churches were very much like many modern Pagan groups: small gatherings in different people's homes—usually hosted and presided over by women; sharing simple lives revolving around love and caring for each other; a communion of bread and wine...All this prevailed up until the year 313, when Emperor Constantine (a right bastard!) proclaimed (via the Edict of Milan) Christianity to be the official religion of the Roman Empire. After that, the simple religion based on the life and teachings of the man Jesus did a 180-degree about-face, and became the creed of a ruthless and ambitious empire that would eventually result in crusades, inquisitions, and Witch-burnings. Poor Jesus must be spinning in his grave!

MT: What feelings or thoughts does the Christmas story conjure up in you?

OZ: Congruence with all the many identical stories in so many cultures of the infant Sun God born at the Winter Solstice from the womb of Night: Krishna, Horus, Mithras, Apollo, etc. Whole books have been written about this subject and I find them fascinating—the universality of this concept: light being born of darkness; the sun (Son) born on the longest, deepest, darkest night of the year. I always loved all the customs of Christmas/Yule as a child and growing up—and I was delighted to eventually discover that they are *all* Pagan in origin; unchanged over millennia. They put me in touch with the continuity of my ancestors—and with all cultures of the Northern Hemisphere who share these traditions.

MT: Ditto—Easter?

OZ: And ditto right back atcha! Even the name of the holiday has remained unchanged from Pagan times, as it is the name of the Goddess of Fertility: Eostra, Estre, Esther, Ishtar, Ostara, Astarte, Isis, Inanna, Aphrodite—the Eastern Star (the planet Venus). To this day we love to decorate Ostara eggs with our two-and-a-half-year-old granddaughter, and hide them for her to find. Again, all the symbols and customs of this day are thoroughly Pagan, commemorating this time the rebirth of life on the Earth—the return of vegetation (the Green Man and Maid), animal babies (the Red Man and Maid; the Horned God), etc. Time to plant our garden!

MT: If you have one, what is your favourite story, parable, teaching, or symbol of Jesus?

OZ: Well, let's see, there's a lot of good ones. The parable of the Good Samaritan is one I often reference in talking to Christians about Pagans (i.e., we Pagans are the kindly neighbours who are not of your religion, but are nonetheless good people). The parable of the Talents is a good one also (though I prefer the Hindu version in which the items are seeds rather than coins, and the wise son plants them, thus multiplying them vastly). And I particularly like the story in which Jesus is tempted by the Devil with Wealth, Fame, and Power—and he rejects all these, saying "Get thee behind me, Satan!" I think modern televangelists should be reminded of this one!

MT: Who do you suppose Jesus was? For example, a simple teacher, a divine prophet, a magician, or wizard etc.

OZ: I like to think of him as a classic Wizard, in the same tradition as countless others in countless other times, places, and cultures. That is, a wise one, a lore-master, and a superb teacher/mentor. But this does not preclude his also being all those other things: a miracle worker, a magician, a divine prophet, a valid deity of the Christian pantheon, and a simple Jewish teacher. I think of him as one of Us (i.e., Wizards). I only wish that his preaching/teaching career had lasted more than three years, that he hadn't been martyred so early, and that he had taken the trouble to write his teachings down (a profound mistake that I am very aware of, and will not emulate!).

MT: And what lesson(s) do you feel the modern-day church needs to hear from the person/teaching of Jesus?

OZ: Reject wealth, fame, and power as temptations of the devil; "Do unto others as you would have them do unto you"; "Love your neighbour as yourself"; "I say unto you, you are gods"; "The Kingdom of Heaven is within you"; "Judge not, lest you be judged."

MT: Is it possible to be both Christian and Pagan? Why?

OZ: Well, many avowed Christo-Pagans seem to think so, and I would not presume to tell anyone else how to define their own faith! So if they say this is what they are, then it must be possible. My own father has reconciled my Paganism with his Christianity by coming to think of me as a "Pagan Christian," and I do think that in most ways (excluding that whole bit about not lusting after women in my heart…) I probably am more "Christ-like" than the vast majority of declared Christians. Certainly more so than those who lust after wealth, fame, and power!

MT: What, if anything, can modern-day Pagans learn from the message/person of Jesus?

OZ: Do not lust after wealth, fame, and power; "Do unto others as you would have them do unto you"; "Love your neighbour as yourself"; "I say unto you, you are gods"; "The Kingdom of Heaven is within you"; "Judge not, lest you be judged." Lead a simple life, treat others right, be inclusive rather than exclusive in your associations and friendships, and illustrate your teachings with really good stories!

MT: And what, if anything, can Christians learn from modern-day Paganism?

OZ: Do not lust after wealth, fame, and power; Do as you would be done by; Love unconditionally; "Everything is alive and everything is interconnected"; divinity is immanent as well as transcendent, i.e., "thou art God/dess"; We are all children of the same mother; revere and honour women, nature, and all things female; "The Kingdom of Heaven is within you"— and so is the Queendom of Earth; cherish diversity; cultivate compassion and empathy; eschew hatred, intolerance, and all desire for retribution, retaliation, revenge or punishment; condemn not, lest you be condemned; attune your life with the cycles of the seasons; grow a garden; lead a simple life; treat others right; be inclusive rather than exclusive in your associations and friendships. And always capitalize the proper nouns and adjectives referring to other people's religions!

MT: Finally, as the headmaster of a Wizard school, I wanted to ask you one more question from that perspective. Is that okay with you?

OZ: Sure, fire away.

MT: Well I believe you teach a certain amount of "illusion" to your Grey School students. In fact, one of my Magician/Illusionist teachers (Jeff McBride) is on your faculty. Yet some Pagans see both magics as complementary, whereas others seem to see them as opposing forces. Do you have anything to say about this?

OZ: I consider illusion magics to be in the category of "special effects" to enhance rituals, storytelling, and other magickal acts. Thus I see them as complementary rather than oppositional to other types of magick. Any Wizard worth his salt in the old days would be expected to perform illusions at the drop of a hat (or the request of a king)! For instance, when I get up at a campfire to tell a story, I may wave my hand over the fire, and colored sparkles will arise from it. Then I'll reach into the fire and pull out a glowing coal, which I'll hold up in my fingertips. Then I'll make a loose fist with my other hand, stick the thumb in my mouth as if it were a pipe, and insert the glowing coal. I may then take a few puffs, with the pipe glowing each time, lighting up my face. And then I'll open my hands to show there is nothing in them. And now that I have everyone's attention, this will lead into a story.

MT: Marvelous. I'd love to be able to see that some day. Well, Oberon, it has been a pleasure and a delight talking to you over these things. I'm sure what you've said will ring many bells for many people. Thank you once again for you time and your wisdom.

OZ: You're more than welcome, Mark.

ABOUT THE AUTHOR

Oberon Zell-Ravenheart co-founded the Church of All Worlds in 1962. First to apply the term "Pagan" to the newly emerging Nature Religions of the 1960s, and through thirty years of publishing *Green Egg,* Oberon was instrumental in the coalescence of the Neopagan movement. In 1970, he formulated and published the theology of deep ecology that has become known as "the Gaia Thesis." Oberon is the primary sculptor of the Mythic Images Collection (www.MythicImages.com), and author of *Grimoire for the Apprentice Wizard.* He is Headmaster of the online Grey School of Wizardry: www.GreySchool.com.

Thirty-One

······

Cassandra Eason

MT: First of all, Cassandra, I'm so grateful to you for your time and being so willing to be interviewed for this project. Before we begin proper, which particular Pagan tradition do you feel is your main oath? You are known as a Druid, but you also write books with a very Wiccan feel and flavour.

CE: Yes, I am a Druidess, and both Druidry and Wicca revere nature and the sanctity of life and believe in harming none by thought, word, or deed. The main difference is that Wicca focuses on a goddess and god icon/ mother and father separately as part of a dual deity structure. The Goddess is often seen as the original creating mother from whom the male god separated, and then they together brought about creation. In Druidry, though there are many Celtic gods and goddesses, these were before the Roman influence—depicted either in animal form such as Epona the horse goddess (whom the Romans also revered), or as nature deities, such as Druantia the silver fir goddess. Druidry often emphasizes ceremonies under the eye of the sun, outdoors in the early morning, while Wicca is more lunar, night-time based with special reverence for the full moon. Together they form a balance, and I believe that we should adapt all forms of nature spirituality and form our own individual belief systems.

MT: So was the figure of Jesus, to a lesser or greater degree, part of your upbringing as a child?

CE: Jesus was a huge part of my upbringing in the working-class industrial Midlands, both in school and in my three-times-on-Sunday visits to church with my mother. At sixty-one, I can still sing all the words of "Jesus Bids Us Shine" and "Jesus Wants Me for a Sunbeam." I used to get very upset as a child that Jesus had been hurt to save me, and I tried very, very hard to be good. I was aware that Jesus was watching me all the time and he would know if I lied. This fear stayed with me till I was about twelve, when I told my first lie and the world did not come crashing down. I suspect my mother and the school planted and encouraged my view of Jesus as a cosmic policeman.

MT: And does he still hold an importance for you?

CE: Jesus is much less significant to me than the Mother Goddess and the Virgin Mary, whom I regard as an expression of the divine mother principle. I am especially drawn to the Black Earth Madonnas from the Middle Eastern tradition that may be found in many French churches, often hidden away.

As I have become older, Jesus has become to me a very wise prophet who tried to make people more caring. That said, in times of stress I still find myself singing hymns about Jesus and my family. I regard it as a sign to back off fast. Amazingly, I was talking to a friend of a similar age who lives in France, and we discovered that we both were able to recall and sing "Jesus Bids Us Shine" and all the "Jesus Loves Me" hymns.

MT: Do you consider Jesus to have been a historical person?

CE: I believe he was a historical person and a great religious icon. Almost all pre-Christian and Neopagan religions have the idea of the sacrifice god who died to give his body so the crops would grow; before that was the sacrificed animal god. The Hanged Man in the tarot, Odin of the Norse gods hanging on the world tree, again reflects the sacrifice principle to attain enlightenment. So I suspect whether or not Jesus was crucified, the Resurrection, a feature of many pre-Christian sacrifice myths, may have been emphasised to fit in with the beliefs of the Pagan peoples and make Christianity more acceptable to them. This was especially so once St. Paul widened the belief base to include all believers, not just those with a Jewish background.

When I walk round a beautiful church or cathedral, the spirit of Jesus often seems very remote except as the child or infant with Mary, where there is an immediate humanising for me. Most poignant for me as a mother of grown children are the heart-rending images of Maria Dolorosa, the aging Mary holding her dead son. Jesus is a sky being, so I relate better to Mary whose ascension to heaven was, I suspect, a convenient device to totally de-sexualise and de-humanise the mother of God.

MT: What feelings or thoughts does the Christmas story conjure up in you?

CE: Always being the old shepherd in a smelly blanket in the Nativity play at school while my blonde-haired, blue-eyed slender friend got the star role. However, I loved the idea of the wise men bringing gifts and the angels coming down. To me, the Christmas story was a fabulous pantomime, and I never really connected the story strongly with the Jesus who saved me and the guilt trip. Angels were like fairies. When I had children of my own, Nativity plays became a chore of providing costumes and trying to get time off to see them in the third row from the back. I think my real problem is because the story still often has a strong Anglo-Saxon blonde, blue-eyed Mary feel instead of the reality of the Middle East. The closest connection for me is T. S. Eliot's poem "The Journey of the Magi." A cold coming we had of it that I read in my late teens.

In recent years, I have related to the story more as the Mother Goddess giving birth to the new sun king, though of course Jesus was not born in midwinter historically.

MT: And Easter?

CE: The Spring Equinox still affects the Christian dating of Easter and was again hugely significant in many pre-Christian religions as the time of the sacrifice and resurrection of the slain god, though others link the sacrifice with the harvest. The hot cross buns come from an older tradition of Mother Goddess equinox cakes; Easter was the time when in the Norse tradition Ostara, the maiden goddess of spring, opened the doors of the new year with her magical white hare (our Easter rabbit). I always found Good Friday such a dark, frightening day as a child; the church was blacked out and there were black drapes and long, boring silences and dirges. I am glad about the revival of the pre-Christian Equinox/Easter fires in some modern churches. But because Easter heralds such a season of hope (in the Southern Hemisphere, of course, the Christian Easter is close to the Autumn Equinox), I associate Easter mainly with spring flowers and Easter bonnets. In the industrial Midlands of my childhood, the flower sellers would sell bunches of Easter primroses and violets, and the crocus in our back yard would come into bloom. I always had a straw hat trimmed with flowers and exchanged my long woollen grey stockings for white socks—even if it was freezing.

MT: If there's one favourite story, parable, teaching, or symbol of Jesus for you, what is it?

CE: My favourite parable would have to be the one about the loaves and fishes because I can relate to that, often feeding my five children and all their friends when the store cupboard was half empty. It seemed such a practical useful miracle, much more so than turning water into wine at a wedding.

It showed Jesus as a caring, hands-on person who was not just interested in being the great guru; he made sure everyone listening to him had something to eat. That was one of the few times I related to Jesus as a person.

MT: Who do you think Jesus was? For example, a Jewish teacher, a divine prophet, a valid deity, a miracle worker, or a magician?

CE: I would say all of these depending on which qualities people need to emphasise. The attraction of Jesus is that he acts as an icon for people who need miracles, for those who want a deity to worship, for a man who could apparently go against the laws of science, walk on water, and say nothing is impossible if you want it enough. But for me, the teacher and prophet images are best, for he never actually wanted a great fuss to be made about him, according to what we read. He was the son of God, but according to many spiritual traditions, anyone created by a god or goddess figure is a son or daughter of God. So, in that sense, he was divine and we are all divine. We are all spiritual beings in a physical body who, as the created, carry the spark of the creator. Jesus had maybe a larger spark than most, but he spoke for us all.

MT: What lesson do you feel the modern-day church needs to hear from the person or teaching of Jesus?

CE: The modern-day church needs to learn from Jesus to get out into life and help people in need, not sit around arguing principles of theology or who should be a churchwarden. People are desperate for guidance and inspiration and the half-empty churches testify that organised religion is not offering that inspiration. This is not to generate more trendy guitar-playing priests but ministers who go out into the everyday life, get their hands dirty, and challenge corrupt politicians as the voice of ordinary people. Church laws created centuries ago should be reassessed in terms of what Jesus who went out among the people would have wanted, given the realities of the modern world.

MT: Is it possible to be both Christian and Pagan?

CE: It is possible to be both Christian and Pagan; Pagans believe in respecting all life forms and harming none, by thought, word, or deed. All gods and goddesses are ultimately one higher divine creative force. Goodness is goodness no matter in whose name you ask for it or try to live a good life. Even within Christianity there have been arguments about whose god is best. I am a Quaker as well as Pagan and Quakers believe there is good or God/the Goddess in everyone.

MT: What, if anything, can modern-day Pagans learn from the message of Jesus?

CE: Modern-day Pagans can learn from Jesus that you have to have the courage of your convictions and that sometimes you do need to operate from within the world in which you live while challenging its injustices through legitimate means. Jesus did turn over the tables of the money lenders, but I would not advise Pagans to follow suit in their local banks.

MT: And what, if anything, can Christians learn from modern-day Paganism?

CE: Christians can learn from the Pagan principle that what you send out you get back three times. So you cannot just confess to a Christian priest or priestess that you are sorry and have your sins wiped out with three Hail Marys. Even if Jesus did die for your sins, you have to try to put things right if you do wrong and live with consequences.

MT: Cassandra, I was thrilled when I heard of your willingness to be interviewed and I'm even more delighted now that I have. It's been fascinating and enlightening. Thank you very much indeed.

CE: You're welcome.

ABOUT THE AUTHOR

Cassandra Eason is a prolific author of many books, including *Pagan in the City* (Quantum/Foulsham UK) and *Angel Magic: Inspiration for Busy People* (Piatkus UK). Contact her via her website: www.cassandraeason.com for spiritual advice and online courses.

Thirty-Two

......

Raven Grimassi

MT: Raven, it's a pleasure and a privilege to be able to interview you for this book. But before we get onto the main subject, perhaps I could ask you to briefly explain your spiritual tradition, Stregheria. Are you able to do so, especially in comparison with, say, Wicca?

RG: Stregheria is a witchcraft system rooted in Old World Italian Paganism. One of the primary markers of Italian witchcraft is the veneration of ancestors, and this is highlighted in Stregheria. My tradition also works with a mated divine pair who are linked to sun and moon as symbols of their natures. Wicca has many parallels to Stregheria, and some of the key ones are traceable to the Aegean-Mediterranean. Therefore they predate modern Wicca. However, in my published works on Italian witchcraft I have used some modern Wiccan elements. I did this because I was not at liberty to share certain things from the Italian material. So the Wiccan elements served as fillers and bridges.

MT: Was the figure of Jesus, to a lesser or greater degree, part of your upbringing as a child?

RG: Yes, the figure of Jesus was present, but not in the mainstream manner. He was a reflection of the Harvest Lord figure, the slain god of the Vegetation Kingdom (who in the case of Jesus died upon a tree). He carried the life force of death and resurrection in his mythos.

MT: And does he [Jesus] hold any importance to you today?

RG: I think he is important by way of raising human consciousness above rigid and blind adherence to the letter of the law as opposed to the spirit of the law. I think this was his underlying message, but it was reinterpreted by the Church to fall back in line with the human machine of dogma and doctrine (a means of control).

MT: In your opinion, was Jesus a historical person? If yes, do you see the "spirit of Jesus" reflected in the modern-day Church?

RG: It is uncertain to me whether Jesus is a historical character or not. But I feel that the teachings attributed to him are not fully integrated into the organization of the Church. I refer to the administration, and to the generating of finances. I think the personage of Jesus would find much of this objectionable (although I certainly understand the need for money to run the machine and an organization to keep things directed). It's just that it seems in conflict with the teachings of Jesus pertaining to worldly involvement versus a sole focus upon a relationship with the Godhead.

MT: Could it be that Paganism reflects his spirit more so than the Church does?

RG: I am not sure exactly what the "spirit of Jesus" is, but I feel that in Paganism the focus is tribal and earth-based, which encompasses reverence for nature and responsibility to community (while at the same time carrying a heightened sense of self-importance). I don't see reverence for nature in the teachings of Jesus, but perhaps I have missed the texts. The cursing of the fig tree has always been a problem for me in this regard.

As to Paganism reflecting the spirit of Jesus, I believe there are elements of the "one truth spoken by many" within Paganism just as there are in Christianity. I feel that Paganism not only teaches tolerance for other beliefs (and allows that other religions are valid paths for their followers) but that the majority of its practitioners also live the philosophy each day.

I think the Church, as an administration, has strayed from the mission set forth by the teachings of Jesus. In some ways this is unavoidable. But the vast majority of Christians I have known hold as humanly close to the teachings of Jesus as possible. In this regard I believe the Church has done well in establishing an understanding of the Faith. Clearly "good works" are performed by the Church, and these are well in keeping with the compassion reflected in the figure of Jesus.

MT: What feelings or thoughts does the Christmas story conjure up in you?

RG: I have always been intrigued by the inclusion of the Magi in the Christmas story. The idea that occultists were the first to recognize something taking place is interesting, and the inclusion of frankincense, myrrh, and gold reflects the sun god's sacrificial theme (a Lord of the Harvest-type thing). I do not regard the presented story as factual, but I recognize the spiritual message upon which the tale is woven.

MT: And Easter?

RG: Here again the idea of a dying and returning god is reflective of earlier Pagan beliefs. But I see such things as metaphorical as opposed to historical. It seems to me that a Pagan mythos is certainly at the foundation of Christian themes, but that is natural in the course of events and reflects the one story told by all.

MT: If you have one, what is your favourite story, parable, teaching, or symbol of Jesus?

RG: One parable has always stood out to me. It appears in Mark 13: 30–31. Jesus comments that the mustard seed is the "smallest of all seeds on earth." Of course we know today that this is not true; the mustard seed is not the smallest seed on earth. However, it does appear to have been the smallest seed in the geographic region where Jesus was speaking. So here we must take into account that Jesus was delivering truths that were customized to fit the understanding and experience of the people within their specific culture (as opposed to "THE TRUTH" in a larger and holistic perspective). I feel this is important because it lifts the New Testament up and away from "the fixed word of God" and into a spiritual context that is inspirational as opposed to dictatorial.

MT: Who do you suppose Jesus was, if he were a historical person?

RG: I feel that the figure of Jesus represents a man who attained "god-consciousness" (the enlightenment that the soul is one with its creator). It is "at-one-with" the godhead moment, a conscious merging with the Source of All Things. I think that it is here that one understands his or her nature as "divine" and "at-one" with the Source (*the Father and I are one, he who has seen me has seen the Father*). But such an enlightened being is sure to be misunderstood by those who do not share the same higher consciousness (and thus the need for parables).

MT: What lesson do you feel the modern-day church needs to hear from the teaching of Jesus?

RG: It seems to me that the teachings of Jesus speak to the spirit of scripture as opposed to the letter of the law. The latter is the game of Pharisees. In this light, I feel the Church needs to understand what Jesus was trying to point out.

MT: Is it possible to be both Christian and Pagan?

RG: No, to me the statement is like saying "I'm a meat-eating vegetarian." Paganism is the belief in many deities, while Christianity is the belief in one. The two views are not compatible or harmonious with each other in terms of practice. The culture of the region at the time of Jesus was certainly opposed to Pagan beliefs and practices, and Jesus was a Rabbi of the Hebrew teachings and as such would have been opposed to Paganism. Now, that being said, I do not think that the essence of the spiritual tenets of Christianity and Paganism are incompatible.

MT: What, if anything, can modern-day Pagans learn from the message/person of Jesus?

RG: That there is something greater than the self, and that we are part of it.

MT: And what, if anything, can Christians learn from modern-day Paganism?

RG: That the Divine Source of All Things doesn't play favorites. There are as many ways to the Source as there are people in the world.

MT: Raven, it's been wonderful talking to you over these questions. Thank you so very much. I really do appreciate it.

ABOUT THE AUTHOR

Raven Grimassi is the author of fourteen books on Wicca and Witchcraft, including *The Wiccan Mysteries*, which was awarded Book of the Year and First Place–Spirituality Book by the Coalition of Visionary Retailers in 1998, and the *Encyclopedia of Wicca & Witchcraft*, awarded Best Non-Fiction, 2001. His other titles include *The Witches' Craft, Wiccan Magick, Hereditary Witchcraft, Beltane, Italian Witchcraft, The Witch's Familiar, Witchcraft: A Mystery Tradition, Spirit of the Witch, Crafting Wiccan Traditions, Book of the Holy Strega*, and *The Cauldron of Memory*. Raven also co-created and co-authored the two oracle kits *The Well Worn Path* and *The Hidden Path* with Stephanie Taylor, illustrated by Pagan artist Mickie Mueller.

Raven is an initiate of several Witchcraft traditions including Brittic, Pictish, Gaelic, and Celtic Traditionalist. He is also a recognized expert on Italian Witchcraft and the foremost authority on the works of Charles Godfrey Leland in this particular field. Raven currently lives in New England with his wife and divides his time between writing, co-directing the

Mystery School known as the Crossroads Fellowship, and developing the Ash, Birch & Willow training system of Old Ways Witchcraft. Having been born on the festival day of the goddess Ceres (Patron of the Mysteries), Raven is devoted to preserving and teaching the Mystery Tradition of pre-Christian Europe.

Thirty-Three

......

Scott Blunt

During the course of writing this book, I've made many wonderful new friends. I'm now going to introduce you to someone Maxine Sanders suggested I talk to, because he had a rather intense Christian background, yet ended up becoming a High Priest of the Alexandrian Tradition. His temple is know as the Temple of Stella Maris and has initiated many over the course of its life. He is also now training for the Priesthood within a Gnostic/Esoteric Tradition of the Liberal Catholic Church.

MT: Scott, it's a pleasure to be able to interview you here. Perhaps I first ought to ask you to explain why you left the Church originally. After all, it was a very big part of your life.

SB: Why did I leave the Church? This is very complicated and involves other people, but there were a number of reasons. I began to have serious doubts about the theology and practice that has grown out of the Charismatic Renewal. I was also working as a Pastoral Lay Assistant and I was just burnt out. A serious situation arose involving the parish priest (not child abuse!), and I saw such wicked and nasty behavior from prominent members of the church who were so power hungry it was unreal! I found I could no longer pray or worship at Mass, and after a while I lost my faith completely.

MT: Well, later on we'll return to this theme and talk about your current training for the Liberal Catholic Priesthood. But first I want to talk to you about the person of Jesus. Was he part of your upbringing as a child?

SB: Yes. Until the age of four, my mother was a member of the Assemblies of God church.

MT: Does the figure of Jesus feel important to you, even if you don't know why?

SB: Yes.

MT: In what ways?

SB: I found myself back in the Christian world as a near-teenage boy and I "gave my heart" to Jesus when I was eleven, a decision that took me on a spiritual journey that is still going on to this day. *He* gets under your skin [laughs]. Although I'm an Alexandrian Witch, Jesus has always been at the back of my mind. Jesus is important to me; his life, his teachings are amazing. I'm not sure I "feel" but I believe he is important for me on my particular spiritual path; I'm still working all this out.

MT: So do you see Jesus as a historical person? And if yes, how is or isn't his spirit reflected in the modern-day Church?

SB: Yes, of course he existed! And I think that the Church can get bogged down with sex. But I do think the Church reflects the "spirit" of Jesus in the way it upholds the dignity and sacredness of the unborn child and the "weak" in society, which is a good thing.

MT: What feelings or thoughts does the Christmas story conjure up in you?

SB: It is not that important to me and my spiritual path. However, I understand why Catholic Christians are anti-abortion, as the Christmas story tells of God entering our human experience in the Incarnation and thus sanctifying the human being from conception to death.

MT: And the same with regard to Easter?

SB: This I find a challenge, as a Witch! The Resurrection cannot be easily dismissed! When I was a practicing Catholic, the Easter Triduum was filled with sorrow, gratefulness, and joy.

MT: So who was or is Jesus to you, Scott?

SB: Jesus, for me, is a manifestation of the Divine. A healer and a teacher. His message is still relevant today for those who seek to work in the Sphere of Tipareth.

MT: And what lesson do you feel the modern-day Church needs to hear from him?

SB: It depends on your definition of "Church"! I think that the Church needs to rediscover that God is love—that's why He sent Jesus…to show His love. I don't mean that in a "fluffy bunny" sort of way but as a revealing of His nature to humans.

MT: I know you're training to be a Christian Priest, but is it really possible to be both Christian and Pagan?

SB: Again, it depends on your definition of "Pagan"! I think that from an occult point of view, we can experience and acknowledge both Sun and Moon, God and Goddess. "All Gods are one God and all Goddesses are one Goddess."

MT: What, if anything, can modern-day Pagans learn from the message/person of Jesus?

SB: I think Pagans can learn the lesson of sacrifice from Jesus's teachings. Many Pagans believe in self, which can lead to selfish attitudes of "I cannot give to others because I need my 'self time.'" Whereas Jesus taught sacrificial love/giving and reaching out to others no matter what the cost to self! Many Christians need to learn this lesson also!

MT: And what, if anything, can Christians learn from modern-day Paganism?

SB: Peace and acceptance of the human experience.

MT: I can see the love and devotion you still hold for Jesus. Before we close this interview, can you now briefly explain what led you to the Liberal Catholic Church and why you're now training for its priesthood?

SB: I started reading *Science of the Sacraments* by Bishop Leadbeater as I was beginning to "work" with the Ray Stones in my Temple. I was amazed by the mix of Catholic Christianity, Angelic ministry, and occult leanings within the book. I began to look for a Liberal Catholic Church, found many and visited one, but didn't go back. When I was a teenager I felt a very strong call to priesthood, but as I am gay, this wasn't possible, even in the '80s. As I read this book, that feeling of being called came back.

When the calling came back, it was stronger and stronger. I then met you through Maxine Sanders, and you put me in touch with an Independent Liberal Catholic Church. I liked it very much and started going to Mass. I felt the same inner connections there that I have in my own temple. I discussed my thoughts about priesthood with my bishop and after a while, he discerned that I did have a vocation. I have been ordained in the Minor Orders and will be ordained as a Deacon very soon. This decision has been a difficult one, as many Witches do not, or will not, try to understand this deep connection I have with Jesus and the Catholic faith. I have not stopped being a Witch; I still run my coven. There has been a wonderful acceptance of me and the Craft within the Church, which is so refreshing.

MT: Scott, it's been wonderful talking with you. You've been on such a wonderful adventure that I believe will continue. I'm sure your ability to hold two traditions in harmony will be an inspiration to many.

ABOUT THE AUTHOR

Scott Blunt is an Initiated and Consecrated Witch and High Priest within the Alexandrian Tradition. He was a Catholic for many years before that, thinking that when he was first initiated in 1995, that was it! He now sees the spiritual journey like the Spiral Dance, where initiates weave in and out, back and forth. As Scott told me, "When the Spiral Dance is danced, the Magic comes full circle—I found Jesus again. I had missed this man in my life for so long…I love the Goddess and our Horned God, but I have Jesus now, too. However, the Dance continues and the Magic leads us on!"

Thirty-Four

......

Kerr Cuhulain

MT: Kerr, it's a real pleasure to be able to discuss the following themes with you, and I do thank you for your time and input. But firstly before I ask you the Jesus-focused questions, can you briefly explain the mission/vision of the Wiccan Order of Knights of which you are Grand Master?

KC: The Order of Scáthach is a Wiccan order of Knighthood founded by me in November 2007. The Order of Scáthach has evolved into a Wiccan tradition embracing the Warrior philosophies as outlined in my books *Wiccan Warrior, Full Contact Magick,* and *Magickal Self Defense.* You might call it "Warrior Wicca." The Order of Scáthach embraces the concept of chivalry and focuses on empowerment, creative expression, and effective magick. The Order of Scáthach is a study group for people interested in Wiccan magick, energy work, and rituals related to the Warrior path. We are constantly developing new rituals and magick and studying our philosophy. All members are expected to participate and contribute.

The Order of Scáthach is named for Scáthach nUanaind, the daughter of Ard-Greimne of Lethra. Scáthach ("shadow"—pronounced "skya"), also known as Scáthach Buanand ("victorious shadow"), is the most famous of female warriors in Celtic mythology. Living on the Isle of Skye (which is named for her), Scáthach ran a martial training academy at which all of the principal heroes of Celtic myth were trained. Her most famous pupil was Cúchulainn, the warrior hero that influenced my choice of magickal name.

Members of the Order of Scáthach must honor and uphold the Wiccan Rede ("An it harm none, do what thou wilt") in all its aspects. Members of the Order of Scáthach must follow "The Rule," which consists of our thirteen warrior precepts and our Code of Chivalry.

MT: Are you able to expound on that Code here?

KC: Certainly. Our thirteen precepts are as follows:

1. Know thyself.

2. Nurture the ability to perceive the truth in all matters.

3. You create your own reality.

4. Develop a sense of Right Action.

5. Do not be negligent, even in trifling matters.

6. Your body is your temple; care for it!

7. Minimal appearance, maximum content.

8. Perceive that which cannot be seen with the eye.

9. Power with.

10. Who dares wins.

11. The Gods cannot help those who will not help themselves.

12. Be creative!

13. Do not engage in useless activity.

Our Code of Chivalry as outlined in the Scáthach Oath of Knighthood reads as follows:

"By the power of earth, water, air, fire, and spirit, before the Gods, the Sidhe, and the Ancestors, I do declare before this assemblage my fealty and allegiance to Scáthach, to its thirteen precepts, and to the rule of law.

So shall I ever defend the values of Sincerity, Courtesy, Compassion, Perseverance, Industriousness, Justice, Loyalty, Courage, Self-Discipline, Humility, Largesse, Truth, and Honor, which in this modern world are so often neglected. I take these values into my heart and soul that they may manifest themselves in my words and deeds.

Standing proud and free, radiating my inner truth, exultant in my power, I raise up my voice and proclaim myself to be a knight of Scáthach and dedicate myself to the mastery and defense of these values. I vow to do my will while harming none. In this I am resolved. This I declare before the Gods, the Sidhe, and the Ancestors.

Biodh Se! (be it so)"

MT: This is truly fascinating. So how does one enter the Order? I presume there's a strict training?

KC: In the first phase of Order of Scáthach training, the Novice is welcomed into the Order with an Acceptance ritual. The Novice studies energy through both mental and psychical exercises, learns and practices psychic skills, and develops their magickal skills. At the end of this first phase, the Novice becomes a Squire at an Armoring ceremony. The second level of training has to do with studying ritual and magickal weapons: We take our Magickal Weapons seriously and train with them. At the end of this second phase, the Squire becomes a Knight at an Arming ceremony. The third phase of training is about teaching and leadership. At the end of the third phase the Knight becomes a Master at a Mastering ceremony. While our Sabbat rituals are constantly changing to reflect the creativity of our members, these initiations are fixed, tying us together with tradition.

There is no liquor in Scáthach circles or rituals. We respect Pagan traditions that use wine, mead, or whiskey in Circle or ritual as the "water of life." This "prohibition" isn't intended as a criticism of their practices. Some of us were formerly involved in relationships with alcoholic partners and their families. Liquor is too easily abused. We've been to too many Circles or gatherings where people came drunk or got drunk and were a disruptive influence and/or a drain on the group's magickal energy.

Scáthach is a drug-free tradition. No drugs will be tolerated, period. Members of the Order of Scáthach will obey the laws and uphold them. We do not waste our time in altered states of consciousness, whether drug induced or not. Being Warriors, we teach ourselves to use flow states, enhancing our awareness. Our position on this subject is well documented in *Wiccan Warrior, Full Contact Magick,* and *Magickal Self Defense.* We will support anyone committed to recovery efforts.

The Order of Scáthach is a family tradition, and children are entirely welcome in Circle and out.

MT: Kerr, one of things I found most interesting about your work is within the area of exposing fraudsters. I came across this reading about you on the WitchVox website. Has the work you've done regarding the exposure of phony and hostile stories by some members of the Christian community had any effect on how you view Jesus himself? Do you ever feel that some Christians have misunderstood his teaching?

KC: First let me emphasize that the people that I wrote about in my Witch Hunts articles are a very small but very vocal minority within the greater Christian community. Most Christians I deal with aren't centered in intolerance and hate like the few I wrote about.

I think that many fundamentalist Christians desperately want the mythology and allegory the Bible contains to be literal history. Yes, I definitely believe that the fundamentalist Christians I wrote about misunderstand his teaching. Myth is a powerful tool, but only if you recognize that it is myth.

MT: Was the figure of Jesus, to a lesser or greater degree, part of your upbringing as a child?

KC: No. My parents would definitely have described themselves as Christians, but they never attended church. My father was a Freemason and very much wanted me to become part of that (I didn't). I was involved in Air Cadets from an early age and went on to Military College. Both institutions had mandatory church parades (you could choose Protestant or Catholic; I went with the former) so I certainly was exposed to conventional Western religious services. Jesus was in no way part of my upbringing.

MT: And so presumably Jesus is not an important figure for you?

KC: He isn't important to me at all. Not to be disrespectful: I recognize that he is a major religious figure, but he has no meaning for me. A lot of what Jesus is supposed to have said is the same stuff that Gautama Buddha said. Truth is truth, no matter where you find it.

I should point out that back when I was a cadet at Military College, I was swarmed by a bunch of "Christians" who knew that I was Wiccan and wanted to show me how "Jesus loved me" (they actually said that) by beating me up to try to force me to give up my Pagan beliefs and become a Christian like them. I still bear the scars. I've never understood how people can tell you to your face "Jesus loves you" and then do things like that. Even though I retired from anti-defamation work in 2005 to focus on the Order of Scáthach, I still get hateful emails on a regular basis from people claiming to be followers of Jesus. Let me say again: I recognize that this is coming from a vocal minority within the Christian community that does not reflect the views of most of that community.

MT: In your opinion, was Jesus a historical person?

KC: Yes, I'm convinced that he was a historical person, although I am equally convinced that his history has been rewritten and parts of it suppressed to mythologize and build a religion around him.

MT: Is historical Jesus, as you imagine him to be, reflected in the modern-day Church?

KC: No, I don't think that all modern-day Christian churches reflect his spirit, and even those that do have many members who don't.

MT: So would you say that Pagan traditions reflect the spirit of Jesus better?

KC: Yes, I suppose that it could be said that many Pagan traditions do reflect what you'd describe as his spirit. I think that my Order of Scáthach does.

MT: What feelings or thoughts does the Christmas story conjure up in you?

KC: The elders of the churches took old Pagan myths and rewrote them with Jesus as the principal figure. The same myth of the birth of the Son/Sun can be found in many older mythologies. They even moved the date of his birth to have it coincide with older Pagan festivals. I *don't* think of Christmas: I always work Christmas/Boxing Day to allow my fellow workers to go and observe these festivals. I celebrate Yule (the winter solstice), not Christmas. Christmas has been turned into a commercial rat race where people are desperately trying to buy each other's affections. People should entirely give up on the gifts (that should give the merchants a heart attack!) and focus on celebrating each other. It should be about people, not property.

MT: The same for Easter?

KC: Yes. After all, Easter is even named after a Saxon Goddess of fertility (Eostre) and the Church came up with an incomprehensible method of fixing the date on different days every year. I celebrate Eostre/Ostara rituals on the vernal equinox, same day every year. The Christian Easter has even less significance for me than Christmas does.

MT: If you have one, what is your favourite story, parable, teaching, or symbol of Jesus?

KC: Can't say that I do. I prefer other teachers.

MT: Fair enough. So who was Jesus to you? For example, was he a simple Jewish teacher, a divine prophet, a miracle worker, or a magician?

KC: He was a carpenter who became a Zionist rebel. It may be that he was a "miracle worker." I can do magick, so it is entirely possible that he figured out how to do so as well. A prophet? Definitely. Divine? In my view, the divine is inseparable from the mundane world, so Jesus is as divine as I am and you are. Thou art God/dess.

MT: What lesson do you feel the modern-day Church needs to hear from the person or teaching of Jesus?

KC: Let's start with Mark 12:33: Love thy neighbour like thyself. I'm guessing that since there's so much violence in the world, there are a lot of people that don't love themselves out there.

MT: Is it possible to be both Christian and Pagan?

KC: You know, I've had a surprising number of people tell me that they consider themselves "Christian Pagans/Witches." I find this hard to fathom. Wiccans consider the divine to be inseparable from the world: Christians don't. Christians do guilt and commandments ("thou shalt not"), Wiccans do personal responsibility ("I will not"). I could go on and on with this. If someone is telling me that they're a Christian Pagan, then I suggest to them that they haven't really made up their mind what they are.

MT: What, if anything, can modern-day Pagans learn from the message of Jesus?

KC: As I said earlier, a lot of what Jesus is supposed to have said is stuff other prophets like Buddha said. I'm not about to suggest that there aren't valuable lessons contained in his teachings, but so many in the Pagan community have had negative experiences with people *calling* themselves Christians that I'm not inclined to directly use *any* of Jesus's teachings. Jesus's lessons are there in what I teach, in that we strive to teach sincerity, courtesy, compassion, justice, courage, humility, largesse, and truth. This said, I don't use Jesus as an example to my students. He's not my prophet. We Wiccans don't DO prophets. If someone asks me, "What is the word of God?" I tell them, "Sit down and listen." The divine speaks to us all. You don't need professional clergy to do it for you. As a priest I should help others to find their path, not force people to follow mine.

MT: What, if anything, can Christians learn from modern-day Paganism?

KC: Get your head out of the sand, welcome to the twenty-first century, and stop praying for someone else to solve your problems. Respect the Earth, celebrate life, and take responsibility for your life. Create your own reality.

Religion isn't a "one size fits all" proposition. Put a dozen people in a field, have them witness the same "epiphany" and one will see Jesus, one will see Mary, one will see Erzulie, one will see Gaia, one will see a UFO, and at least one will be looking around, bewildered, saying, "What are you all looking at?" We all are looking at the same thing, but because we come from different educational, social, and cultural backgrounds, we see things differently. Let's celebrate our differences and get along.

MT: Finally, has your work as a corrector of false opinions about Paganism and Wicca had any effect on how Christians see their own Lord? For example have any ever written to you to express a more loving view of their Christ?

KC: Yes, a few have. Mostly I've heard from Christians who already believed that and wanted to write to assure me that they weren't like the hateful, ignorant people I wrote about. I knew that already, but it was nice to hear from them. Not one of the people that I wrote about ever wrote back to say they'd recanted or reconsidered. A few of them wrote back to threaten me. None of them followed through with those threats.

MT: Kerr, thank you. It's been a fascinating discussion. I'm very grateful to you for giving me so much of your time.

KC: You're very welcome, Mark.

ABOUT THE AUTHOR

Kerr Cuhulain retired from the Vancouver Police Department in November 2005 after serving twenty-nine years with them. Kerr is currently working as a police dispatcher. He has been a Wiccan for thirty-nine years and has been involved in anti-defamation activism and hate crime investigation for the Pagan community since 1986. Kerr is the author of the books *Law Enforcement Guide to Wicca, Witch Hunts, Wiccan Warrior, Full Contact Magick,* and *Magickal Self Defense,* as well as the ebook *Modern Knighthood,* with more on the way. He is also the author of a column on anti-defamation issues and hate crimes on The Witches' Voice website called "Witch Hunts." Kerr is the former Preceptor General of Officers of Avalon, an organization representing Neopagan professionals in the emergency services (police, firefighters, emergency medical technicians). He is also the founder of an order of knighthood, the Order of Scáthach.

Thirty Five

......

Gill Edwards

I first came across Gill Edwards when I had one of those moments in a bookshop when a particular book seemed to glisten, shine, and demand being picked up from the shelves. The book was *Wild Love*, and it was exactly what I needed to read at that point in time. I wholeheartedly recommend all of Gill's books; they explore the most profound spiritual themes with depth, elegance, and practicality. Absent is the "pie in the sky/life's a bed of roses" romanticism. Her books' lessons are relevant, human, and life changing. After reading *Wild Love* I wrote to Gill and we became friends. I stayed with her a few times, and she took me on exciting hikes over the incredible Cumbrian hills, where we'd discuss all things from faith to relationships. In the time I knew Gill, I came to see her as a remarkable woman—even fearless. Sadly, she departed this world in November of 2011. However, her legacy and spirit live on in all the treasures she has left us.

Dear Gill, you were an angel on earth, a ray of god-light, and a sweet voice of all-embracing love. Bless you and all your loved ones.

MT: Gill, first of all may I say how delighted I am that you agreed to this interview. Thank you so much for giving me this time.

GE: You're welcome, Mark.

MT: Before we get on to the actual theme of Jesus, perhaps I might invite you to first expound a little on your spiritual tradition which you term New Age/Metaphysical. What do those terms mean to you?

GE: I'm rather ambivalent about the term "New Age," as some people associate it with being irrational and flaky. Since I come from a scientific background, I see myself as fairly balanced between my left and right brain. But the term "New Age" broadly means that this era is a time of a global shift in consciousness, a spiritual awakening. Most New Age teachers also agree that everything is sacred and that the physical world is an aspect of the divine. I'm a panentheist who sees God as both immanent and transcendent. It is a non-dualistic viewpoint. "Metaphysical" means that I teach about the links between the visible and invisible realms, and how thought and consciousness get "downloaded" into physical reality.

MT: Thank you for clarifying those terms and, yes, I would also see myself as a panentheist. So Gill, was the figure of Jesus, to a lesser or greater degree, part of your upbringing as a child?

GE: Yes, I grew up in a broadly Christian (C of E) family, though religion was not part of our everyday life. My mother was once a Sunday school teacher, but I later learnt that she became disillusioned with the Church's approach to women—the "churching" of women and exclusion of women as priests—and so dropped out of any participation. We only went to church very occasionally, such as on Christmas Eve, as my parents liked carol singing!

MT: I can relate very much to your disillusionment with establishment Christianity. But did Jesus as a figure have any impact?

GE: Yes. Growing up in a Christian country, Jesus is the figure who represents love, enlightenment, and higher potential to me—just as it would have been Buddha if I lived in Thailand. Jesus always felt like a very benign figure, even if the Church did not.

MT: So do you see Jesus as a historical person?

GE: Yes, I believe that Jesus was a historical figure. Channelled sources whom I trust have confirmed that is the case, and I have never questioned that anyway.

MT: By "channelled," you mean spiritual mediumship?

GE: Channelling differs from mediumship in that channels access higher consciousness, often from beings who have never been physical. Mediums talk to "dead people," who are often not much wiser than they were when physical!

MT: Ha ha, fabulous. And how do you see Jesus?

GE: I see Jesus, above all, as a representative of unconditional love—and also as a symbol of our higher potential. "All that I have done, you shall do and more" feels like such a crucial phrase—an affirmation that Jesus was simply a wayshower, showing us what we are all capable of when we are aligned with our higher selves and that he wasn't different or special. I certainly don't see Jesus as the only son of God—that feels like one of the most destructive myths of Christianity, and one which I'm sure Jesus would not have wanted to be propagated.

MT: Do you see Jesus's spirit reflected in the modern-day Church?

GE: Some aspects of the Church reflect what I see Jesus as representing, but so often the Church seems to spread fear, judgment, and divisiveness rather than unconditional love and oneness. Perhaps the greatest "loss" as the Church reinterpreted Jesus's teachings was the loss of the immanence of God.

MT: Would you say that Pagan traditions and concepts reflect the spirit of Jesus better?

GE: Pagan traditions are very good at reconnecting us with the immanence of God within humanity, nature, and all things. I suspect that Jesus was a feminist, and yet patriarchal religion distorted his work—promoting the old idea of a judgmental father figure in the sky who was transcendent rather than immanent, and gradually leading to seeing the earth as a "fallen" place, the body as less than sacred (St. Francis's ranting against and beatings of his own body come to mind) and thus leading inevitably and ironically towards a secular society. The Pagan traditions have held on to the divine feminine.

MT: Gill, one of the most alluring Jesus stories of all is the Christmas story. What thoughts or feelings does it conjure up in you?

GE: The Christmas story feels like a story of hope and light being born. It is the old celebration of winter solstice and the "return of the light," and I see this as metaphorical as well as literal. It is a story of love and rebirth, and of the sometimes hostile environment into which love can find itself—the fearful ego that can dismiss or push love away. And yet somehow, love manages to live and survive, and even thrive. The Christmas story makes me feel warm inside, and connects me with hope and love.

MT: And the same for Easter?

GE: The Easter story has a quite different effect on me because of its focus on crucifixion and the cross. Although the cross can be seen as a symbol of the way we get crucified by the conflict between our negative ego and higher self, I don't find it a positive image! The fact that Jesus was resurrected and seen after his death just makes me think "so what?" Everyone survives death, and countless people have been seen after death by those who are open and heart-centred or clairvoyant. So what is the big deal? I don't like the idea that this somehow made Jesus special, as if he was the only person who had ever survived death in his light body. (If he had returned to his *physical* body after the crucifixion, that would make him different!) I think his message was that everyone is eternal, but then it got twisted into seeing him as special—and tragically, it became a story that glorifies self-sacrifice and martyrhood. The *life* of Jesus was the point, not his death!

MT: If you have one, what is your favourite story, parable, teaching, or symbol of Jesus?

GE: I have always loved the Sermon on the Mount. "Ask and it is given. Seek and ye shall find. Knock and the door shall be opened." By "coincidence," this mystical passage was assigned to me at school on the only occasion when I read in front of the whole school assembly, and it had a profound impact. I pondered its meaning for a long time, and it was only when I began to read channelled teachings such as Seth that I came across the idea that we create our own reality—and began to understand that the Sermon on the Mount was about the immanence of God, and also that we live in a loving Universe. "Ask and it is given." The channelled source Abraham has written a book by that title, saying that it sums up how the Universe works. We get what we focus upon. We get what we desire. We get what we believe in and expect. And even when we attract problems into our lives, in a loving Universe, there are always gifts and lessons to be learnt—so nothing is ever wasted. Nothing can ever go wrong. This is the basis of what I teach and write about today, and how I live my life.

MT: Gill, do you think Jesus was a teacher, a prophet, a miracle worker, a magician?

GE: A spiritual teacher, healer-shaman, miracle worker, and magician—yes, all of those. I see him as divine only in the sense that we are all divine.

MT: What lessons do you feel the modern-day Church needs to hear from the person of Jesus?

GE: Firstly, the lessons of unconditional love—beyond blame, beyond guilt, beyond judgment, and beyond fear. And secondly, the immanence (as well as transcendence) of God/Spirit/All That Is. The problem is that we connect with our inner power that way, and I think this is what the Church has always been afraid of! It has always tried to hold on to its power and put priests between us and God. People are fed up with this, and unless the Church hears this message very soon, it will die.

MT: Is it possible to be both Christian and Pagan?

GE: Well, if you are Christian in the sense that you follow the mystical teachings of Jesus, then yes. If it means being fundamentalist and seeing Christianity as the exclusive "one path" to God, then no.

MT: What, if anything, can modern-day Pagans learn from the person of Jesus?

GE: Not sure about this. I suspect that what Jesus taught is already there in Paganism.

MT: What can Christians learn from modern-day Paganism?

GE: That everyone and everything is sacred and divine—including nature. A forest can be our cathedral, and can whisper the greatest of wisdom to us, if only we listen. Connecting with the divinity in nature can help to reconnect us with our own divinity too. Nature has so many lessons to teach. As Seth once said, "No apple tree tries to grow violets"—which is a lovely reminder that we only need to be ourselves, instead of constantly striving to be different or perfect.

MT: I love the image of a forest cathedral. How wonderful. Gill, it's been so marvelous talking with you. Thank you, and many blessings on all your future work.

ABOUT THE AUTHOR

Gill Edwards was a clinical psychologist, also trained in metaphysics, shamanism, energy psychology and energy medicine. She authored *Living Magically*, *Life Is a Gift*, *Wild Love*, *Conscious Medicine*, and other books, and ran Living Magically workshops in the UK and abroad since 1991. Gill saw her life's work as helping to reawaken the divine feminine within ourselves and society – with a focus upon our emotions and intuition, our connectedness with nature, and the 'cosmic dance' between the visible and invisible realms. She physically left this world in November 2011, but she is still with us in many other ways.

Conclusion

......

In a sense, there can be no conclusion to this book for it is (hopefully) going to spark the *beginning* of something new, something that might build bridges of understanding between two very different worlds. Pagan and Christian readers will have had many surprises. For Pagans, Jesus now no longer needs to be that figure of the past, ignored or avoided. The divine baby thrown out with the dirty bath waters can be retrieved. And Christians can now see the Pagan world in a very different light, a much more positive light. In fact, I suspect many Christians will (like myself) have learned a tremendous amount about Jesus Christ from the Pagan elders who've contributed essays and interviews. A conclusion seems somehow strangely wrong.

Yet, on the other hand, there *is* a way to conclude this book *for me*. You see, writing this book has been a remarkable journey—a journey into new territories and one which has changed me considerably. It represents an adventure that began back when I was hugely disillusioned with Christianity (not Jesus) and during a point in my life when I was considering giving up the Christian path altogether. I'd lost my job as a priest and along with that my home, income, pension, and so much more. The officialdom of the Church to which I belonged had not helped at all. In fact some from within it went out of their way to cause trouble for me and my family. It was my Druid friends who were the true saviours during that period. However, as things developed, and as I continued to refuse to ditch Jesus, I started to meet a much more open and progressive kind of Christian. I joined the Progressive Christianity Network Britain and then the USA-based Progressive Christian Alliance and made some wonderful friends. On top of this I discovered the Independent Sacramental Movement and found fellow clergy who were also open to what they could learn from the Druidic and Pagan paths. At last I had found fellow Christians among whom I could be myself. Gradually my belief in the priesthood that was first recognised and authorised in me back in 1996 was rekindled and set alight, but in a very different way.

I have now found a home, an open Christian community where I can continue to offer myself as a broad-minded and eclectic priest while also remaining connected and immersed within the nature-based world. It is called the Open Episcopal Church, and I am delighted and proud to be joining them soon within a colourful and sacramental service. Within that service, a priest and a priestess of the Pagan way will also have a role, to give a divine masculine/divine feminine blessing at the end of the ceremony. I imagine that will be the first time in history when Pagan clergy have had such a role within a Christian Ordination.

·····

But what about my conclusions with regard to Jesus and Christ? Well, let me put it this way: I was still a huge admirer of Jesus when I began the research. That's why I first floated the idea of the book. Now, after nearly three years of work, I can say that I've fallen back in love with him in an even deeper way than before. However, I'm going to remain vague with regard to some of the Christological questions this book has brought to the surface.

Yes, I see Jesus as a fully human being, but I also see him (through the historical-metaphorical Jesus Christ) as a gateway to the Divine experience. I believe in the Cosmic Christ, and that he is akin to Buddha nature. In other words, we all have a spark of him within us. I can say the creeds of the Church as long as I am not required to believe them literally, and I see the Church as a dispenser of Grace, but I also see other religions as dispensers of Divine Grace.

My deepest prayer is that this incredible man who lived a humble peasant's life in a rundown province of the mighty Roman Empire some two thousand years ago—a man of peace who ironically became the object of war and hatred—gradually becomes a symbol of unity. And not just unity within the various sects of Christianity, but unity between Christian and Pagan. I do not wish either path to abandon their own long-cherished beliefs, neither do I want them merge into some putrid ecumenical greyness. No, I want them to do Jesus a favour and place him back within his own first-century Jewish context. Then we can see how his message was adapted, moulded, and mythologized, so that finally his message can become the universal message it deserves. Jesus can be the saviour of Christians, but he can also be a teacher for Pagans and members of non-Christian paths.

Epilogue

......

A Druid Magician and the Son of God

The following words were written by a man who has become a brother to me in various ways. Indeed it was through him that I discovered the Druidic path. Rob Chapman is a magician in the same sense as me (a conjurer) and yet is also an esoteric magician. A Druid for many years, Rob uses illusionary magic to take people deep into the mystery of being. He and I met after he read one of my books and decided to get in touch with me. I was so enthralled by his grasp of stage magic combined with Druid wisdom that I asked if I could attend a Druid ritual. That day was a pivotal point in my spiritual development. It was Rob who, as Druid Chief, initiated me into the Bardic mysteries in an old wet womb-like Welsh mountain cave. As was the custom, each Druid there presented me with a token of my initiation. Rob's was a small wooden pendant necklace with the Druidic Awen symbol burned into the wood. However when I turned it round I noticed it also had a Celtic Cross burned on the other side. I looked up at Rob and with a wink he said, "Whichever path you choose, in the future,

you'll always be my brother." That is a characteristic of the Pagan
men and women I've been privileged to know—a thoroughly generous
openness, a realistic faith that only wants the best for you, and a great
respect for all the gods of the world.

I grew up with the church, even wanted to be a vicar at some point in my life. Yet as time ticked by, I felt myself drawn to the more esoteric paths, a journey which has brought me to the point I find myself at now, which is within the Druid tradition. Druidry is a nature-based spiritual path that gives you a framework to explore your own personal beliefs in relationship to the land you live upon. Therefore there are Pagans, Christians, Jews, and Muslims all looking at their own personal connection with spirit and the divine. For me this is a wonderful thing, and very much at the heart of my feeling toward the church; I never felt that there was a place for personal understanding and connection to Jesus and God through the established church. You could voice an opinion, but at the end of the day "truth" is handed to us by the trained clergy. Therefore I have never really been able to find that personal connection through the church.

Yet Jesus as a character holds an interest for me. I do not believe that he was the Son of God, more an individual that had a message from spirit. Unfortunately I believe that message has been long distorted into political power, rather than a gift to humankind for a better way of being. I do not even know if I believe him to have really existed or whether his life story is just another parable like those he chose to teach by. But does that matter? I think not. The heart of what is important is the message that is given by the story. When I look at the story of Jesus I see the life of a person who made the ultimate sacrifice for the message he felt about so strongly. But this does not make him unique. In fact, it has led to one of the greatest guilt trips ever. Many people have given their lives to the cause they believe in, and even today we have people that do this. We do not always agree with their cause; governments will label them as terrorists and disturbers of the peace. Jesus the anarchist is not an unfair statement. In his life there was great acceptance of people, there was a lack of judgement. He treated all as equal, healing the poor, the sick, and the tax collectors alike. If I think of Jesus as an anarchic anti-establishment defender of the meek, I find a character that resonates. Not the Son of a single divinity, but a son of humankind, who dared to put his head above the parapet, accepting the risks that entailed.

If I look at Jesus from the perspective of my profession as a mystery entertainer, magician, and hypnotist, I discover for myself a couple of things. The first is that there is no emotional connection there at all, which echoes what I have just said, but then there is also the curious performer in me that wants to know how he did his thing. Was it a power from God? In truth all the power that ever existed is here, in this moment, now, be it from God or wherever. I believe in magic, but also am very aware that even in a short time the deed of the performer can become the work of mystics, inflated by the word. People have come up to me telling me that they remember the way I levitated a person in the middle of a room. Now I do not do levitation effects with people, I have hypnotised people to not be able to see an object I am standing on and this gives to them the impression that I am floating. Yet people from the audience will come up saying that they remember me floating. Which says to me that when we look at the miracles and wonders of Jesus, we have to allow for the distortion of perception, the altering of reality. Not as so many say over the last two thousand years, but in what will have been a very short period of time. After a month's time I hear from people that an effect I performed is being reported as an act with true supernatural origins. If we bring the element of hypnosis into this, then we can see how an individual wanting to get over a message, using illusion, suggestion, and hypnosis could quite easily in, say, six months have very tall tales of his achievements being told all over the place. We as human beings make myth, we have the gift of magic, to take something ordinary and make it extraordinary. If some of the performance magicians around today were to go and perform their magic and not tell you it was a trick, in truth there would be a lot of people believing it was real. Someone once said to me, "I know it is all a trick, but you are not like the others—you do real magic." That is someone in this century asking the question. Take that back a couple of millennia and you can see how Jesus as a Holy man could have had the influence that he did. Holy men have always used magic and showmanship to show the masses their powers and the might of Gods. Also, trance as a part of religious practice is as old as belief. The Bible has many references to people falling into sleep, falling into trance; indeed, God put Adam to sleep to remove a rib, Satan used suggestion to influence Eve. Paul speaks of being in trance whilst in the Temple (Acts 22:17). Indeed, Acts is full of accounts of the apostles gazing into the eyes of people who are then healed. This man was listening to Paul speak, and when he fixed his gaze upon him and saw that he had faith to be made well, said with a loud voice, "Stand upright on your feet." The man leaped up and began to walk (Acts 14:9–10).

This then leads us to the point that, yes magic trickery was known of at the time, but hypnosis as we see and think of it is a concept of the last few centuries. In the time of Jesus, the ability to influence people through touch, eye contact, and the spoken word would have been an amazing performance to behold and one that again would easily be retold and embellished at a quick pace.

So Jesus as a mystic with a message who had skills that we would now associate with magicians is, I feel, a realistic image. Living in a universe where all things stem from one point—be it a big bang, the divine, or God creating the world in seven days—means Jesus really did do his thing through the power of God. However, each and every one of us does what we do because of that one moment where it all began.

I would love to be able to sit down with Jesus and hear what he has to say about the world we live in and the way the Church has developed since his passing. I feel that our history of persecutions, holy war, and torture would turn his soul. A man who taught "love thy neighbor" would see a history of hate and fear. Indeed, I am sure over a drink or two he would laugh out loud at how his actions had been distorted and changed. Who knows, he may even be willing to share a trick or two.

In compiling these few thoughts, I come to a closer idea of my relationship with Jesus the man, the myth, the rebel. And it is a relationship of sorrow; my heart draws a tear for a way of life that could be so beautiful. A man died for that which has become dogmatic and soulless. His message has become a power-based religion so far removed from what I feel was its original. I would want to take the man in my arms and use his own words.

"Forgive them ... they know not what they do."

ABOUT THE AUTHOR

Rob Chapman is a mystery entertainer; Druid of the Order of Bards, Ovates, and Druids; and a initiate of the Alexandrian tradition of the Craft. He has spent several years running public events and retreats as a founder of the Earthworks Druidic Community, which unfortunately is no more. At present, he is putting his energies into developing his performance work and is married to the lovely Rowena.

Bibliography

······

Baldet, Jacques. *Jesus the Rabbi Prophet.* Rochester, VT: Inner Traditions, 2005.

Berry, Thomas. *The Great Work: Our Way into the Future.* New York: Bell Tower, 1999.

Besant, Annie. *Esoteric Christianity.* Wheaton, IL: Quest Books, 2006.

Bloom, William. *Psychic Protection.* London: Piatkus, 1996.

Bonwick, James. *Irish Druids and Old Irish Religions.* (reprint) New York: Dorset Press, 1986.

Borg, Marcus. *Meeting Jesus Again for the First Time.* New York: Harper-Collins, 1994.

Borg, Marcus, and N. T. Wright. *The Meaning of Jesus.* London: Harper-One, 1999.

Borgeaud, Philippe. *The Cult of Pan in Ancient Greece.* Translated by Kathleen Atlass and James Redfield. Chicago: University of Chicago Press, 1988.

Boulton, David. *Who on Earth Was Jesus?* New Alresford, Hampshire: O-Books, 2008.

Calhoun, Peter. *Soul on Fire.* New York: Hay House, 2006.

Chilton, Bruce. *Rabbi Jesus.* New York: Doubleday, 2000.

Chopra, Deepak. *The Third Jesus.* London: Rider, 2008.

Churcher, John. *Setting Jesus Free.* New Alresford, Hampshire: O-Books, 2009.

Clifton, Chas S. *Her Hidden Children: The Rise of Wicca and Paganism in America.* Lanham, MD: AltaMira, 2006.

Copenhaver, Brian, ed. *Hermetica.* Cambridge: Cambridge University Press, 1992.

Crossan, John Dominic. *Jesus: A Revolutionary Biography.* San Francisco: HarperCollins, 1995.

Crowley, Aleister. *Magick.* London: Routledge & Kegan Paul, 1985.

Cunningham, Jim, ed. *Nudity & Christianity.* Bloomington, IN: Author House 2006.

Cunningham, Scott. *Wicca: A Guide for the Solitary Practitioner.* St. Paul, MN: Llewellyn Worldwide, 2004.

Deren, Maya. *Divine Horsemen.* London: Thames and Hudson, 1953.

DiZerega, Gus. *Pagans and Christians: The Personal Spiritual Experience.* St. Paul, MN: Llewellyn Worldwide, 2001.

Draco, Melusine, ed. *The Coven of the Scales: Collected Writings of A. R. Clay-Egerton.* London: Ignotus Press, 2002.

Ehrenreich, Barbara. *Dancing in the Streets.* New York: Metropolitan Books, 2006.

Eliade, Mircea. *Shamanism: Archaic Techniques of Ecstasy.* New York: Pantheon Books, 1964.

Eliot, T. S. *Four Quartets*. San Diego: Harcourt Brace Jovanovich, 1943.

Farrar, Janet, and Stewart Farrar. *A Witches' Bible*. London: Hale, 1984.

———. *The Witch's God*. Blaine, WA: Phoenix Publishing, 1989.

Ford-Grabowsky, Mary. *The Making of a Prophet: Matthew Fox at 60*. Self-published, 2000.

Fortune, Dion. *Applied Magic*. Wellingborough, Northamptonshire: The Aquarian Press, 1962.

———. *Mystical Meditations on the Collects*. York Beach, ME: Weiser, 1991.

Fox, Matthew. *The Coming of the Cosmic Christ*. New York: HarperCollins, 1988.

———. *Confessions: The Making of a Post-Denominational Priest*. San Francisco: HarperSanFrancisco, 1996.

———. *Creativity: Where the Divine and the Human Meet*. New York: Jeremy P. Tarcher, 2002.

———. *The Hidden Spirituality of Men: Ten Metaphors to Awaken the Sacred Masculine*. Novato, CA: New World Library, 2010.

———. *One River, Many Wells: Wisdom Springing from Global Faiths*. New York: Jeremy P. Tarcher, 2000.

———. *Wrestling with the Prophets*. New York: Jeremy P. Tarcher, 2003.

Godwin, Joscelyn. *The Theosophical Enlightenment*. Albany, NY: State University of New York Press, 1994.

Golub, Deborah. "Cultural Variations in Multiple Personality Disorder," in Lewis M. Cohen, Joan N. Berzoff, and Mark R. Elin, eds., *Dissociative Identity Disorder: Theoretical and Treatment Controversies*. Northvale, NJ: Jason Aronson, 1995.

Grant, Kenneth, and Steffi Grant. *Zos Speaks*. London: Fulgur, 1998.

Graves, Robert. *The White Goddess*. London: Faber and Faber, 1981.

Greer, John Michael. *The Druidry Handbook.* York Beach, ME: Weiser, 2006.

Harpur, Tom. *The Pagan Christ.* Toronto: Thomas Allen Publishers, 2004.

Harvey, Graham, and Charlotte Hardman, eds. *Pagan Pathways.* London: Thorsons, 1995.

Harvey, Graham. *Contemporary Paganism.* New York: New York University Press, 1997.

Herrmann, Steven. *William Everson: The Shaman's Call, Interviews, Introduction, and Commentaries.* New York: Eloquent Books, 2009.

———. *Walt Whitman: Shamanism, Spiritual Democracy and the World Soul.* New York: Eloquent Books, 2010.

Higginbotham, Joyce, and River Higginbotham. *ChristoPaganism: An Inclusive Path.* Woodbury, MN: Llewellyn Worldwide, 2009.

Hogart, R. C. *The Hymns of Orpheus.* Grand Rapids, MI: Phanes Press, 1993.

Hutton, Ronald. *Triumph of the Moon.* Oxford: Oxford University Press, 1999.

Iamblichus. *De Mysteriis,* trans. Thomas Taylor. London: Bertram Dobell & Reeves and Turner, 1895.

Meyer, Marvin, and Richard Smith, eds. *Ancient Christian Magic: Coptic Texts of Ritual Power.* San Francisco: HarperSanFrancisco, 1994.

Meyers, Robin R. *Saving Jesus from the Church.* New York: HarperCollins, 2009.

Mikalson, Jon D. *Athenian Popular Religion.* Chapel Hill, NC: University of North Carolina Press, 1983.

Morien (Owen Morgan). *The Light in Britannia.* London: Whittaker & Co., 1887.

Nolan, Albert. *Jesus Before Christianity.* London: Darton, Longman, and Todd, 1977.

O'Laoire, Sean, Fr. *Souls on Safari*. Tuscon, AZ: Wheatmark, 2006.

The Order of Bards, Ovates, and Druids. *Gwers of the Bardic Grade*. Lewes, UK: OBOD, 2001.

Pagels, Elaine. *Beyond Belief*. London: Pan, 2005.

Paladin, Lynda. *Painting the Dream: The Visionary Art of Navajo Painter David Chethlahe Paladin*. Rochester, VT: Part Street Press, 1992.

Pollack, Rachel. *Tarot Wisdom*. Woodbury, MN: Llewellyn Worldwide, 2008.

Roberts, Richard. "The Chthonic Imperative: Gender, Religion and the Battle for the Earth" in Joanne Pearson, Richard H. Roberts, and Geoffrey Samuel (eds.), *Nature Religion Today: Paganism in the Modern World*. Edinburgh: Edinburgh University Press, 1998.

Sahajananda, John Martin. *You Are the Light: Rediscovering the Eastern Jesus*. New Alresford, Hampshire: O-Books, 2003.

Scharding, Michael, ed. *A Reformed Druid Anthology*. Online publication: Drynemetum Press, 2004.

Starhawk. *The Spiral Dance*. San Francisco: Harper & Row, 1979.

Townsend, Mark. *The Gospel of Falling Down*. New Alresford, Hampshire: O-Books, 2007.

———. *The Magician's Tale*. New Alresford, Hampshire: O-Books, 2008.

———. *Path of the Blue Raven*. New Alresford, Hampshire: O-Books, 2009.

Trible, Phyllis. *God and the Rhetoric of Sexuality: Overtures to Biblical Theology*. Philadelphia: Fortress, 1978.

Van Alphen, Markus. *Jesus Christ and His True Disciples*. The Esoteric Christianity E-Magazine, 2007.

Waite, A. E. *The Pictorial Key to the Tarot*. Stamford, CT: US Games Systems, 1990.

Wallace, Mark. *Finding God in a Singing River.* Minneapolis, MN: Augsburg Fortress, 2005.

West, Kate. *The Real Witches Handbook.* London: Thorsons, 2001.

Weyler, Rex. *The Jesus Sayings.* Toronto: House of Anansi Press, 2008.

Wojtyla, Karol. *Love and Responsibility,* trans. H. T. Willetts. San Francisco: Ignatius Press, 1993.

Further Reading

......

–The Historical Jesus–

Borg, Marcus, and N. T. Wright. *The Meaning of Jesus.* London: Harper-One, 1999.

Borg, Marcus. *Meeting Jesus Again for the First Time.* New York: Harper Collins, 1994.

Boulton, David. *Who on Earth Was Jesus?* New Alresford, Hampshire: O-Books, 2008.

Chilton, Bruce. *Rabbi Jesus.* New York: Doubleday, 2000.

Churcher, John. *Setting Jesus Free.* New Alresford, Hampshire: O-Books, 2009.

Crossan, John Dominic. *Jesus a Revolutionary Biography.* San Francisco: Harper Collins, 1995.

Funk, Robert W., Roy W. Hoover, and the Jesus Seminar. *The Five Gospels.* New York: HarperOne, 1993.

Mead, G. R. S., *The Hymn of Jesus.* London: Watkins, 1907.

Meyers, Robin R. *Saving Jesus from the Church.* New York: HarperCollins, 2009.

Murphy, Catherine M. *The Historical Jesus for Dummies.* Hoboken, NJ: Wiley Publishing, 2008.

Nolan, Albert. *Jesus Before Christianity.* London: Darton Longman and Todd, 1977.

Pullman, Philip. *The Good Man Jesus and the Scoundrel Christ.* Edinburgh: Canongate Books, 2010.

Spong, John Shelby. *Jesus for the Non-Religious.* New York: HarperCollins, 2007.

Weyler, Rex. *The Jesus Sayings.* Toronto: House of Anansi Press, 2008.

–Christ and Cosmic Christ–

Besant, Annie. *Esoteric Christianity.* Wheaton, IL: Quest Books, 2006 edition.

Chopra, Deepak. *The Third Jesus.* New York: Harmony, 2008.

Fox, Matthew. *The Coming of the Cosmic Christ.* New York: HarperCollins, 1988.

Harpur, Tom. *The Pagan Christ.* Toronto: Thomas Allen Publishers, 2004.

O'Laoire, Sean. *Souls on Safari.* Tuscon: Wheatmark, 2006.

Pagels, Elaine. *Beyond Belief.* London: Pan, 2005.

Sahajananda, John Martin. *You Are the Light: Rediscovering the Eastern Jesus.* New Alresford, Hampshire: O-Books, 2003.

Tolle, Eckhart. *A New Earth.* London: Penguin Books, 2006.

Endnotes

......

–Dedication–

1. Gus DiZerega, *Pagans and Christians: The Personal Spiritual Experience* (St. Paul, MN: Llewellyn Worldwide, 2001), 214.

–Foreword–

2. Steven Herrmann, *William Everson: The Shaman's Call, Interviews, Introduction, and Commentaries* (New York: Eloquent Books, 2009), 94.

3. Ibid., 95.

4. See Matthew Fox, "Otto Rank as Mystic and Prophet in the Creation Spirituality Tradition," at www.matthewfox.org.

5. Herrmann, *William Everson*, 100.

6. I tell the story in Matthew Fox, *Creativity: Where the Divine and the Human Meet* (New York: Jeremy P. Tarcher, 2002), 173. See also: Lynda Paladin, *Painting the Dream: The Visionary Art of Navajo Painter David Chethlahe Paladin* (Rochester, VT: Part Street Press, 1992).

7. Herrmann, *William Everson*, 105.

8. Steven B. Herrmann, *Walt Whitman: Shamanism, Spiritual Democracy, and the World Soul* (New York: Eloquent Books, 2010), 255.

9. Ibid., 255, 256.

10. Ibid., 256.

11. Ibid., 42.

12. Ibid., ix.

13. Ibid., 258.

14. Ibid., 287, 288.

15. Mary Ford-Grabowsky, *The Making of a Prophet: Matthew Fox at 60* (Self-published, 2000), 70, 71.

16. Barbara Ehrenreich, *Dancing in the Streets* (New York: Metropolitan Books, 2006), 21, 22, 28, 29.

17. I have described some of these experiences in Matthew Fox, *Confessions: The Making of a Post-Denominational Priest* (San Francisco: HarperSanFrancisco, 1996) and I have treated some of the intellectual gifts I have received from earth-based spiritual teachings in Matthew Fox, *Wrestling with the Prophets* (New York: Jeremy Tarcher, 2003), chapters 6, 7, 8. So much of pre-modern Christian mysticism was creation-centered and earth-based as well, thus Hildegard of Bingen, Meister Eckhart, and Thomas Aquinas among others carry deeper similarities to earth-based religions than to heady modern anthropocentric theologists.

18. Matthew Fox, *One River, Many Wells: Wisdom Springing from Global Faiths* (New York: Jeremy Tarcher, 2000), 119.

19. I treat this subject at some length in Matthew Fox, *The Hidden Spirituality of Men: Ten Metaphors to Awaken the Sacred Masculine* (Novato, CA: New World Library, 2010)

20. Thomas Berry, *The Great Work: Our Way into the Future* (New York: Bell Tower, 1999), 190.

–Introduction–

21. Albert Nolan, *Jesus Before Christianity* (London: Darton Longman and Todd, 1977), 3.

–Chapter One–

22. Janet and Stewart Farrar, *The Witch's God* (Blaine, WA: Phoenix Publishing, 1989), 52.

–Chapter Two–

23. Robin R. Meyers, *Saving Jesus from the Church* (New York: HarperCollins, 2009), 10.

24. Jacques Baldet, *Jesus the Rabbi Prophet* (Rochester VT: Inner Traditions), 1.

25. Marcus Borg, *Meeting Jesus Again for the First Time* (New York: Harper Collins, 1994), 28, 29.

26. Gospel of Mark 14:50.

27. Gospel of Matthew 3:13–17.

28. Mark's use of the Greek language is far more basic and "primitive" than Luke or Matthew, who will state a parallel Jesus quotation with far more eloquence than Mark. Mark also occasionally uses an unusual word or phrase where Matthew uses a more common one. This clearly makes more sense if Matthew was revising Mark, rather than the other way round. An internet search for "Marcan Priority" will give you ample examples of the reasons why this is the most commonly held position among scholars.

29. John Dominic Crossan, *Jesus: A Revolutionary Biography* (San Francisco: HarperCollins, 1995), xviii, xix.

30. Many archaeologists and theological scholars now believe that Jesus was actually born in Nazareth, or perhaps Bethlehem of Galilee, a small town not far from Nazareth. They use both biblical and archaeological evidence to support their theory. This is a huge subject, but one example is this: throughout the Bible, Jesus is referred to as 'Jesus of Nazareth,' not 'Jesus of Bethlehem.' In John there's even a passage questioning Jesus's legitimacy because he's from Galilee and not Judaea where the long-awaited messiah was expected to come from (7:41–43).

31. A large number of modern scholars hold that Jesus may have been a direct follower in John the Baptist's movement, and later went his own way with a less desert-based/aesthetic message and a more urban-based/grace-filled one.

32. Flavius Josephus was a first-century Jew and Roman citizen who wrote the *Antiquities of the Jews* in 93 CE. Here Jesus is mentioned twice, the first passage being called the *Testimonium Flavianum,* where it says: "About this time came Jesus, a wise man, if indeed it is appropriate to call him a man. For he was a performer of paradoxical feats, a teacher of people who accept the unusual with pleasure, and he won over many of the Jews and also many Greeks." It must be said that there are concerns about the authenticity of certain parts of Josephus and it is widely held by scholars that at least part of the work had been altered by a later scribe.

33. A biblical example can be found in Matthew 12:24–30, where the Pharisees accused Jesus of casting out demons by the power of Satan/Beelzebub. A non-biblical example can be seen in the *Babylonian Talmud* (late first or second century CE) Babylonian Sanhedrin 43a–b: "On the eve of the Passover they hanged Yeshu and the herald went before him for forty days saying [Yeshu] is going forth to be stoned in that he hath

practiced sorcery and beguiled and led astray Israel. It is taught: On the eve of Passover they hung Yeshu and the crier went forth for forty days beforehand declaring that '[Yeshu] is going to be stoned for practicing witchcraft, for enticing and leading Israel astray. Anyone who knows something to clear him should come forth and exonerate him.' But no one had anything exonerating for him and they hung him on the eve of Passover. Ulla said: Would one think that we should look for exonerating evidence for him? He was an enticer and G-d said (Deuteronomy 13:9) 'Show him no pity or compassion, and do not shield him.' Yeshu was different because he was close to the government."

–Chapter Three–

34. Borg, *Meeting Jesus*, 10.

35. Baldet, *Rabbi Prophet*, 120.

36. Borg, *Meeting Jesus*, 32, 33.

37. Visions: See Numbers 12:6 and Jeremiah 23:28.

    Dreams and their interpretation: See Genesis 41:12–13 and Daniel 2:16, 19; 7:15–16; 8:15–16.

    Direct communications/meetings with God or angels: See Genesis 32:1–33:11 and Exodus 33:7–34:35.

    Miracles of healing/dead raising: See 1 Kings 17:17–24 and 2 Kings 4:18–37.

    Miracles of creating/multiplying substances: See 2 Kings 4:1–7 and 2 Kings 4:42–44.

38. Borg, *Meeting Jesus*, 35, 36.

39. Bruce Chilton, *Rabbi Jesus* (New York: Doubleday, 2000), 106, 109.

40. Peter Calhoun, *Soul on Fire* (New York: Hay House, 2006), xiii.

41. Ibid., 8.

42. Robin R. Meyers, *Saving Jesus from the Church* (New York: HarperCollins, 2009), 124.

43. See Phyllis Trible, *God and the Rhetoric of Sexuality,* Overtures to Biblical Theology (Philadelphia: Fortress, 1978).

44. Scott Cunningham, *Wicca: A Guide for the Solitary Practitioner* (St. Paul, MN: Llewellyn Worldwide, 2004), 5.

45. DiZerega, *Pagans and Christians,* 93.

46. Ibid., 94.

47. John Churcher, *Setting Jesus Free* (New Alresford, Hampshire: O-Books, 2009), 19, 20.

48. Ibid., 19.

49. Meyers, *Saving Jesus,* 123.

50. Ibid., 92.

51. Ibid., 52.

52. For example see Luke 6:1–4, Luke 7:36–8:3, and Matthew 11:19.

53. Baldet, *Jesus the Rabbi Prophet,* pp. 112, 113: He gives evidence of how Jesus clearly had something of a bias towards the *am ha-eretz*—the "country people" or "people of the earth" of the looked-down-upon northern province of Galilee.

54. Albert Nolan, *Jesus Before Christianity* (London: Darton Longman and Todd, 1977), 37.

55. Ibid., 41.

56. DiZerega, *Pagans and Christans,* 94.

57. Fr. Sean O'Laoire, *Souls on Safari,* (Tuscon, AZ: Wheatmark, 2006), 36, 37.

58. Martha and Mary, Luke 10:38–42.

59. Mary Magdalene, Luke 8:2–3, Mark 15:40, Matthew 27:56, John 19:25, and Luke 23:49.

60. Nolan, *Jesus Before Christianity*, 57.

61. Gospel of Luke 10:30–37.

62. Gospel of Luke 7:1–10.

63. Gospel of Matthew 15:22–28.

64. Rex Weyler, *The Jesus Sayings* (Toronto, ON: House of Anansi Press, 2008), 314.

65. Brother John Martin Sahajananda, *You Are the Light: Rediscovering the Eastern Jesus* (New Alresford, Hampshire: O-Books, 2003), 43.

66. Ibid., 45.

67. Ibid., 45.

68. Ibid., 47.

–Chapter Four–

69. Janet and Stewart Farrar, *A Witches Bible* (London: Hale, 1984), 177.

70. Baldet, *Rabbi Prophet*, 41.

71. Borg, *Meeting Jesus*, 29.

72. See Gospels of Mark 10:18 and Luke 18:18–19.

73. Nolan, *Jesus Before Christianity*, 122.

74. Meyers, *Saving Jesus*, 14.

75. The Gospel of Thomas translation by Thomas O. Lambdin (Coptic version), Saying 3.

76. Thomas resembles the hypothetical Q both in content and the fact that it is just a collection of sayings. Because of the close parallel between much of Thomas and the synoptic Gospels, some scholars suggest that Thomas is actually based on Q or is

actually Q itself. However, these remain only speculations, as there is no conclusive evidence that Q ever existed.

77. To put the argument very simply, it's all about how someone becomes "justified" and "saved" from sin in order to get to heaven after death. The "Works" answer is that we work for our salvation through good deeds, observing holy traditions, and being obedient to God through the Church's laws, etc. The opposing "Faith" answer is that we are saved through our faith in God alone, as long as we believe in Jesus's sacrificial death and are repentant of our sins. In my opinion both arguments are flawed (but that can wait for another book!).

78. See the Gospel of Thomas, Sayings 24 and 26.

79. Elaine Pagels, *Beyond Belief* (London: Pan, 2005), 32.

80. Ibid., 41.

81. Ibid., 57.

–Chapter Five–

82. Rachel Pollack, *Tarot Wisdom* (Woodbury, MN: Llewellyn Worldwide, 2008), 147.

83. See Josephus, Pliny the Younger, Tacitus, etc. An Internet search on any of these names in relation to Jesus will bring up much fascinating information.

–Chapter Six–

84. Deepak Chopra, *The Third Jesus* (London: Rider, 2008), 23.

85. Marcus Borg and N.T. Wright, *The Meaning of Jesus* (London: HarperOne, 1999), 146.

86. Ibid., 147.

87. Ibid., 147.

88. Justin Martyr, Dial, with Trypho, ch. lxix; ANF. i, 233.

89. Mark Townsend, *Path of the Blue Raven* (New Alresford, Hampshire: O-Books, 2009), 79.

90. William Bloom, *Psychic Protection* (London: Piatkus, 1996), 63.

91. DiZerega, *Pagans and Christians*, 213.

92. Mark Townsend, quoted from *Pagan Dawn,* Imbolc/Spring Equinox edition, 2010 No: 174.

93. The Order of Bards, Ovates, and Druids, *Gwers of the Bardic Grade* (Lewes, UK: OBOD 2001), Gwers 14.

94. Ibid.

95. Mark Townsend, *The Gospel of Falling Down* (New Alresford, Hampshire: O-Books, 2007), 71–77.

–Chapter Seven–

96. My research for this book has enlightened me to the fact that when the accounts of the resurrection are submitted to the "criteria of historicity" (even by the most progressive of biblical scholars), they pass most of the tests.

97. Tom Harpur, quoted (with permission) from the author's website, www.tomharpur.com

98. Annie Besant, *Esoteric Christianity* (Wheaton, IL: Quest Books, 2006 edition), 66.

99. Ibid., 60.

100. Bp. Markus Van Alphen, *Jesus Christ and His True Disciples* (The Esoteric Christianity E-Magazine, 2007).

101. Matthew Fox, *The Coming of the Cosmic Christ* (New York: HarperCollins, 1988), 111.

102. St. Francis of Assisi—1224 CE, From "The Canticle of the Sun."

103. Fr. Richard Rohr, *The Cosmic Christ* (audio CD) (Southport, UK: Agape Ministries, 2000).

104. Ibid.

105. Ibid.

106. Genesis 1:26.

107. Wisdom 6:12 (NRSV).

108. Ibid., 6:16.

109. Ibid., 7:22b–25b.

110. Ibid., 7:27.

111. Proverbs 8:22 (NRSV).

112. Ibid., 8:27–31.

113. 2 Corinthians 12:1–10 (NRSV).

114. Gospel of John 1:1.

115. Gospel of John 1:3, 4 (NIV).

116. Matthew Fox, *Radical Prayer, Love in Action* (audio CD) (Louisville, CO: Sounds True, 2003).

117. Ibid.

118. Fr. Richard Rohr, *The Cosmic Christ* (audio CD) (Southport, UK: Agape Ministries, 2000).

119. Ibid.

120. Ibid.

121. O'Laoire, *Souls on Safari*, 130.

–Part Two–

122. Janet and Stewart Farrar, *A Witches' Bible: The Complete Witches' Handbook* (London: Hale, 1984), 122.

–Chapter Fifteen–

123. References: *Shamanism: Archaic Techniques of Ecstasy* by Mircea Eliade (New York: Pantheon Books, 1964).

–Chapter Seventeen–

124. T. S. Eliot, *Four Quartets* (Harcourt Brace Jovanovich, 1943), 35.

125. Dion Fortune, *Mystical Meditations on the Collects* (York Beach, ME: Weiser, 1991).

126. See John Michael Greer, *The Druidry Handbook* (York Beach, ME: Weiser, 2006), 9–43 for a history of the Druid Revival.

127. This is the basic creed of the Reformed Druids of North America (RDNA). See David Frangquist, "Outline of the Foundation of Fundamentals," in Michael Scharding, ed., *A Reformed Druid Anthology* (Drynemetum Press, 2004), 33–34.

128. James Bonwick, *Irish Druids and Old Irish Religions* (repr. Dorset Press, 1986), 3–5.

129. Morien (Owen Morgan), *The Light in Britannia* (Daniel Owen, 1887).

130. See Joscelyn Godwin, *The Theosophical Enlightenment* (State University of New York Press, 1994) for a readable history of these schools of thought.

131. For a useful exploration of these issues, see Philippe Borgeaud, *The Cult of Pan in Ancient Greece,* tr. Kathleen Atlass and James Redfield (Univ. of Chicago Press, 1988) and Jon D. Mikalson, *Athenian Popular Religion* (University of North Carolina Press, 1983)

132. John 3:30

133. John 10:10.

134. See the discussion in Godwin, *Theosophical Enlightenment.*

–Chapter Eighteen–

Editor's note: Sources used for this essay follow:

135. *Holy Bible*, Revised Standard Version.

Maya Deren, *Divine Horsemen* (London: Thames and Hudson, 1953).

Part 4 of Chapter 1 provides a description and analysis of the process by which the dead become ancestral deities.

Dion Fortune, *Applied Magic* (Wellingborough, Northamptonshire: The Aquarian Press, 1962).

Chapter III, "The Group Mind," explores the theory behind artificial elementals and god-forms.

Deborah Golub, "Cultural Variations in Multiple Personality Disorder," *Dissociative Identity Disorder: Theoretical and Treatment Controversies,* edited by Lewis M. Cohen, Joan N. Berzoff, and Mark R. Elin (Northvale, NJ: Jason Aronson, 1995).

Iamblichus, *De Mysteriis,* trans. Thomas Taylor. Hastings, UK: Cthonios Books, 1895.

–Chapter Nineteen–

136. See for example, Vivianne Crowley, "Wicca as a Modern-Day Mystery Religion" in Graham Harvey and Charlotte Hardman (eds.), *Pagan Pathways* (London: Thorsons, 1995), 83, 90.

137. Fortune, *Mystical Meditations,* 32.

138. Mead, G. R. S., *The Hymn of Jesus* (London: Watkins, 1907), 17.

139. Ibid., 18.

140. Ibid., 19.

141. Ibid., 21–23.

142. Robert Graves, *The White Goddess* (London: Faber and Faber, 1981), 30–31.

143. Kenneth and Steffi Grant, *Zos Speaks* (London: Fulgur, 1998), 125–26.

144. http://www.hermetic.com/bey/mundus_imaginalis.htm (last accessed February 22, 2010).

145. Mead, *Hymn of Jesus*, 23.

146. Ibid., 25.

147. Ibid., 52.

148. Ibid., 55.

149. Ibid., 23.

150. Aleister Crowley, *Magick* (London: Routledge & Kegan Paul, 1985), 125–27.

151. R. C. Hogart, *The Hymns of Orpheus* (Grand Rapids, MI: Phanes Press, 1993).

152. Mead, *Hymn of Jesus*, 24.

153. Ibid., 25.

154. Brian P. Copenhaver, ed. *Hermetica* (Cambridge: Cambridge University Press, 1992). See the use of metaphor in the discourse of the mixing bowl, 15–17, or the method of teaching employed 18–20.

–Chapter Twenty–

155. Pope John Paul II, *Theology of the Body*, Pauline Books, 1997, 76.

156. Fox, *Hidden Spirituality:* Here he explores the Green Man as a powerful male metaphor for fertility and generativity, recalling Hildegard of Bingen calling Jesus "a green man."

157. "The Torah indirectly alludes to Aaron's nakedness in the ceremony of his washing and investiture (Leviticus 8:6f). This rite of initiation into the priesthood took place in about 1000 BC." Michael A.Kowalewski, The Naked Baptism of Christ, in *Nudity & Christianity*, ed. Jim Cunningham (Author House 2006), 431.

158. John 19:23–26 (Young's Literal Translation).

159. John 20:7 (New International Version).

160. "Naked on the Cross" by Michael A.Kowalewski, in *Nudity & Christianity*, ed. Jim Cunningham (Author House, 2006), 349, quoting St. Jerome, Epistle 58 AD Paulinum.

161. Pope John Paul II, *Theology of the Body*, 76. Christopher West, writing on a website dedicated to John Paul's *Theology of the Body*, states: "The TB calls us to look deeply into our own hearts, to look past our wounds and the scars of sin, past our disordered desires. If we're able to do that we discover God's original plan for creating us as male and female still 'echoing' within us. By glimpsing at that 'original vision,' we can almost taste the original experience of bodily integrity and freedom—of nakedness without shame. And we begin to sense a plan for our sexuality so grand, so wondrous, that we can scarcely allow our hearts to take it in." http://www. theologyofthebody.net/index.php?option=com_content&task =view&id=27&Itemid=48.

162. Karol Wojtyla, *Love and Responsibility*, trans. H.T. Willetts (San Francisco: Ignatius Press, 1981), 176–92.

163. See "Was Jesus Married?" by Bill McKeever at http://mrm.org /jesus-married.

164. See Bruce Chilton *Mary Magdalene: A Biography* (Image, 2006) for an accessible but well-researched book by a biblical

theologian that supports a possible relationship between Mary and Jesus.

165. It is important to note that the crucifix was not used as a Christian symbol until the fifth century.

–Chapter Twenty-One–

166. A. E. Waite, *The Pictorial Key to the Tarot* (Stamford, CT: US Games Systems, 1990), 156.

–Chapter Twenty-Two–

167. Rex Weyler, *The Jesus Sayings: The Quest for His Authentic Message* (Toronto, ON: House of Anansi Press, 2008).

168. The Gnostic Gospels, such as the Nag Hammadi Library, contain texts that show every evidence of being authentic writings of the followers of Jesus, but were condemned and banned by the orthodox church hierarchy. Indeed, the Gospel of Thomas is considered by experts and Christian historians to be the source for the material in the Gospels of Matthew, Mark, and Luke. The political and religious battles that led to this outcome are well documented in Pagels's important study, *The Gnostic Gospels* (New York: Vintage Books, 1981).

169. Thomas 3, 51, 109, 113. Matthew 13:44. Mark 13:21. Luke 10:16. Mary 4:3–4. According to Pagels in *The Gnostic Gospels,* Jesus "rejects as naïve ... the idea that the Kingdom of God is an actual event expected in history," and saw it instead as "a state of transformed consciousness." (137).

170. Thomas 3, 20, 51, 113. Matthew 13:31–32, 24:26. Mark 4:30–32. Luke 13:18–19, 17:23.

171. Thomas 96–97. Matthew 13:33. Luke 13:20–21.

172. Thomas 2, 92, 94. Matthew 7:7–8. Mark 11:24. Luke 11:9. John 14–16. Mary 4:7. Dialogue of the Saviour 70. Apocryphon of James.

173. Thomas 2, 3, 5, 6, 92. Mark 4:22. Matthew 10:26. Luke 12:2. 1 Corinthians 12:7–11. Dialogue of the Saviour 44. Gospel of Mary.

174. Wiccan Charge of the Star Goddess can be read at http://www .wicca-spirituality.com/charge-of-the-star-goddess.html.

175. (Serving two masters— i.e., being less than fully committed to the Divine, seeking both earthly success and spiritual reward) Thomas 47. Matthew 6:24. Luke 16:13. (Letting the dead bury the dead—i.e., leaving the affairs of the material world to those who do not seek Divine life) Matthew 8:22. Luke 9:59–60. Apocryphon of James.

176. Thomas 24, 33. Mark 4:21. Matthew 5:14–16. Luke 8:16, 11:33. John 8, 11, 12. Gospel of Mary. Dialogue of the Saviour 14, 34.

177. Dr. Martin Luther King: "No one can be free until all are free."

178. Thomas 14, 45. Mark 7:15. Matthew 7:16, 12:33, 15:11. Luke 6:43–45. James 3:12.

179. Thomas 45. Matthew 7:16–20. Luke 6:43–45.

180. Thomas 48, 106. Mark 11:22–23. Luke 17:6. 1 Corinthians 12:10.

181. Every act of affirmation, positive thinking, visualization, and prayer is a form of magick: they aim to make miracles.

182. (Know yourself) Thomas 3, 70. Dialogue of the Saviour 30, 35. Apocryphon of James. Book of Thomas the Contender. "To know yourself is to know God"—attributed to Jesus, Joseph Smith, Judaism, Taoism, Islam, Hinduism, Buddhism,

Baha'i writings … and likely every spiritual teacher and tradition throughout history.

183. "… popular or everyday use of ritual power [magick] was proscribed by the church authorities (though the use of ritual power per se was just as characteristic of the legitimate church ritual)." *Ancient Christian Magic: Coptic Texts of Ritual Power,* ed. Marvin Meyer and Richard Smith (San Francisco: HarperSanFrancisco, 1994), 18.

184. Oxford Dictionary and Online Etymology Dictionary

185. Ibid.

186. Merriam-Webster Dictionary and Online Etymology Dictionary.

187. Thomas 14. Mark 6:7–13. Matthew 10:1–14. Luke 9:1–6.

188. Thomas 25. Matthew 5:43–48. Luke 6:25–37.

189. In its original Greek, the biblical word for sin is *hamartia.* It's an archery term that means missing the mark. In other words, sin doesn't mean a flaw in your being nor a crime against God. To sin is to make a mistake, to miss the target (i.e., the Divine).

190. The Wiccan Rede: "Do as ye will, an ye harm none."

191. Thomas 14. Matthew 5:38–44, 6:12–15. Luke 6:29, 11:4. Mark 3:28–30.

192. Thomas 26. Matthew 7:3–5. Luke 6:41–42.

193. Matthew 23:12. Mark 12:38–40. Luke 17:10, 20:45–47. Peter 5:5. Romans 12:3–8, 12:16. Apocryphon of James.

194. Thomas 22, 37, 46. Matthew 18:2–6, 18:3, 19:14. Mark 10:13–16. Luke 18:15–17. John 3:5.

195. (Blessed are the hungry) Thomas 36, 64, 69. Matthew 5:6, 22. Luke 6:21, 12:22–34. (Eat what is before you) Thomas 14. Luke 10:7–9.

196. Thomas 95. Matthew 4:11, 5:41–42. Luke 6:30, 14:12–14. Romans 12:20.

197. Thomas 2, 36, 92, 94. Matthew 6. Mark 11:24. Luke 11:11– 13. Mary 4:7. Papyrus Oxyrhynchus 654:2.

198. Wiccan Three-Fold Law: "Whatever you do, for good or ill, will return to you three times over."

199. Matthew 23. Luke 11:46. Gospel of Mary.

200. Thomas 39, 102. Luke 11:52, 12:1–3. Matthew 23:13–15.

201. Buddhism, Hinduism, yoga, etc. See also Teaching 19: Personal Experience of God.

202. Frequent in Thomas, Mark, Matthew, Luke, Mary. Dialogue of the Saviour 76.

203. The Dialogue of the Saviour 76, Sylvanus 117: 19–22 and 30–32.

204. Thomas 39. Matthew 10. Gospel of Nazareth 7. P. Oxy. 655. Ignatius's Letter to Polycarp.

205. Genesis 3:14–15.

206. Knowledge: The Apocryphon of James 8:23–27, The Gospel of Thomas: 39, The Apocryphon of James 8:23–27. Self-knowledge: Gospel of Thomas: 3, 70, 111; The Book of Thomas the Contender 138:14–18; The Apocryphon of James 12:19–22; The Gospel of Truth 24:32–25:19, The Gospel of Philip 61:33–35, 76:17–22; The Teachings of Silvanus 92:10–12.

207. Pagels, *The Gnostic Gospels.*

208. Thomas 114. (Having female disciples) Luke 8:1–3, 24:10. 2 Timothy 4:19–21. Gospel of Mary.

"In its earliest years the Christian movement showed a remarkable openness toward women. Jesus himself violated Jewish convention by talking openly with women, and he included them among his companions."—Elaine Pagels, *The Gnostic Gospels*, 73.

209. Men have their own powers and gifts, but in Western history that has never been denied, so there's no need for that discussion here.

210. "Second-century followers of Carpocrates in Alexandria, for example, credited their teachings to Mary, Martha, and Salome. Marcion, who researched the historical Jesus, appointed women as priests. Valentinus in Egypt supported women prophets and healers. Early Jesus followers included women and practiced healing that later Christians considered heretical magic."—Rex Weyler, *The Jesus Sayings*, 158.

"All initiates, men and women alike, participated equally in the drawing; anyone might be selected to serve as priest, bishop, or prophet." Pagels, *The Gnostic Gospels*, 49.

211. Luke 10:42.

212. Gospel of Thomas 1, 18, 19, 85, 111. John 8:52. Matthew 16:28. Mark 9:1. Luke 9:27.

213. Thomas 3. Gospel of Mary. Apocryphon of James. Book of Thomas the Contender.

214. Not accepting worship: John 5:41, John 6:15.

Be Christ: The Gospel of Thomas 108; The Apocryphon of James 2:28–32, 7:10–15, 8:30–36; The Gospel of Philip 61:29–31, 67:26–27; The Teachings of Silvanus 90:29–30, 103:12–15; The Gospel Of Mary 8:15–20, 18:15–18; Mark 10:21 and various other exhortations to "take up my cross and follow me."

215. Matthew 13:11–17. Mark 4:10–12, 4:33. Luke 8:10. Thomas 13, 62. Gospel of Mary. Apocryphon of James.

"Members of the inner circle suggested that what the bishop and priests taught publicly were only elementary doctrines.

They themselves claimed to offer more—the secret mysteries, the higher teachings."—Elaine Pagels, *The Gnostic Gospels*, 47.

216. Tom Harpur, *The Pagan Christ* (Toronto: Thomas Allen Publishers, 2004).

–Part Three–

217. From a conversation I had with Raymond Buckland.

218. From a conversation I had with Vivianne Crowley.

219. Quoted by St. Augustine in *City of God* 19.23. *Christianity and the Roman Empire*, Ralph Martin Novak. (Harrisburg, PA: Trinity Press, 2001.) 133–34.

GET MORE AT LLEWELLYN.COM

Visit us online to browse hundreds of our books and decks, plus sign up to receive our e-newsletters and exclusive online offers.

- Free tarot readings • Spell-a-Day • Moon phases
- Recipes, spells, and tips • Blogs • Encyclopedia
- Author interviews, articles, and upcoming events

GET SOCIAL WITH LLEWELLYN

Find us on
Facebook
www.Facebook.com/LlewellynBooks

Follow us on

www.Twitter.com/Llewellynbooks

GET BOOKS AT LLEWELLYN

LLEWELLYN ORDERING INFORMATION

Order online: Visit our website at www.llewellyn.com to select your books and place an order on our secure server.

Order by phone:
- Call toll free within the U.S. at 1-877-NEW-WRLD (1-877-639-9753)
- Call toll free within Canada at 1-866-NEW-WRLD (1-866-639-9753)
- We accept VISA, MasterCard, and American Express

Order by mail:
Send the full price of your order (MN residents add 6.875% sales tax) in U.S. funds, plus postage and handling to: Llewellyn Worldwide, 2143 Wooddale Drive Woodbury, MN 55125-2989

POSTAGE AND HANDLING:
STANDARD: (U.S. & Canada)
(Please allow 12 business days)
$25.00 and under, add $4.00.
$25.01 and over, FREE SHIPPING.

INTERNATIONAL ORDERS (airmail only):
$16.00 for one book, plus $3.00 for each additional book.

Visit us online for more shipping options.
Prices subject to change.

FREE CATALOG!

To order, call
1-877-
NEW-WRLD
ext. 8236
or visit our
website

CHRISTOPAGANISM

JOYCE & RIVER HIGGINBOTHAM

An Inclusive Path

ChristoPaganism
An Inclusive Path
Joyce and River Higginbotham

Witches praying the rosary? Catholics reading Tarot cards?

For some, it's blasphemy. For others, it's a launching pad to enlightenment. But for interfaith experts Joyce and River Higginbotham, it's a new reality begging for intellectual study. More and more, Pagans and Christians are incorporating each other's practices into their own belief systems, forging hybrid spiritual paths that borrow from both earth- and scripture-based religions. Standing in two worlds at once, ChristoPagans are sparking a new conversation about the nature of faith and the evolving spiritual needs of a chaotic world. With scholarly poise, the Higginbothams wade into this provocative religious pairing, deftly navigating its minefield of heresy and personal bias.

Free of political agenda but ripe with open-minded curiosity, *ChristoPaganism* launches a whole new dialogue on the subject of personal belief.

978-0-7387-1467-7, 336 pp., 7 ½ x 9 ⅛   **$19.95**

CHRISTOPHER PENCZAK

THE

M·Y·S·T·I·C

fOUNDATION

UNDERSTANDING & EXPLORING
THE MAGICAL UNIVERSE

The Mystic Foundation
Understanding & Exploring the Magical Universe
CHRISTOPHER PENCZAK

The sheer number of mystical traditions in the world can be overwhelming to seekers new to the metaphysical world. Summing up the universal truths underlying many mystic institutions, *The Mystic Foundation* is an initial step toward understanding the wisdom of each.

This nondogmatic primer outlines the mystical teachings of Paganism, Christianity, Islam, and other spiritualities spanning Eastern and Western traditions. Penczak transforms complex subjects and ideas—such as the powers of creation, life forces, elements, the world beyond, spirit entities, sacred space and time, magick, and metaphysical skills—into easy-to-understand concepts. Each chapter features exercises—including meditation, aura cleansing, chakra balancing, and psychic travel—to help seekers "go within" and ground themselves in a variety of mystic beliefs. By the end of the book, readers will have a solid foundation in mysticism for choosing a path of their own.

978-0-7387-0979-6, 336 pp., 7 ½ x 9 ⅛   **$15.95**

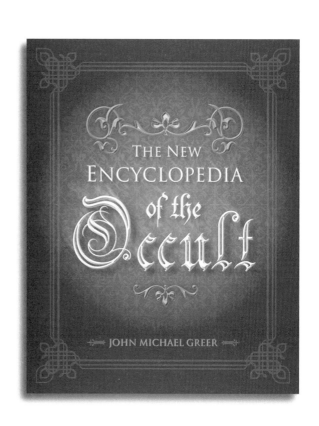

The New Encyclopedia of the Occult
JOHN MICHAEL GREER

From "Aarab Zereq" to "Zos Kia Cultus," it's the most complete occult reference work on the market. With this one text, you will gain a thorough overview of the history and current state of the occult from a variety of North American and western European traditions. Its pages offer the essential knowledge you need to make sense of the occult, along with references for further reading if you want to learn more.

You will find the whole range of occult tradition, lore, history, philosophy, and practice in the Western world. *The New Encyclopedia* of the Occult includes magic, alchemy, astrology, divination, Tarot, palmistry, geomancy, magical orders such as the Golden Dawn and Rosicrucians, Wiccan, Thelema, Theosophy, modern Paganism, and biographies of important occultists.

978-1-56718-336-8, 576 pp., 8 x 10   **$32.95**

SPIRIT
of the
WITCH

Religion & Spirituality in Contemporary Witchcraft

RAVEN GRIMASSI

Spirit of the Witch
Religion & Spirituality in Contemporary Witchcraft
RAVEN GRIMASSI

Find peace and happiness in the spiritual teachings of the Craft

What is in the spirit of the Witch? What empowers Witches in their daily and spiritual lives? How does a person become a Witch?

In *Spirit of the Witch*, Raven Grimassi, an initiate of several Wiccan traditions, reveals the Witch as a citizen living and working like all others—and as a spiritual being who seeks alignment with the natural world. He provides an overview of the Witch's view of deity and how it manifests in the cycles of nature. Seasonal rituals, tools, magic, and beliefs are all addressed in view of their spiritual underpinnings. Additionally, he shows the relationship among elements of pre-Christian European religion and modern Witchcraft beliefs, customs, and practices.

978-0-7387-0338-1, 264 pp., 6 x 9   **$12.95**

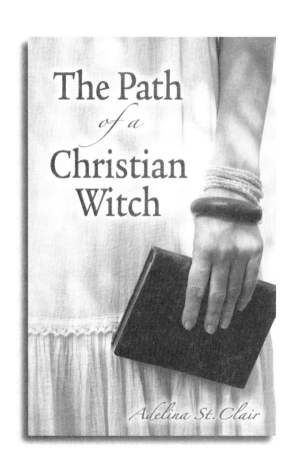

The Path
of a
Christian
Witch

Adelina St. Clair

The Path of a Christian Witch
Adelina St. Clair

Is it possible to be a Christian Witch?

At a time when the merging of spiritual systems can be controversial and challenging, this inspiring book offers guidance and insight into blending faiths in today's world.

Raised in the Catholic faith, Adelina St. Clair spent many years questioning and soul-searching before she found a way to merge aspects of Wicca and Christianity into a vibrant, loving belief system. Filled with personal anecdotes, this book tells the story of St. Clair's journey of self-discovery and revelation, illuminating the fusion of spiritual beliefs in a way that no formal text ever could.

A unique mix of memoir and how-to, this book addresses major contradictions in belief, such as monotheism, Goddess worship, magic, and the teachings of Christ. Through real-life examples and daily rituals, it shows how one woman incorporated her Christian identity into a Wiccan practice.

978-0-7387-1982-5, 216 pp., 5³⁄₁₆ x 8   **$15.95**

RAVEN DIGITALIS

PLANETARY
SPELLS & RITUALS

Practicing Dark & Light Magick
Aligned with the Cosmic Bodies

Planetary Spells & Rituals
Practicing Dark & Light Magick
Aligned with the Cosmic Bodies
Raven Digitalis

Raven Digitalis, who's fast becoming a recognized and highly influential voice in the Wiccan/Pagan community, returns with a unique and dynamic spell-book reflecting his signature approach to magick and spirituality.

Organized by the planets, Sun, and Moon, these powerful spells are aligned according to the astrological energies. Digitalis introduces fifty-five profound rituals that can be easily customized according to one's magickal and spiritual path. From personal growth to practical concerns, you'll find spells to sharpen intuition, summon ancestors, honor Saturn returns, relieve depression, manifest abundance, reveal the truth, undo social conditioning, purge impurities, help the dying cross over, and much more.

978-0-7387-1971-9, 336 pp., 6 x 9   **$19.95**